Appreciating Melodrama

Appreciating Melodrama

Theory and Practice in Indian Cinema and Television

Piyush Roy

BLOOMSBURY
NEW DELHI • LONDON • OXFORD • NEW YORK • SYDNEY

BLOOMSBURY INDIA
Bloomsbury Publishing India Pvt. Ltd
Second Floor, LSC Building No. 4, DDA Complex, Pocket C – 6 & 7,
Vasant Kunj, New Delhi, 110070

BLOOMSBURY, BLOOMSBURY ACADEMIC INDIA and the Diana logo are trademarks of Bloomsbury Publishing Plc

First published in India 2022
This edition published 2022

Bloomsbury Academic
An imprint of Bloomsbury Publishing Plc

ISBN: HB: 978-93-54354-86-1; eBook: 978-93-54354-88-5
2 4 6 8 10 9 7 5 3 1

Typeset in Manipal Technologies Limited
Printed & bound in India by Replika Press Pvt. Ltd.

Bloomsbury Publishing Plc makes every effort to ensure that the papers used in the manufacture of our books are natural, recyclable products made from wood grown in well-managed forests. Our manufacturing processes conform to the environmental regulations of the country of origin.

For

Thakuba (Aditya Prasanna Madhual), Aai (Malatilata Rout),
Julki apa and Pramila Panda aunty

॥ संप्रेषण का कोई भी माध्यम कला है और संप्रेषण का संदेश ज्ञान है। जब संदेश का उद्येश्य उत्तेजना उत्पन करता हो तब कला के उस रूप को हीन कहते हैं। जब संदेश निश्वार्थ प्रेम, सत्य और महान चरित्र की रचना करता हो, तब वह कला पवित्र मानी जाती है ॥

निर्देशक चंद्रप्रकाश द्विवेदी, उपनिषद् गंगा, एप. 8, ऊपवेद (2012)

Any means of self-expression is an art and the message of self-expression is knowledge. When the purpose of the message creates agitation, that form of art is considered inferior. Bad arts are used only to satiate the hunger of the body and the thirst of the eyes. When the message creates selfless love, truth and great character that art is considered to be sacred.

Director Chandraprakash Dwivedi, *Upanishad Ganga*, Ep. 8, Upaveda (2012)

Contents

Foreword

Appreciating Melodrama by Piyush Roy is a timely intervention, as it challenges the Western critique of Indian films as 'melodrama' and subverts the Western 'standard' in an against-the-grain appraisal of Indian cinema and television. It establishes continuity in Indian dramatic modes through the application of the theoretical framework provided by the 2,000-year-old aesthetics of the Indian *Natyashastra* attributed to the sage Bharata. In providing a chronological study of landmark films from Bombay (now Mumbai) and regional cinema, this study epitomises the development and continuing success and appeal of Indian films in the subcontinent and amongst a global audience. By utilising the '*Rasa*' theory, which embodies *navarasas* (nine universal human emotions) and *bhavas/anubhavas* (feeling/mood/sentiment/expression), this book gives primacy to character depiction in popular films, which have impacted Indian and international audiences through time, in a balanced argument without demonising or valorising Indian cinema.

The book's historical and mythological overview of Indian aesthetics/poetics establishes the continuity of Sanskrit forms in classical literature, oral tradition and folk culture in India through time. The book challenges the premise of Hollywood-led assertions of the 'norm' that has informed the canonisation process of academic film studies syllabi. In tracing the journey from drama to cinema, the significance of traditional regional theatre and popular culture in a national television epic series, it establishes the links between diverse performance art forms and thus consolidates the position of silver and small screen productions as integral to Indian aesthetic perception and response. While highlighting the overlap between parallel films and the popular masala film industry, it makes a distinction between cognitive realism and affective realism, as it affirms the efficacy of the Indian melodrama in its continuing appeal with its audiences from pre- to post-Independence times. The foundational *rasa/bhava* theory highlights the honesty and integrity of culture-specific creativity and practice that problematises established ideas of Western binarism and a place and space for the validity and appeal for Indian cinema.

This book opens up a fresh area of scholarship with its refreshing revisionist approach. It moves away from European–American recommended 'standards', questioning notions of the 'norm' as it dismantles the prevalent canon. It comes in the wake of the Black Lives Matter movement and the decolonisation of the curriculum project that have rocked the establishment and renowned institutions worldwide in a postcolonial affirmation of Indian techniques and performance traditions that utilise the song and dance, emotion, action and dialogue kaleidoscope of the masala film. This nuanced appreciation of the stereotypical and stylised clinches the 'universal' and timeless nature of the guidelines offered by the *Navarasa* theory of the *Natyashastra*. It augments and enriches the Hollywood-led film canon, widening current critical debates, and opens new doors to further research, and new perspectives in a reader/audience-response theoretical approach can give primacy to emotionalised performance and its undeniable appeal. This perceptive and in-depth study allocates a pride of place to effective melodrama and its makers, allowing the reader/critic to see Indian films in a new light and encouraging a global reassessment of film studies.

Dr. Bashabi Fraser, CBE
Professor Emerita of English and Creative Writing
Director, Scottish Centre of Tagore Studies, Edinburgh Napier University
Honorary Fellow, Centre for South Asian Studies, University of Edinburgh

Preface

Indian cinema is fast becoming the most-watched and arguably a very influential national cinema of the 21st century. Against this backdrop, *Appreciating Melodrama* is a highly original contribution to the field of Indian film studies and beyond, offering a comprehensive insight into the history and development of the defining features of Indian cinema. Its originality lays in the diversity of its subject matter and sources. For the first time (in a single English publication), an interdisciplinary academic work engages with the key films of all four major regions of cinema in India (West/Marathi, North/Hindi, South/Telugu, East/Odia), covering a period of a hundred years and multiple genres. Within this broad sweep, it pays specific attention to the conscious and subconscious processes that underpin the development of *rasa* traditions in Indian filmmaking by, in part, interrogating the creative and technical voices behind them.

The extensive use of interviews is a major strength of the study. The breadth of the project allows it to embrace a diverse collection of interviewees from across the industry, both geographically and professionally. Notable subjects include the Indian auteurs K. Vishwanath and Shyam Benegal, prominent actors like Sarat Pujari and Om Puri and iconic screenwriters such as Salim Khan and Kamlesh Pandey. Eminent Indian cinema directors based in different regions are vital sources for Roy, including individuals such as S.S. Rajamouli (the director of *Bahubali*), Nirad Mohapatra and Prashanta Nanda (Odia cinema), Paresh Mokashi (Marathi), Anjali Menon (Malayalam), Srijit Mukherji (Bengali) and Chandraprakash Dwivedi (Hindi). By mining the experiences of such instrumental figures, Roy creates an engaging portrait of Indian cinema. This methodology also adds a sense of the personal to the study; some of these directors, technicians and 'movie legends' are taking part in academic research for the first time, making their contributions original and individual. Complex insights emerge without excluding a non-academic audience.

For those interested in the more technical aspects of Indian film, the analysis is thorough and compelling. The author's detailed critical reviews of the devices and acting choices deployed in contemporary drama are enhanced by the observations of key players in the productions. Crucially, *Appreciating Melodrama* combats the often-patronising attitude towards the masala style of narrative and its melodramatic performances. It casts these creative choices in a new light by introducing a *rasa*-based theoretical model through which to view expressive performances, particularly within musical sequences. This provokes thoughts on how audiences can identify the layers of explicit and implicit emotions (*rasa*) in song-, dance- and dialogue-oriented scenes, showing that *rasa*-based analyses of Indian cinema should be a vital cornerstone of contemporary film criticism.

Having begun his career as a journalist and then editor of *Stardust* magazine, Roy's intimate knowledge and enthusiasm for Indian film shines through this book. He remained a prolific author and prize-winning journalist even while completing his PhD at Edinburgh University, where I had the privilege to serve as his supervisor. Given the immense breadth of his knowledge, which he shared every week in the popular Indian Film Club screenings and discussions which he organised for the University's Centre for South Asian Studies, it was clear from the start that Piyush's research would become a milestone in Indian film criticism. It will hopefully lead to Indian film being taken more seriously as an art form, at the same time helping us to move away from the Eurocentric bias in the interpretation of the visual arts. Roy's ambitious project will be a valuable resource for anyone involved in the study of drama and film and its practice. Its careful analysis provides a vital and original contribution to the academic field of film studies. It will also be a provocative and engrossing read for those in related fields in academia and the millions of Indian film enthusiasts around the globe.

Dr. Crispin Bates
Professor of Modern and Contemporary South Asian History
University of Edinburgh, UK
Director of the Centre for South Asian and Indian Ocean Studies
Sunway University, Malaysia

Acknowledgements

A profound moment in my journey from writing on cinema (as a critic) to writing about cinema (as a film historian) was the dawn of an opportunity to also start making cinema, encouraged by friends and fellow cinephiles during my doctoral pursuit at the University of Edinburgh. Thanks are due to those friends and mentors. The journey helped inculcate empathy into my critical outlook towards reviewing movies. Subsequently, making films in the Indian context with local technical talent and exploring vernacular idioms of expression, performance articulation and conditionings towards one's expectations from cinema and movie-watching made me further appreciate and better engage with the narrative purpose and achievements of the unique aspects—song, dance and emotion and signature aesthetics, *bhavas* and *rasas*—in India's varied onscreen storytelling traditions across mediums. I also realised that there has been a serious lack in acknowledgement and acceptance of the same in popular review and writings, because of a critically dismissive attitude towards Indian cinema's most distinct, high engagement attributes, as unrealistic distraction and melodramatic escape, for their not confirming to the established Euro–American canons about 'the recommended best' in film lists, study, criticism and making.

This book, conceived as a researched argument highlighting the role of civilisational aesthetic traditions in the shaping of artistic expression, brings into critical consideration voices and perspectives of those who make movies in the Indian context. The aim is to introduce discussions on alternate and empathetic parameters of review. Hence, it was essential to go beyond cross-textual academic endorsements to actually engage with the real makers of celluloid masterpieces in the Indian context, along with their fans and interpreters. This would not have been possible without liberal time commitment for qualitative, open-ended discussions with each of my interviewees, most of whom are valuable contributors in their respective fields to the art, craft and review of films.

I would like to thank pioneer auteur of Indian parallel cinema movement of the 1970s, Shyam Benegal, veteran Hindi filmmaker and television director Lekh Tandon, who began his prolific direction career in the 'Golden Age of Hindustani Cinema' (1950s) and made some popular television serials in the 1980s and 1990s. The director and lead actor of the still-watched, much-quoted historical TV series *Chanakya* and producer–director of *Upanishad Ganga*, Chandraprakash Dwivedi, and multinational-award-winning veteran Telegu and Tamil cinema director of musical classics, K. Vishwanath, for their exhaustive insights into the *Natyashastra* traditions of Indian cinema. They have also made some memorable shows in the 'Golden Age of Indian Television/ Doordarshan' (1980s/1990s).

Thanks are due to S.S. Rajamouli, producer–director of epic Telegu cinema blockbusters, including the Bahubali film series, and Nirad Mohapatra, maker of one of the most critically acclaimed Odia films of all time, *Maya Miriga*, for sharing insights on the influence and achievement of *rasas* in their works. Popular maker of *masala* movie potboilers in the 1980s–1990s, Deepak Shivdasani, and multinational-award-winning 21st-century Bengali cinema auteur, Srijit Mukherji, and writer–director of popular new-age Malayalam language dramas, Anjali Menon, for their insightful conversations on *rasa*-evoking practices in their respective regional language movie industries and own filmmaking styles. Experimental Indian filmmaker Kamal Swarup, filmmaker and chairman of the Kerala State Chalachitra Academy, Kamal and director of *Harishchandrachi Factory*, Paresh Mokashi, for their insights on the influences and the influence of Dadasaheb Phalke around the birthing of Indian feature films at the beginning of the 20th century. The life and times of the 'father of Indian cinema', Phalke, have been the focus of some of their most acclaimed film works, along with offering valuable insights on region-specific sociocultural influences on the 'Silent Era of Indian Cinema' (1898–1930).

Together, each of the above acclaimed filmmakers, representing and working in some of India's largest and most prolific cinema industries like Hindustani (Hindi/Urdu), Telegu, Tamil, Odia, Malayalam, Marathi and Bengali, have enriched the arguments in this book with pan-Indian cinema perspectives on moviemaking in the space of a single book compendium.

Thanks are due to the legends of Indian movie acting like Amitabh Bachchan, Hema Malini, Om Puri, Tom Alter, Vikram Gokhale and Bollywood's new millennium 'superstar actor-with-a-difference', Vidya Balan, each of whom, in my interactions for interviews published in the *Stardust* magazine, have offered personal insights on elements shaping their own and Indian movie acting styles. This has lent some valuable practice-based attestation to the book's recommendations on how to observe and appreciate the layers in 'emotive acting'. I am grateful to pioneer Odia filmmaker-actor Gopal Ghosh, Odia cinema's first superstar Sarat Pujari and its most successful producer-director and lead actor of multi-starrer post-1970s *masala* blockbusters, Prashanta Nanda, for sharing their personal journeys and insightful anecdotes from the birth to the evolution of Odia cinema as a significant regional film industry in East India.

My long conversations with Indian cinema's first female superstar playback singer from the 1940s, Shamshad Begum, veteran choreographer Saroj Khan, popular Hindi cinema script writers Salim Khan and Kamlesh Pandey, and actors and acting gurus Kishore Namit Kapoor and Anupam Kher have enriched the book's highlighting of *bhava* and *rasa* elements in every sphere of the film craft, from story conceptualisation to performed interpretation and choreography, apart from being the essence of all song and music endeavours.

I express my gratitude to senior critics, writers and lovers of Indian cinema, such as Ali Peter John, Mark Cousins, Surya Deo, Rajiv Vijayakar, and Professor Rachel Dwyer (School of Oriental and African Studies, London), for their analytical discussions on the many queries emerging from my initial research. Thanks especially to Surya Deo for sharing archival newspaper records of the first reviews of the first Odia film, *Sita Bibaha* (1936).

My heartfelt gratitude to former director of the National Film Archives of India (NFAI), Pune, P.K. Nair, for many valuable resource leads, and its present director Prakash Makdum for research access to film magazine archives and the viewing of all existing silent Indian films in the NFAI collection for study and review. Most posters and photographs used in the book are courtesy the National Film Archives of India.

Special thanks to the founder and creative director of Swastik Productions Pvt. Ltd., Siddharth Tewary, maker of the first major 21st-century adaptation of the Mahabharata epic as a mega television series telecast on Star Plus India Pvt. Ltd. (2013–2014), for hosting me on the show's sets at Umargam in Gujarat and allowing extensive access to all its cast and crew. Thanks also to episode director Mukesh Singh, production manager Kuntal Shukla and actors Sourabh Raaj Jain and Saurav Gurjar.

The book is the published outcome of my doctoral thesis submitted to The University of Edinburgh, titled 'The Aesthetics of Emotional Acting: A *Rasa*-Based Review of Indian Cinema and Television' (2017). It would not have been possible without the guidance and critical suggestions of and many discussions with my supervisors Prof. Crispin Bates and Dr. Paul Dundas. Prof. Bates has constantly encouraged me to convert the findings of my over three years of field work in India and many interviews of archival value conducted as a film journalist and Editor of *Stardust* into a book; he also conducted the manuscript's first edit. Prof. Dundas, every one of your questions on my every submission has further refined the researcher in me. Thanks are also due to my doctoral thesis examiners, Prof. Bashabi Fraser (poet, post-colonial writer–academic and director of The Scottish Centre for Tagore Studies) and Dr David Sorfa (Programme Director of Film Studies, The University of Edinburgh), whose critical inputs and incisive reviews have enriched the book's final arguments.

The actual realisation of the thesis to book, however, would not have been possible without Shambhu Sahu, who represented the work to publishers. His enthusiasm for the work, clubbed with a researcher's interest in the study of cinema, patience and diligent guidance through the publishing process will be forever cherished, as will the beginning of a new association with my publishers, Bloomsbury India. Thank you, Chandra Sekhar (Publisher, Academic Books, Bloomsbury India) and Shreya Chakraborti (Editorial Manager) for your faith in the book's academic promise and necessity, and Ankita Deshpande (Editor), for a truly meticulous edit and some valuable questions and perspectives to ponder and review. The processes of learning are, indeed, never over or enough.

Thanks are also due to Prof. Saugata Bhaduri and Prof. Indrani Mukherjee from Jawaharlal Nehru University, Delhi, and Sara Martínez from Book Permissions Springer Nature, Germany, for facilitating the reproduction of excerpts from the chapter 'Gendered *Bhavas*: Perpetuating Notions of "Ideal" Male and Female Behaviour Through Specific Emotions Highlighted in Acting in *Mayabazar*', authored by me in their co-edited book publication, *Transcultural Negotiations of Gender Studies in (Be)longing* (2015). Thanks to John Cerullo, Senior Executive Editor, Rowman & Littlefield/ Globe Pequot, Applause Books/Backbeat Books, for facilitating permissions towards reproducing excerpts from my authored book, *Bollywood FAQ: All That's Left to Know About the Greatest Film Story Never Told* (2019).

I am thankful for the participant and moderator feedback on some of the book's chapters presented as work-in-progress seminar talks at various international conferences in the UK ('MOVING ON: South Asian Screen Cultures in a Broader Frame' conference, University of Westminster, London [2014]; BASAS [British Association of South Asian Studies] annual conferences at Royal Holloway, University of London [2014] and University of Cambridge [2016]; 'The Rest and The West: RipOff or Resourceful Creativity?' Innovation over Imitation in Popular Cinema Beyond the West, conference, University of St. Andrews [2016]; and the Centre for South Asian Studies seminars at The University of Edinburgh [2015]).

I am forever grateful for my foundational and lifelong sources of inspiration, the four people to whom this book is dedicated—my paternal grandfather Aditya Prasanna Madhual, maternal grandmother Malatilata Rout, aunt Manjula Madhual (Julki apa) and Prof. Pramila Panda from REC Rourkela, who, since my childhood, through their long and short stories sourced from the diversity of human existence, local literature, Indian mythology and history, did perhaps subconsciously inculcate within me a shared love for the art of storytelling, local lore and storytellers irrespective of the medium of communication, be it novels, classical dance, theatre or film.

A good story is of fundamental essence to the 'art' of a film. How it is told constitutes the craft of filmmaking. Why a particular story is selected for cinematic telling from a plenitude of options and experiences that make human life, and how it is told, is courtesy the context, culture and movie-watching memories and their influences on a filmmaker. This book is a humble effort at appreciating the above by engaging with voices that represent, shape and create content across a diversity of Indian language cinemas that make up the world's largest and most prolific national film industry. I hope the book also fosters the development of an empathetic understanding of some fundamental, common, stated and unstated civilisational notions about 'creating art and its criticism' that have held the unity in Indian cinema's vibrant and plural creative masala mix.

List of Illustrations

Tables

Figures

Images

Introduction: Bharata to Bollywood

> The conception of art as an activity and an independent spiritual experience, freed of practical interest, which the intuition of Kant perceived for the West, was already in 10th century India, an object of study and controversy[1].
>
> Raniero Gnoli, Indologist

> The *rasa* philosophy or wisdom goes back for many thousands of years and somewhere in the collective subconscious it has become ingrained in Indian filmmakers, myself included. Yet, in the various contradictory philosophies of film criticism, an orthodoxy has crept in, leaving the *rasa* theory unkindly looked upon in some critical and academic circles. This could be considered intellectually fascist[2].
>
> Srijit Mukherji, filmmaker

Indian cinema, popularly known as 'Bollywood'[3], is arguably, along with yoga, spices, the Taj Mahal and Gandhian thought, one of the most universally recognised Indian contribution and introduction in global culture today. Despite 'its predominant narrative styles not conforming to the first world European and/or American cinema narrative structure' (Thomas 2010: 22–24), its diverse regions of filmmaking and the many contradictions surrounding the appreciation of its indigenous aesthetics, Indian cinema is acknowledged as an influential national cinema. It functions as an important socio-cultural tool of entertainment, engagement and influence for its audience. Simultaneously, it has also emerged as an industry of immense global reach and financial worth. It is mainly led by five of India's largest language cinemas—Hindi, Tamil, Telegu, Malayalam and Bengali—but films in the remaining 18 official Indian languages (listed in the eighth schedule of the Indian Constitution) and those outside of it, such as Bhojpuri and English, together account for the Indian film industry's annual output of nearly 2,000 films a year. Today, Indian movies are screened in theatres and cinemas in over 100 nations from the

United States to Australia and United Kingdom to South Africa. They have also been enjoying an increasing distribution presence in the dubbed film circuits of Africa, the Middle East and South America; the subtitled showcasing of movies through online and OTT platforms like YouTube, Hotstar, Netflix and Amazon Prime has further increased viewership for regional language movies across and beyond India. International ticket sales of some post-2010 Hindi, Telegu and Tamil films, such as *Dangal* (The Wrestle, 2016), *Bahubali 2: The Conclusion* (2017) and *2.0* (2018), have generated an income share at times rivalling their earnings from distribution within India.

India has been the largest moviemaking nation in the world for over three decades. It is, more-over, increasingly viewed as the world's second-most important film industry after Hollywood and arguably more important than the European film industry (Epstein 2011). Since Sony Pictures' 2007 Diwali festival debut with the film *Saawariya* (The Lover, 2007), Hollywood studio majors like Disney, Fox Star, Sony Pictures and Viacom 18, with a decade plus presence in the Indian film market, have been making or distributing films in Hindi and regional Indian languages. Fox Star and Viacom 18 have made films in other Indian language cinemas like Tamil, Telegu and Bengali, while Indian film production companies like Reliance Big Pictures are co-producing Hollywood films. By 2003, within five years of being granted an industry status by the Indian Government, 30 film production companies were listed on the National Stock Exchange. Half of the Best Hindi Film nominees at the 2011 Filmfare Awards had at least one foreign national heading one of its technical teams. The International Indian Film Academy (IIFA) awards, which began at London's millennium dome in 2000, have emerged as one of the biggest global event exports of any national film industry, having been hosted by cities in Africa, Asia, Europe and North America in the two decades since their inception. Numbers have always been Indian cinema's biggest advantage. Post 2000, it has been acknowledged as the most viewed cinema worldwide, peaking to 2.6 billion cinema admissions in 2012, in contrast to Hollywood's 1.36 billion (McCarthy 2014).

Another record of sorts was achieved in 2011, when just the making of a video of a yet to be shot Tamil film song '*Why this Kolaveridi?*'

went viral on YouTube. It garnered over five million hits in a week and crossed the one-crore mark in 10 days, highlighting one of India's larger regional language cinema's potential global appeal.

The distances between industries may be shrinking, collaborations between technicians increasing and appeal of Indian cinema widening, but the genre continues to confuse viewers outside of India. Much of Indian cinema, especially its popular 'all India form' often erroneously identified with Bollywood, remains initially amusing and perplexing to non-Indian audiences and critics in its 'epico-mythico-tragico-comico-super-sexy-high-masala-art form in which the unifying principle is a techni-colour-storyline' (Rushdie 1996: 148–149; Stadtler 2005: 517). Its aesthetics are Indian cinema's strongest identifier, differentiator and attraction for traditional fans. However, in the absence of fair appreciation models of its defining attributes, both within India and in the West, it continues to suffer a crisis of recognition (Dudrah 2006; Ray 1976; Thomas 2008).

India has one of the lowest percentages of admissions for Hollywood films, which is still less than 10 per cent (KPMG India 2016)[4]. This implies that India's film-going audience (despite having access) watches fewer American movies than many other audiences in the world. A majority of the Indian audience appear to return to familiar films or to those they have grown up watching after occasional partaking of other world cinema aesthetic experiences. According to Rachel Dwyer, leading professor of Bollywood Studies in the UK, 'It is the only cinema apart from Hollywood, which is more popular than Hollywood in the country it is made. And that is something unique about Indian cinema' (2015). What is that unique attraction in its telling? What is that missing appeal in other national cinemas that is present only in Indian cinema for its fans and consumers? This necessitates a researched engagement. There is a need, given the 'inadequacy of existing Euro-American film theory models' (Booth 1995/2000; Hogan 2009; Lutgendorf 2007; Thomas 2008), for contributions towards an empathetic criticism of Indian cinema, to strengthen emerging arguments for appreciating Indian cinema on terms of reference that engage with its diversity rather than dismissing it with an essentialisation as is often encountered in practice.

Indian Cinema: Definitions and Divisions

Describing all Indian language cinemas with the term Bollywood, which originated as a reference to films made in Bombay or Mumbai's Hindi film industry, is a minor indicator of the above-mentioned tendency towards essentialisation. Bollywood has now mutated into a brand and genre in itself, both in media reference and academic discourse. Hindi cinema or Bollywood has, however, been equally passionately and convincingly claimed as the dominant narrative form and storytelling convention in all Indian cinema (Rajadhyaksha 2003; Yadav 2001: 42). This has been evidenced in films from India's regional cinemas, which share the Bollywood format of a blend of numerous emotion-evoking modes such as action, comedy and 'melodrama'[5]. They use larger-than-life characters, spectacle, songs, dialogue and dance to weave together an integrated whole that prioritises the establishment of an affective or emotional connect over an appeal to the intellect of its audience. Using the phrase 'Bollywoodisation of Indian cinema' to describe this influence of cinematic storytelling, Rajadhyaksha (2010) identifies it as the most homogenising influence and recognisable factor amongst all Indian mainstream language cinemas. It is termed as commercial cinema too, because of its profit-based motivations. This body of cinema will henceforth be referenced as 'popular cinema' in the book.

The other major category within Indian films, based on aesthetic criteria and a notional privilege of being driven purely on artistic motivations by critics and/or 'anglophone Indians' (Kesavan 2012: 13), is the off-beat or art-house cinema. Its corpus is primarily comprised of the emotionally understated, realistic, appealing-to-the-intellect (intellectual/thought-provoking) films that were made from the late 1960s onwards, subsequent to auteur Satyajit Ray's successful international debut with the Apu films (1955–59) trilogy[6]. These films were often made using state funding. The greatest differential of this category of cinema was its subscription to the canons of Euro-American film theories with a perceived (and often stated) total rejection of popular cinema's filming codes. Predominantly located within Bengali and Malayalam cinema, the number and influence of these films increased after the emergence of director Shyam Benegal's pioneering New Wave cinema in Hindi (*Ankur*, The Seedling, 1974), coupled with intermittent bursts in Odia, Assamese, Kannada and, most recently, English (Hood 2000; Rajadhyaksha and Willeheim 1994). For categorisation purposes, these films will be called 'parallel cinema' in the book, and not art-house as they are often referred to, in agreement with actor–scriptwriter Salim Khan's argument that since filmmaking is an artistic exercise, all cinema is art, with the sole distinction being whether it represents good or bad art[7].

These artistic and commercial categorisations did not always exist in Indian cinema discourses or film criticism. For instance, many acclaimed films from the Golden Era of Hindi Cinema (1950s–1960s) can be considered as forbearers of both subsequent popular and parallel cinema making styles. The classics of that era, such as *Mother India* (1957) and *Mughal-e-Azam* (The Great Mughal, 1960), which Salim Khan refers to as art films, were commercial blockbusters featuring most of the popular cinema attributes listed above. Also, many New Wave cinema directors of the 1970s and 1980s, after making their mark through films in the parallel cinema category, having received critical acclaim and with access to larger funds, shifted to the popular style of filmmaking in the 1990s in order to take their films to a bigger audience. Finally, the post-2000 entry of blockbuster Indian films like *Lagaan* (Taxation, 2001), *Kabhi Khushi Kabhie Gham* (Sometimes Happiness, Sometimes Sadness, 2001) and *Devdas* (2002) in non-South-Asian diaspora spaces in Europe, and *Muthu* (1995) in Japan, has been in their art-house, mini-theatre and/or camp circuits. Films regarded as popular in India, when selected for screening in first-world international film festivals like Cannes, Toronto and the like, were received as art-house cinema (Brunow 2010; Sriniwas 2010). The borrowed categories of aesthetic divisions inspired by Euro-American distribution are thus incomplete and non-absolute. The accompanying appreciation parameters that have come to define filmmaking styles within Indian cinema have been consistently rejected by most of its films. Some of the finest actors have frequently acted in both these forms to equal acclaim and great filmmakers and stars have worked alongside them, kindling Indian cinema's current global spread. Actor turned acting guru Anupam Kher states, 'Just because realistic acting looks fascinating, it does not mean that the acting done by mainstream actors in India is easy to do. It is easy to simplify and do realistic acting. It is very difficult to do dramatised acting' (2015). If Raj Kapoor's socialist melodramas made Indian cinema popular in the erstwhile USSR, China and Eastern Europe in the 1950s, Amitabh Bachchan's angry young man *masala* films widened its appeal in the Middle East and Africa in the 1970s. Shah Rukh Khan's post 1990s' aspirational candyfloss romances have inspired cultural engagements like Bollywood-style dance classes in Europe beyond its South Asian diaspora (Dudrah, Mader and Fuchs 2015). For 'holding the largest audience from diverse places and cultural backgrounds in the contemporary world of cinema' (Mader 2010), Khan was the subject of a multidisciplinary international conference organised by the University of Vienna in 2010 focussing on the contribution of his stardom to the increasing popularity of Hindi cinema post-2000 among mainstream Euro-American audiences. His 2015 bestowal of an honorary doctorate by the University of Edinburgh, a first for an Indian cinema star, is a big step forward in the acknowledgement of the discipline of film studies and the place of Indian cinema within it.

Traditionally, Indian cinema had been accessed through unofficial channels of distribution across the globe. Since 2000, it has increasingly been distributed in Europe and the United States with Western audiences getting an opportunity to seriously engage with it in art-house and mainstream cinema spaces with subtitles. The reception has not always been one of uncontested enthusiasm, but the playing field at least is more even than before. Indian film and music critic Rajiv Vijayakar states:

> If you are giving somebody a burger everyday, he is going to eat only the burger, until you feed him something else like a *biryani*. Even then, he would not be able to make a choice between whether his burger was better or the *biryani*. He may not even like the *biryani* instantly. He has to keep eating the *biryani*, until he develops a taste for it and only then will he be able to decide whether they are both equally good or which one is better (2012).

Around the beginning of the first millennium C.E., Bharata *muni* in the ancient Indian dramatic textbook of the *Natyashastra* had also used a similar taste and reception analogy to frame one of the most seminal ideas of Indian aesthetic appreciation—the *rasa* theory of aesthetic taste and appreciation. This theory will provide the focus in this book as the latter investigates the former's use and viability for the analysis and appreciation of Indian cinema.

The *Natyashastra*: Essence and Origin

The origin of the *rasa* idea, after two millennia of scholarly deliberations by critics and Sanskritists in India and the West, can be traced back to the 2000-year-old textbook of Sanskrit drama, the *Natyashastra*. It is considered to be the foundation of Sanskrit drama and the first most exhaustive, comprehensive and encyclopaedic practical manual of dance, acting, music and theatre in India. Deliberating at length on stagecraft and the performing arts, it describes and categorises the different kinds of drama, acting and direction, along with the varied aesthetic experiences of the audience. According to South India's prominent 20th century dramatist–scholar Adya Rangacharya, *Natyashastra*'s creator, Bharata *muni*, 'has not only defined for us characters on the stage, but even characters in the auditorium (i.e. the audience)' (1966: 73), based on the nature of their reactions to onstage acts. Schwartz sums up its scope and significance as 'part theatrical manual, part philosophy of aesthetics, part mythological history, part theology' (2004: 12) and part psychological in its 'analysis of the mental states of spectators watching a performance, and the nature and effects of the pleasures derived thereof by them' (Raghavan 1940: 73–81).

Though the *Natyashastra* is attributed to the mythical Bharata *muni*, art historian Kapila Vatsyayan acknowledges a counter view that the name could have been an acronym for the three syllables—Bha (*Bhava* or mood/state of mind), Ra (*Raga* or melody) and Ta (*Tala* or rhythmic timing)—essential for any artistic performance (2007: 6). This acronym of 'Bharata' then possibly went on to become a common name for sages, dramatists or actors working over a couple of centuries to formulate the foundational principles of Sanskrit dramaturgy that have come to define the *Natyashastra* in its present form. However, when the name

Bharata is used in this book, it is intended to refer to an individual and not as an abstract term.

The *Natyashastra* compendium of dramatic lore, in accordance with the traditional Indian practice of prescribing the authorship of any ancient work (e.g., the Vedas) to the gods or sages of yore, in its first chapter ascribes its authorship to Lord Brahma, the creator in Hinduism's Trinity of Gods that feature Lord Vishnu as the preserver and Lord Shiva as the destroyer. Its genesis was in response to a request by the gods to create something that would educate and inspire its readers about the nature and behaviour of the world by imitating its conduct through various stages and situations, to be rendered by physical and other forms of acting, by depictions communicating the emotions of the entire triple world[8]. Since the work was intended to be entertaining and enlightening at the same time, its presentation had to be pleasing to the eyes and the ears so that it was accessible to all, from the evolved immortals of the celestial world to the demons of the netherworld, along with the entire diversity of the human race in between. As a result, Brahma composed the fifth Veda, known as the *Natyaveda*[9], incorporating elements from all the arts, sciences and ethics. He took 'the words from *Rig Veda*, music from *Sam Veda*, movements and make-up from *Yajur Veda* and emotional acting from *Atharva Veda*' (NS 1.17–18; Rangacharya 1966: 1) and gave it to Bharata[10], and his sons or pupils to practice and perform the lessons of a good, civilised and moral life for the entertainment and enlightenment of all. Dance already existed when drama was created, with Shiva being the acknowledged god of dance. However, when Shiva saw the first performance of drama, though appreciative of Brahma's creation and the efforts of Bharata and his actors, he thought it was too plain. Brahma then asked Bharata to take inspiration from Shiva's *tandava* (cosmic dance) and created the *apsaras* (celestial nymphs) to perform them with grace (*lasya*), since he felt that no male other than Shiva could perform the graceful aspects of his *tandava* as elegantly. Experiencing the aesthetic appeal of Shiva's dance movements, Bharata incorporated dance to beautify drama and transformed it from a *suddha purvaranga* (simple drama display) to a *chitra purvaranga* (beautiful dramatic presentation), thus giving birth to the concept and realisation of the first operatic Sanskrit dance drama (Raghavan 1940: 2–4).

Within the fable on the origin of drama is embedded a significant guiding principle that has become the raison d'être of all Indian performance forms including cinema: the integral role of music and dance in any dramatic performance. According to Srijit Mukherji:

> Bharata's *Natyashastra* tells of a storytelling tradition through music and songs, which is why I am personally unapologetic about using music and songs to take my story forward. The West might have denounced and forsaken the musical genre in the 1940s and 1950s, but for me, music and songs is as much of a tool as a trolley shot, a jump cut or a particular sound design. We tend to stress unnecessarily on a song or music being a song or a music when it could very well be another cinematic tool for the storyteller, which it is for me, and which it has been for the Indian sub-continent. That is why the use of music has been one of the biggest unifying factors for Indian cinema (2015).

This should not be confused with an unequivocal recommendation of the musical format without any reservations. Bharata warns in his review of *Amrutamanthan* (The Churning of the Ocean), the first ever drama performed in the mythical land of the gods, that music and dance should not be overdone or else both the performers and the viewers will feel the strain (Raghavan 1940: 3). This divine claim to its origins endorses the influential and divine status of the *Natyashastra* in the Indian aesthetic scheme, but it does not exactly aid in ascertaining a credible upper limit to the date of its authorship. The broad consensus amongst modern (post-1900) commentaries is that it existed before the beginning of the Christian era. Bharatanatyam dancer and scholar Padma Subrahmanyam contends that the *Natyashastra* is pre-Ramayana, since there is no mention of its hero, Rama, in the drama treatise (2010: 21). Its lower limit is a more assured, pre-Kalidasa, pre-450 CE period. This has been endorsed by the eminent Sanskrit dramatist himself in his reference to the Bharata legend and in his attribution to the sage of the idea of the eight *rasas* in his 5th century CE romantic drama *Vikramorvasi* (Urvashi Won by Valour, Kane 1994: 43).

The Theory of *Rasa*

One of the most intriguing aspects of Bharata's exhaustive treatise is its theory of aesthetics, developed by later commentators into the Sanskrit drama's influential *rasa* theory. Though *rasa* has many literal meanings such as taste, extract, juice, essence and ultimately bliss, in the *Natyashastra* it is used to signify the essence of an emotion as a sentiment or the final emotional state of 'relish/satisfaction/reaction/aesthetic experience'[11] achieved by a spectator while watching and experiencing a performing art. According to Kane, 'This also is the most seminal contributor principle, which when extensively deliberated removes all perceived notions of neglect of [any proper] aesthetic appreciation in Indian drama traditions given its [obvious] fondness for ethics and frequently enveloping frameworks of metaphysical speculation' (1994: 8).

According to Bharata, *rasa* is born in the union of the play with the performance of the actors and is to be realised by the audience. Its articulation by Bharata, however, suffers from the established predilection of ancient writers for concise definitions and summary explanations, followed by limited illustrative articulation. This ensures that later commentaries are valuable sources for analysis and interpretation. Since the *Natyashastra*'s prime focus is dramatic representation and not the *rasa*—which is first described in the context of drama as a means to appreciating dramatic art and not vice versa—Bharata dedicates only two (chapters six and seven) of its 36 chapters to a summary listing and description of the *rasas* and their constituting *bhavas* (Rangacharya 2010). Scholars like Subrahmanyam have opted to view this only summary introduction to *rasa* as an indicator of the fact that the concept was already in practice at the time of the writing of the *Natyashastra*, with its practitioners being aware of its significance in any performative form. By listing it at the beginning of his treatise, Bharata was only reinforcing its already acknowledged pre-eminence before deliberating at length on other lesser-known aspects and attributes of the dramatic art.

The *Natyashastra* in Review: Commentators and Commentaries

The *rasa* idea, however, has been consistently evolving and extensively engaged with to become Sanskrit drama's most debated subject, to be acknowledged, used and/or challenged by dramatists, writers and critics for over two millennia for various interpretations[12]. Evolving insights within subsequently emerging Indian philosophical systems have further shaped and influenced the application and understanding of the *rasa* concept in aesthetic appreciation (Vatsayan 2007). This can be attributed to two reasons: first, Bharata's cursory enunciation of a *sutra* of immense psychological insight and significance that immediately demanded a clearer articulation by its every subsequent commentator; and the second, the unquestioned acknowledgement by all commentators of the *Natyashastra* on the status of the *rasa* concept as a cornerstone of aesthetic appreciation. They systematically worked towards converting it into a fundamental aesthetic conception for all Indian art forms, starting with drama and dance, followed by poetry, literature and now cinema. There are many treatises expounding the theory of *rasa*, but this book will situate its understanding and interpretation of the concept to its most authoritative source, the *Natyashastra* (as translated by Ghosh in 1961 and Rangacharya in 2010) and its most influential commentary by 11th century CE Kashmir philosopher and aesthetician Abhinavagupta, titled *Abhinavabharati* (as discussed by Gnoli in 1956). The *Abhinavabharati*, according to all its subsequent medieval commentators and modern Sanskrit scholars, marks the highest critical and intellectual achievement in the history of the evolution of the '*Rasa* School of appreciation' (Sarma 1994: 6–8). It is the only source that reviews the lost original works and views of most pre-10th century commentators of the *Natyashastra* like Bhattalolata, Sankuka, Bhattanayaka and Bhattatauta (Vatsayan 2007: 138). Abhinavagupta, also wrote an influential commentary on Anandavardhana's pathbreaking '*dhvani* theory'[13] (*Dhvanyaloka* 9th century CE), which suggested that the dominant *rasa* of an aesthetic work could also be located the essence of its creator's aesthetic suggestion.

Bharata's text comes first since it is universally accepted as the generator of the concept of *rasa* and provides the earliest and most fundamental, if succinct, template, based on which all subsequent discussions and commentaries were made. However, *Abhinavabharati* lent a strong metaphysical foundation to the *rasa* concept, making it an accepted truism in Sanskrit poetics, 'never to be set aside by rival systems and improved only in detail by later speculations' (De 1959: 177). Gnoli highlights its subsequent rising status in *rasa* criticism stating:

> Abhinavagupta's conclusions in *Abhinavabharati* with rare exceptions were accepted by all later Indian aesthetic thinkers to be unanimously considered the most important text in the whole of Indian aesthetic thought (1956: xiii).

Lal and Nandy acknowledge its influence on all Indian theatrical forms, the predecessors of their respective regional language cinemas, observing that:

> His [Abhinavagupta] framework has, over the centuries, been in dialogue with the tacit aesthetic frames that inform the various modes of popular self-expression, ranging from *Kathakali* (South India) to *Ramleela* (North India) to *Jatra* (East India) (2006: xvi).

Moreover, after Abhinavagupta, there was a major lull in the analysis of Bharata's *rasa sutra* in terms of the addition of any radical new contribution or theoretical shift. Jagannatha's late 17th century *Rasagangadhara*, the last major medieval century interpreter of Bharata's *rasa sutra*, also indicates the strong influence of Abhinavagupta, who is paraphrased in many parts of the text (Sarma 1994: 81). Formal articulations on Sanskrit drama principles in the English language did not commence until the mid-19th century appearance of English translations of ancient Sanskrit dramas and the occasional surfacing of manuscripts of the *Natyashastra*, starting with William Jones' first translation in English of Kalidasa's *Abhijnana Shakuntalam* (The Recognition of Shakuntala, 5th century CE) in 1789 and followed by

H. H. Wilson's *Theatre of The Hindus* (1826). A critical re-engagement with Sanskrit aesthetics in the modern era happened only after M. Hiriyanna's pioneering and imaginative *Art Experience* (1919), which has since guided a generation of 20th century scholars (Ghosh, Pandey, Gnoli, Krishnamoorthy, Raghavan, Sankaran, Rangacharya, Gerow and others) to 'carry his observations as a talisman for investigating the contours of Indian aesthetics' (Vatsayan 1997: xii). Other contributions included the updated 20th century commentaries and translations of the *Natyashastra*[14], *Dhvanyaloka* and *Abhinavabharati*, and their interpretations of the *rasa* theory. Highlighting the paradigm shifting status and influence of Hiriyanna's work, art historian Kapila Vatsayan observes:

> No longer is it necessary to understand Indian aesthetics by referring to Plato, Aristotle and others. Nor is it any longer necessary to prove that there is a long and most sophisticated philosophic discourse on aesthetics (Vatsayan 1997: xii).

K.C. Pandey's *Comparative Aesthetics 1 & 2* (1950) constitutes one of the first notable post-independence compendium commentaries. While discussing the *Abhinavabharati* in the background of the history of Indian aesthetic thought, Pandey's work studies the problems in aesthetics from the viewpoints of different dramaturgists and poets in the background of Eastern (Sanskrit drama) and Western (Aristotle's Poetics) thought. A comparative analysis of the various commentators of the *rasa* school is also the focus of Kane, De and Krishnamoorthy's critical engagement with the evolution of the *rasa* theory. Kane's *The History of Sanskrit Poetics* (1994) provides a chronological overview of the commentaries on the *Natyashastra*. Its approach, however, is more encyclopaedic and informative than argumentative. S.K. De's *Some Problems of Sanskrit Poetics* (1959) is fairly argumentative; yet, it locates a decline in the study of Indian aesthetics in the post-Abhinavagupta period to the confusion of its medieval commentators. From the many rules, canons, meandering divisions and sub-divisions of the *Natyashastra* and its commentaries, as discussed by Kane and De, K. Krishnamoorthy's *Essays in Sanskrit Criticism* (1974) narrows down the *rasa* doctrines and points of view to those relevant to contemporary aesthetic criticism. Edwin Gerow's *Indian Poetics* (1977), a seminal overview on Indian aesthetics by a Western scholar, engages the relevant themes of the *rasa* theory in an aesthetic analysis in the context of the 20th century commentaries of interpreters such as Gnoli, De, Kane, Krishnamoorthy and others. Gerow, in *Rasa and Katharsis* (2002), compares attitudes of appreciation between Sanskrit and Western drama concepts and explores the translatability of the Indian *rasa* aesthetic to film analysis. He tests the applicability of its categories for film classification by using a limited sample of Indian and European art house films. He does this by noting a film's dominant themes before attempting to locate their closest *rasa* counterpart from the *navarasas*. These works have helped broaden our understanding of the canon of Indian aesthetics at the deepest level, enabling us to explore and expand the scope of their universal ideas and ideals to newer artistic mediums like cinema.

This book refers to Gnoli's *Aesthetic Experience According to Abhinavagupta* (1956) as its primary reference text for reading the *Abhinavabharati*, along with the English translations of the *Natyashastra* by M. M. Ghosh and Adya Rangacharya. Apart from making a strong case for the contemporary relevance of the *rasa* interpretations of Abhinavagupta, they argue for the study of Indian aesthetics on its own terms, instead of locating it within comparable Western theatre frameworks.

Drama to Cinema: A Tradition in Perpetuity

These ancient yet still relevant guidelines were appropriated by Indian cinema—the latest in India's vibrant tradition of fine arts—and evolved into unique on-screen expositions. Thus, Indian filmmakers unconsciously became the heirs of great Sanskrit dramatists[15]. Since early Indian cinema grew out of theatre, 'the producers and directors were always conscious of the spectator as audience-in-performance aware of the range of *rasas* built into the structure of the play' (Mishra 2009: 441). For instance, the almost mandatory format of interspersing of songs in film narratives has been conclusively sourced 'to the Indian tradition of music and song as part of dramatic expression going back two thousand years to the Sanskrit theatre' (Morcom 2007: 3). According to American Indologist Philip Lutgendorf:

> The *Natyashastra* format of alternately spoken and sung performance, which gave great emphasis to poetic and musical expression of emotion, survived the demise of Sanskrit drama towards the end of the first millennium [following the Mughal invasion] and became characteristic of a range of regional folk dramatic forms using vernacular languages; it was transferred to the urban proscenium stage by the theatre troupes of the nineteenth century, [and] after the introduction of film sound to India in 1931, [became] the standard format for commercial cinema (2011: 235).

Sanskrit drama lost royal patronage in most of North India post 1100 CE, given the different artistic sensibilities of its new Muslim rulers, but it did not vanish from the Indian landscape. Dramas and commentaries continued to be written in Sanskrit. But they were not performed as often as during the Gupta age or the era of Harshavardhana; this did lend credence to claims that Sanskrit theatre was actually dying in the medieval period of Indian history (Barnouw–Krishnaswamy 1980: 70–71). The more modest, adaptable, travelling avatars like the *jatras* of Bengal, *nautanki* of North India, *terukkuttu* of the South and other regional and folk drama forms that needed no stage or state patronage continued to thrive in the rural space. Looked down upon by the educated and not preserved in any written form until the late 19th century CE, these forms of drama enjoyed a much more active life in relatively modest venues through constant enactment, unlike Sanskrit dramas. The latter were constantly written and commented upon but were seldom enacted and were primarily limited to the private theatre of local maharajahs, nawabs (e.g., the 19th century revival of Kathak under Wajid Ali Shah of Oudh) and joint family zamindar *baris* of cultured aristocracy like the Tagore family of Bengal.

Local saints of the 14th–17th century Bhakti movement[16] (Ravidas, Sankardev, Chaitanya Mahaprabhu, Vallabhacharya, Surdas, Mirabai, Kabir, Tulsidas, Tukaram, Dhyaneshwar, Namdev, etc.) contributed to the flow of dance and music through devotional songs (e.g., Chaitanya's *kirtans* and Lalan Fakir's *baul* songs in Bengal) as their preferred mode of discourse and worship. The Islamicate[17] traditions of *dastaans* (epic Persian adventure sagas like *The Arabian Nights*) and the performance traditions of Sufi mysticism further amalgamated with North India's *katha* style of performance narrations by *Kathakas* (bards cum storytellers) to give birth to two of the Indian subcontinent's most loved medieval century cultural forms that still enrich and inspire its filmic dance (*Kathak/Natwari*) and music, especially the light classical song genre of *ghazals* and *qawwalis*.

The Sanskrit theatre traditions meanwhile continued to be patronised in the Hindu kingdoms of the East—e.g., the Ganga dynasty's introduction of the performance of Jayadeva's *Gita Govinda* as a ritual service in Puri's Jagannath Temple in Odisha from the 13th century (Dhar 2007: 43–45)—and in South India—e.g., Kerala's *Koodiyattam* and *Kathakali* temple dance forms—where it remained relatively insulated from the Muslim cultural invasion. This can be evidenced in the locating of most of the 19th century manuscript discoveries of the *Natyashastra* in South India apart from the momentous discovery of the first manuscript of the Kashmiri Abhinavagupta's *Abhinavabharati* in modern times in Kerala (Vatsayan 1996). Art historian Kapila Vatsayan has recorded the discovery of various manuscripts of the *Natyashastra*'s root text in different parts of the subcontinent from Nepal to Bengal and Kashmir to Kerala in vernacular scripts like Newari, Devanagari, Grantha, Tamil and Malayalam between the 11th and 18th centuries. She argues that the rest of India too participated in the continuing transmission of the *Natyashastra* 'as a living vibrant tradition where the practice and performance and its crucial discourse were complementary and mutually supportive' (Vatsayan 2007: 36–37). Scholar of South Asian theatre history Kathryn Hansen locates a consciousness about Sanskrit drama traditions in the Indian subcontinent's performative tradition, noting that 'most of the generic labels for folk theatre in North India like *mancha, lila, jatra* and the like are derived from words meaning stage, play, show, processional theatre' with an element of spectacle, which was integral to some of the greatest Sanskrit dramas[18]. The *Jashn* of Kashmir, *Gitinatya* of Odisha, *Swang* of Punjab, *Kathakali* of Kerala and *Gandharva/Sangeet natak* of Maharashtra also share a similar generic nature of being staged performances with theatrical acting.

The *Natyashastra*'s prescriptions of theatrical art as practised in the times of Kalidasa thus had 'remained an invisible law' (Bowers 1969: 18) that bequeathed to the Indian sound film of 1931 'a river of music that had flowed through unbroken millennia of dramatic tradition' (Barnouw–Krishnaswamy 1980: 72). Indian filmmakers also introduced songs to counter the influence and appeal of foreign-made films. This eventually became a successful survival strategy; it made Indian cinema's song-interspersed format a signature attribute of its cinematic storytelling that has come to define its uniqueness amongst world cinema. Any subsequent experimental or sustained rejection of this song-and-dance format has failed with the Indian audience, for being 'foreign or un-Indian'[19] like the Hindi parallel cinema movement that had peaked in the 1970s and withered away by the 1980s. According to Om Puri, one of the movement's influential lead actors:

> Indian art house [parallel] cinema directors made one mistake. They eschewed the song-and-dance format because they felt it was below them. I feel that they should not have resisted the format because we Indians have always used music to communicate – be it in the street theatre, *nautankis*, and *jatras*. They should not have hesitated to use music as a tool to make the [Indian] audience understand and connect with their films (2006: 14).

Puri's observation contradicts the myopic limiting of the origins of Indian cinema's song-and-dance spectacles by many Indian film theorists exclusively to Bombay's Parsi theatre of the 19th and early 20th century. This oversimplified notion of apportioning the history of all Indian melodrama to Parsi theatre is 'akin to finding the origins of tragedy in Europe, erroneously, in its 19th century-opera, for instance' (Hogan 2008: 41). Even if one assumed this view to be true, then how would one explain the similar *rasa*-evoking attributes in the cinemas of South India, Bengal or Odisha, which did not have the specific Parsi theatre backdrop? The narrative style of these language cinemas was inspired by their region's respective folk theatres, as discussed above. Senior Bollywood critic and film writer Ali Peter John explains:

> Only Parsi theatre cannot be the mother influence of all Indian or Hindi cinema. It only appealed to makers in Bombay and that too just a handful of them like those educated in English. Parsi theatre was the only source of entertainment at that time for the elite so whatever they saw there, those who did not have original ideas copied them and put them on screen. The whole group of Golden Age [of Hindi cinema] filmmakers like Bimal Roy, and others, who brought about the idea of social relevance in Hindi films, worked independent of any Parsi theatre influence. There is something charmingly Indian about even his [Bimal Roy] most commercial film *Madhumati* [1958]. Not everyone working in the Hindi film industry in the 1950s-70s was educated, but they were aware of the idea of the *navarasas*. In the south, the foundation and knowledge of the *Natyashastra* was much stronger as South cinema is theatre... (2012).

Thus, what arguably works for the proponents of Indian cinema's Parsi theatre traditions is their sole focus on Mumbai's Hindi cinema, whose early adventure films and Shakespeare-based plays did gain inspiration from Parsi theatre's song-interspersed presentations. Writers and actors moving from Mumbai's declining Parsi theatres to films, forming the new creative industry's initial talent pool, brought the influence of their acting backgrounds to the new medium. Moreover, three of the silent cinema and early sound era Mumbai studios, Imperial, Minerva and Wadia Movietone, were owned by Parsis. Stating the usage of 'Parsi theatre' as a separate drama categorising terminology to be a misnomer, veteran Bollywood director Lekh Tandon explains:

> The term, Parsi theatre, should not be construed as a separate theatre category. The Parsis only put in their money and managed the administration of these theatre productions. Once these gained in popularity and turned into successful theatre ventures because of the honesty, integrity, business acumen and entrepreneurship skills of their Parsi owners and managers, they started to be called as Parsi theatres by their audience and reviewers, primarily for them being owned by members of the Parsi community. But the source of many of their performances and themes still happened to be Sanskrit plays and Indian epics (2015).

However, two of Hindi cinema's other early film genres, mythologicals and devotionals, in their performance and presentation styles were closer to then influential and successful Marathi musical theatre led by Bal Gandharva. Popularly known as the *Gandharva* era when boys essayed female parts on stage, these musicals, both in their staging and choice of subjects, adhered to tenets of Sanskrit dramaturgy and were designed to evoke *rasa* realisation amongst fans or *rasikas* (Jadhav 2011). Their acting style, stories, costumes and set design, according to Marathi cinema director and maker of *Harishchandrachi Factory* (Harischandra's Factory, 2009), Paresh Mokashi, 'were imitated by Dadasaheb Phalke when he started making India's first indigenous feature film, *Raja Harishchandra* (1913)' (2010) and 'by his successors from the silent movies to the early talkies' (Rangoonwalla 1979: 12).

The *Natyashastra* postulates that an ideal play should evoke all the principal *rasas*—the more the better, since a drama, and likewise a film, is meant for and seen by persons of different tastes—perhaps best explains the distinctive *masala*[20] nature of most Indian films and their intended audience's ease in relating to its format of multiple emotions, genres, plot and mood transitions. And even where one *rasa* is dominant, Malayalam cinema writer–director Anjali Menon observes, 'Other *rasas* may enter and leave. That openness in our dramatic structure, which we see in all our movies is a bequest of India's theatre traditions. So, one needs to understand what Indian theatre was all about to understand why our films are the way they are' (2015). A damning criticism often voiced by Indian viewers is that a film lacks the anticipated range of emotions[21]. This differentiation in expectation from a cinematic narration predictably baffles Western film critics, who are uninitiated and unaware of the *rasa* theory and its aesthetic anticipation from a performance[22]. Western films are often referred to as cold and 'no close copy of Hollywood has ever been a hit' (Thomas 1995: 162). According to scriptwriter Anjum Rajabali:

> Hollywood films are considered "dry" here. That is, not enough emotions. When you Indianise a [Western/Hollywood] subject, you add emotions. Lots of them. Feelings like love, hate, sacrifice, or revenge, pangs of separation. But, in a Hollywood film if a hero and

> heroine were to separate and you had five scenes underlying how they are suffering because they miss each other, people might find that soppy and corny too. Not here. Our mythology, our poetry, our literature is full of situations where lovers pine for each other. Take the *Mahabharat* and you will see what I mean. Every situation has feelings, dilemmas, other kinds of conflicts, confrontations, sacrifices, moral issues coming up all the time, etc (Ganti 2004: 183).

This centrality of emotion to the Indian arts, including Indian cinema, can be directly traced to the centrality of the *rasa* theory in Indian tradition. 'Just as Aristotelian ideas of unity and Romantic theories of expression have influenced European drama and films, the theory of *rasa* has had effects across Indian arts' (Hogan 2008: 3). Yet, using *rasa* as a tool of aesthetic analysis for evaluating a film's structure, purpose, acting achievements and artistic merit remains a rare undertaking in mainstream film reviews, and only a handful of films have been brought under its ambit in academic engagement.

Love, Disgust and Wonder: The Shifting Affections in Indian Film Criticism

The beginning of the study of Indian cinema as a subject of critical engagement almost coincides with the release of *Raja Harishchandra* (King Harishchandra) in the early 20th century. Its director, the now acknowledged 'premier pioneer' and 'father of Indian cinema' Dadasaheb Phalke, was an avid critic and commentator of the cinema of his day and released a *Making of Raja Harishchandra* featurette after his film. The featurette and his writings focused on educating his viewers about the new medium and its possibilities. His precedent was actively followed and extended to a critical analysis of the emerging creative medium and its signature narration attributes by many of his successors. These include Bengali auteur Satyajit Ray[23], Bollywood showman Subhash Ghai, litterateur and Tamil cinema script writer M. Karunanidhi, whose writings on and off the screen strengthened the mid-20th century Dravida language and identity movement, and Anurag Kashyap, one of the most influential filmmakers from the post-2000 independent Indian cinema movement. Outside the filmmaking fraternity, the first burst of serious film criticism on Indian cinema in English is attributed to the caustic and critical Baburao Patel, whose *Filmindia* (one of the earliest film magazines published in India in the 1930s) spared none. He went from being a filmmaker and an editor of note to an elected member of the Indian Parliament. According to writer–playwright Saadat Hasan Manto:

> Baburao wrote with eloquence and power. He had a sharp and inimitable sense of humour, often barbed. There was a tough-guy assertiveness about his writing. He could also be venomous in a way, which no other writer of English in India has ever been able to match (Manto 2003: 123).

India's oldest surviving film magazine, The Times of India group's *Filmfare*, and The Indian Express group's film weekly, *Screen*, while cultivating the first dedicated stream of film journalists, further enriched the literature on Indian cinema writing in English. Their archives remain one of the most valuable documents of the Golden Years of Indian cinema, when, as senior journalist Raju Bharatan recalls, 'a lot more was written on cinema than its celebrities' (Dubey 2006). *Stardust, Star & Style, Cine Blitz, Movie* and *g* were some of the notable film magazine additions in the 1970s and 1980s that went beyond their fanzine premise to periodically print critical reviews of seminal films of the day and offer an appreciation of the craft of its directors and actors. The scope for film journalism widened in popular media with the growth and maturing of the film industry and the emergence of review columns in mainstream dailies as regular serious engagements with cinema writing. Most of the above-mentioned magazines also started increasing the breadth of their reviews and commentary on cinema to include analytical pieces on the best, the influential and the challenging. Baburao's influence and success, though not repeated, did set a template for writing on mainstream popular cinema with acerbic potshots by most elite/upper-middle class and/or anglophone Indian critics[24]. This can be evinced in the critiques of the immediate successors of Baburao's writing legacy, film historian Firoze Rangoonwalla or Marxist critic Chidananda Das Gupta, with a preferential bias in favour of reviewing all Indian films using the canons of Euro-American film theories, models and notions of review. This was affected by either 'apologetically'[25] playing down or 'ironically'[26] ignoring the Indian aesthetic traditions that had been shaping and defining Indian cinema narratives since its inception.

A major factor in the relegation to the background of any serious engagement with the indigenous aesthetics of Indian cinema was the tremendous international reception and celebration of Satyajit Ray's Bengali cinema debut with his films in the Apu Trilogy (1955–59). Those films also marked the first serious academic engagement in the West with any form of Indian cinema and its filmmakers. This engagement went beyond its status as an exotic or 'incomprehensible other' as it drew plaudits from both emerging film theorists (e.g., Andre Bazin) and globally acclaimed directors like Akira Kurosawa and Martin Scorsese. The possibility of reviewing Indian cinema as a worthy equal alongside First-World, European and/or Hollywood cinema made both its governmental sponsors and mainstream film critics campaign for more Ray-like, realistic cinema that conformed to Western canons of filmmaking. It emerged by positioning itself as a parallel entity distinct from private/studio-made mainstream or popular cinema. While it is unfair to assume that Ray and his cinematic successors did not adhere to the aesthetic traditions of Indian cinema, their films did nonetheless look and feel less melodramatic than the mainstream popular Indian cinema coming out of Mumbai (then Bombay)/Bollywood. Moreover, the volumes of popular cinema's formulaic productions diffused the worth of many of its auteur filmmakers and made sweeping generalisations, like categorising all Indian cinema within a generic title of 'Bollywood'; an easy and arguably lazy way to study them within First-World cinema discourses. By using dominant canons of Western filmmaking often in 'convenient and deliberate ignorance'[27] with their inherent aesthetic standards, Indian popular cinema was, whenever 'taken seriously'[28], subjected to an 'impertinent and unfair criticism'[29]. As a consequence, any film in the popular format was declared inferior irrespective of its merits, as were, by extension, its unique culture and performance-tradition-specific attributes. These came to be reviewed as faults to many—'loose and fragmented narratives, realism irrelevant, psychological characterisation disregarding, elaborate dialogue prizing, music essential, spectacle privileging, audience emotion exciting fare' (Thomas 1995: 162)—in comparison with the restrained and realism prizing Euro-American narrative models. According to director Srijit Mukherji:

> If you say that only a particular kind of cinema is cinema and make a distinction between high and low art, and in the same breadth you are condemning the caste system, which has been plaguing our country for years, you are somewhere not being intellectually consistent. For instance, when you condemn a religion or a philosophical thought which says that all other philosophies are wrong or false and it is the only true and one way of reaching God as a fundamentalist view, and at the same time you are applying a similar thought process in cinema, and calling only a kind of cinema is "cinema" and the rest are not, then you are demeaning the art and trivialising a pursuit which integrates the best bits of science, art and commerce to come together in one unified creative form... What I have experienced in my personal journey until now is that there exists this high-brow intellectual orthodoxy regarding certain canons of Western mode of treating cinema, the parameters of which obviously do not apply in the Indian context. Yet, year after year we tend to evaluate or judge a lot of Indian cinema based on those parameters. The parallels are fascinating if you look at the definition of orientalism by Edward Said, you will understand that much of the intellectual writing is the result of a political position of these people in a very post-colonial paradigm. Hence, these obviously are intellectually suspect, as they look down upon and patronise basically a lot of creative output from this part of the world based on notions, parameters and yardsticks set by the West. We need to formalise and recognise the fact that the West does not evaluate a Harry Potter movie on the same parameters as a *Schindler's List* [1993]. But unfortunately, when it comes to this part of the world, we start putting everything on the same plane and then denouncing one and uplifting the other, which is pathetic (2015).

Western film criticism, taking its cue from this defensive apology and the 'guilty pleasure' taken in popular Indian cinema as expressed by its own critics, especially in the English language media, either indulgently exoticised popular Indian cinema as baroque and pastiche or superficially dismissed it as simplistic, escapist, populist, massy (mass-market), low-brow cinema, comparing it unfavourably with its more 'confirming parallel cinema'[30]. According to British critic, former Edinburgh International Film Festival director and documentary filmmaker Mark Cousins:

> Many [critics/filmmakers] in America and France feel that because they sort of invented cinema, they kind of own it in some way. It is hard for the Western world to believe that other countries and continents have not only taken it all [of cinema] but run with it very well. It also has a real lack of interest, a blindness, a blinkered attitude towards other cinemas… Indian cinema kind of blossomed after independence. Indian cinema of the 1950s, 60s and 70s was a riot of ideas and dramas. But because Britain and the West had cut India off in terms of its expectations, and in terms of its curiosity, it then sort of did not want to know about the triumph of the Hindi cinema. I would also argue that Western film culture and Indian film culture were out-of-phase in some way. By the time of the great Bollywood films of the 1970s, we had in the West, Martin Scorsese, Francis Ford Coppola, and the like. Their films were also about the angry young man just as *Zanjeer* [Chains, 1973] was, or *Sholay* [Embers, 1975] was. But we were so fascinated by our angry young man, our Robert DeNiro that we did not pay any attention to [Amitabh] Bachchan [also known as Indian cinema's angry young man] (2014).

John W. Hood in *Essential Mystery: The Major Filmmakers of Indian Art Cinema* (2000) articulates this biased mindset of considering India's parallel category of cinema to be aesthetically superior to its popular counterpart when he lists the former category's complete dissociation and playing down of popular Indian cinema attributes to be its greatest virtue and value. The cinema of Ray and his successors like Ritwik Ghatak, Mrinal Sen, Adoor Gopalakrishnan, Shyam Benegal, G. Aravindan, Buddhadeb Dasgupta, Govind Nihalani and Ketan Mehta is, according to Hood, 'free to experiment with form, style, structure and more polished actors given to greater realism, in the absence of stereotypical roles' (2000: 5). The films of now unanimously acclaimed popular Hindi cinema auteurs like Guru Dutt, Bimal Roy, Raj Kapoor and Mehboob Khan are dismissed by Hood with a cursory acknowledgment of their having 'a notable degree of artistic sophistication' (2000: 3). Under Hood's aesthetic parameters, these acclaimed popular Indian filmmakers still remain inferior to their more artistic parallel cinema counterparts, who shoot with 'a more widely developed aesthetic sense like restrained pace, no or fewer song and dance, short narratives, no melodrama' (2000: 3–8). Hence, it is not surprising that in contrast to a plethora of writings on Indian parallel cinema filmmakers since the 1970s, one finds only occasional scholarly engagement in the book with the auteurship of Raj Kapoor, Bimal Roy, Mehboob Khan, Guru Dutt or Gulzar (a filmmaker from India's 'middle-of-the-road' cinema genre)[31]. Studying this category of filmmakers in monograph studies or as research-led academic book explorations is a post-2000 phenomenon led mostly by post-1990s critics or journalist-turned-academics like Nasreen Munni Kabir, Anupama Chopra, Rinki Bhattacharya and Saibal Chatterjee, amongst others. While Rachel Dwyer's critical analysis of the films of Yash Chopra remains that rare serious academic treatment of the works of a popular director who does not belong to the Golden Era of Indian Cinema, the Dudrah, Mader and Fuchs edited *SRK and Global Bollywood* (2015), the first research-driven book-length review of the legacy of an Indian superstar, remains a lone achievement in the academic genre of Indian star studies.

Rangoonwalla's informative but often derisive *A Pictorial History of Indian Cinema* (1979), while attempting a chronological recording of all Indian cinema, takes an extremely critical position of popular cinema makers. It sees 'rays of hope' only in the works of Satyajit Ray and his legacy's torchbearers like Mrinal Sen, Shyam Benegal and others. The opening line of the book states the writer's bias: 'It may sound ridiculous to say that motion pictures in India "began in a hotel"[32] and are still there, but both the past and the present [the late 1970s] give enough evidence of that' (Rangoonwalla 1979: 10). The book does, however, discuss popular Indian cinema specific genres, raises valid concerns about the high number of purposeless films being made in the mainstream format and provides a listing of landmark filmmakers and films in Hindi and major regional language cinemas up to late 1970s. In *Seeing is Believing* (2008), senior film critic Chidananda Das Gupta, while terming Bollywood 'a variety performance', regrets its 'use of a vocabulary not understood abroad (i.e., the Euro-American West)' (Das Gupta 2008: 55–56). This attitude contributes little towards a fair understanding of the indigenous or different narrative attributes and motivations of Indian cinema that continue to shape much of film criticism within India. It is then conveniently invoked as a legitimate excuse for ignoring its popular cinema in serious film analysis studies in the West. According to Kesavan:

> The truth is that it is not Bombay's cinema but our understanding of what a good film ought to be that is derivative. For anglophone Indians whose definitions of fictional art are derived from books and films in English (or French or Russian or Japanese), the Bombay film begins to seem like second-rate mimicry or a guilty pleasure. Salman Rushdie, in whose fiction Bombay cinema plays a large part, makes this case bluntly: "Most Hindi movies were then and are now what can only be called trashy..." The real problem that the anglophone Indian has with Bombay's films isn't their tackiness: it is the absence of realist conventions. He might adore Priyanka Chopra and worship Shah Rukh Khan, but he can't help notice that their films are made up of stock elements that seem out of sync with rational modernity, which is underwritten by the rules of realism. A film culture where the musical is so completely the norm that a film without songs is remarked on is obviously a local aberration, an aesthetic dead-end. Paradoxically, the Hindi film's success in film markets other than India confirms this conclusion. To be popular in the Middle East, Central Asia, parts of Russia and Africa is to be a cinema for backward peoples as yet undisciplined by realism, reason and modernity. A cinema that doesn't bear witness to the real world is either escapist entertainment that you can enjoy in an ironic way or something you choose to watch because you were socialised into this cinema as a child and watching Hindi movies is your way of staying connected to that lost hinterland, that Bharat-which-is-not-India. To think in this way is understandable but wrong... Something is lost, of course, when the Bombay film-maker forsakes the cultural and linguistic intimacy of realism, but, as [films like] *Sahib, Biwi aur Ghulam* [Master, Madam and Servant, 1962] teaches us, much is also gained. So, Rushdie's right — and he isn't. Much of the output of Bombay's film industry is trashy, but the aesthetic that makes the bad films is also responsible for the good ones (Kesavan 2012: 13–16).

It is the reassessment of this aesthetic, and the offering of clarity on its misperceptions along guidelines that are empathetic to its arguably non-realist conventions, that is the focus of this book.

A Representative Overview of Critical Compilations/Writing on Indian Cinema

Shaped predominantly by critics and rarely by researchers, the first books on studies of Indian cinema set the discourse of two irreconcilable streams—parallel and popular—but primarily engaged with history. They charted compilation lists, encyclopaedias, star biographies and occasional directorial oeuvre analyses. This can be seen in a representative sample of some of the first book publications on Indian cinema, namely Firoze Rangoonwalla's *Indian Filmography, Silent and Hindi Film: 1897–1969* (1970), Rajendra Ojha edited *75 Glorious Years of Indian Cinema: 1913–1988* (1988), *B. V. Dharap's Indian Film* annuals spanning from 1920–1985 and *The 100 Luminaries of Hindi Cinema* (1996) by ex-*Movie* magazine editors Dinesh Raheja and Jitendra Kothari. Instead of educating the audience about the uniqueness of Indian cinema aesthetics, their primary concern was to present an authentic and educational chronology of the major events in the film industry's evolution in the 20th century. Amongst these elaborate journalistic introductions to the Indian film industry, Erik Barnouw and S. Krishnaswamy's *Indian Film* (1980) can be viewed as the first major academic book on Indian cinema. Though chronological in structure, the book, which was released in the 50th year of Indian cinema, presents a detailed study of the processes, performance and products of the Indian film industry from three of its major centres of production, Mumbai, Kolkata and Chennai. It begins with the late 19th century, when cinema was first introduced into India months after the first public screening of a film in France. Inter-cut with brief biographies on leading filmmakers and the socio-political influences on the medium, it highlights Indian cinema's 'extraordinary hold over its audiences, offers an understanding of its song and dance traditions, multi-lingual nature of enterprise, secular foundations, financial structure and Maharajah like superstars' (Barnouw–Krishnaswamy 1980: vii). The book also acknowledges Indian cinema's foundations in the subcontinent's Sanskrit drama traditions. The revised second edition additionally documents the growth in the Indian parallel cinema movement from the period of the declaration of Internal Emergency (under Prime Minister Indira Gandhi in 1975) to Satyajit Ray's completion of 25 years of filmmaking (1979). Published at a time when serious/academic research on Indian cinema was negligible, this edition is concluded by Barnouw and Krishnaswamy with a contented note that they find themselves in a relatively more gratifying atmosphere of film research at the turn of the 1980s. This is acknowledged by Lal and Nandy in their introduction to *Fingerprinting Popular Culture* (2006), where they date the beginning of proper research of popular cinema in Indian intellectual and academic circles a little after and in response to the Indian Emergency. Lal and Nandy note that by the late 1980s this 'powerful, pan-Indian, politically meaningful kitsch had even the most incorruptible film analysts reluctantly admit to its ability to say something even if unwittingly, incompetently, inartistically' (2006: xxv).

Since its publication in the 1990s, *Encyclopaedia of Indian Cinema* (1999) by Ashish Rajadhyaksha and Paul Willeheim remains a valuable and exhaustive pioneer compendium among all major lists on Indian cinema to date. It retains the chronological presentation of popular writing; its seminal contribution is its brief yet illuminating introductions to over a thousand landmark Indian films (many for the first time) from all the subcontinent's regional cinemas from 1913 (*Raja Harishchandra*) to 1992. The compendium's critical reviews, ranging from the psychoanalytic to the technological, echo the 1990s' emerging portrayal of Indian cinema as an influential national cinema.

The turn of the 20th century brought a renewed focus on compilation lists of influential 20th century Indian films to educate new audiences outside of South Asia and especially in the West. This accompanied a growing consumption of Indian cinema across the globe via collections of CDs/DVDs and in the form of satellite telecasts. Primary amongst the compilations are *Stardust*'s *The 100 Greatest Films of All Time* (2000)[33], Ashok Banker's *Bollywood* (2001), Gulzar, Govind Nihalani and

Saibal Chatterjee edited *Encyclopaedia of Hindi Cinema* (2003), Subhash K. Jha's *The Essential Guide to Bollywood* (2005) and Rachel Dwyer's *100 Films* (2005). These review a broadly overlapping list of landmark Hindi films in terms of their plot and performance, impact at the time of release, directorial achievements and overall influence in retrospect. While the first two titles additionally offer an appreciation of the quality of the music and lyrics in a film's overall achievement, Banker arrives at his era-specific list of critically acclaimed trendsetters based on their impact at the time of release and subsequent legacy of influence on the Hindi film industry. The *Encyclopaedia of Hindi Cinema* uses explorative essays by reviewers and interviews with senior film industry veterans to engage in a critical discussion on the need for and desirability of the Indianisation of universal cinematic storytelling tools. These tools include editing, sound, special effects, stunts, scripts, costumes, music, lyrics, the flashback technique and similar narration-specific attributes, to create a unique inimitable brand of cinema. All these publications, however, limit their purview to Hindi films only.

Back to the Basics

From an informative, documentary-like chronology of landmark events and influential meaning-makers (filmmakers, actors and music directors), the study of Indian cinema in more than 100 years of the industry's existence has expanded beyond just a collation of multidisciplinary engagements. Academic writing on Indian cinema, while consistently widening the scope of its encyclopaedic research, has been engaging with film production and reception, the ideologies that shape its meanings and the increasing spheres of its influence (local and global). The rise in postcolonial and transnational scholarship calling for a reassessment of 'the hegemony of Western and Hollywood cinemas in media, film and cultural studies... for new theoretical and methodological approaches to Indian cinemas' has further contributed to popular Indian cinema being 'finally acknowledged' with its signature filmmaking attributes by academics and film critics in India and the West since the 1990s (Desai and Dudrah 2008: 1). This has not only opened film theory to a huge body of cinematic work (over 50,000 feature films have been made since the advent of sound in Indian cinema in 1931, with over 15,000 in Hindi cinema), but, as Lutgendorf suggests, has introduced possibilities for exploring an Indian style of filmmaking, setting new directions in film criticism, genre and culture studies. He contends:

> That this enormous and influential body of popular art is now beginning to receive scholarly notice suggests the need for, at least, systemic realignment (as when a big new planet swims into our ken); a more audacious suggestion is that its 'different universe' might make possible an Einsteinian paradigm-shift by introducing new ways of thinking about the space-time of cinematic narrative... as the distinctive conventions of this art form, which have tenaciously resisted the influence of Western cinemas, did not arise in a cultural vacuum (Lutgendorf 2011: 228–229).

Between Rangoonwalla, Das Gupta and Hood's valorising of Indian parallel cinema and Rajadhyaksha, Dwyer and Banker's illuminating reviews of popular Indian cinema, coupled with new ethnography-based insights into audience appreciation of Bollywood, the evolving Indian film form's signature storytelling practices, performance cultures and continuance in essence of ancient aesthetics did somehow get pushed to the periphery of academic scholarship. This has also been the case with its actual meaning-makers—directors, actors, music directors, lyricists, singers and technicians—amidst a surge of audience experience and engagement-driven research that has been shifting the focus in contemporary Indian film studies from creation to consumption. As modern tools and parameters of social sciences such as psychoanalysis, ethnography, nation, identity and economics of filmmaking compete to provide better elucidation, Ravi Vasudevan notes: 'The filmic dimension of film studies seems to have been lost in the process of trying to understand the political economy and sociology of the cinema institution' (2011: 24). Attributing this skew in focus to most prominent Indian cinema scholars coming from a social science instead of film studies background, Wright comments:

from casting, acting, direction and screenplay to the shaping of his purpose for and expectations from the film form. This influence becomes even more significant in the context of Phalke's work. In the making of his first film, *Raja Harishchandra,* he personally led every department of filmmaking, not only as a producer–director but also as the first writer, cameraman, make-up man, costume designer, art director and cine-laboratorian. In Phalke's singular obsession for laying the foundation of a *swadeshi* cinema industry, his stated preferences (over the then prevalent Shakespearean and Parsi theatre style possibilities) and intentions for engaging *only* with the *Natyashastra*'s expectations from a dramatic art will be identified and discussed. Given the survival of only a few clips and one feature film from Phalke's prolific oeuvre of a hundred films, shorts and documentaries, the ephemeral nature of scattered historical sources and a dependence on Phalke's writings to evidence his indebtedness to the *Natyashastra*, this chapter will study his life's work and review his bequest in a biographical narrative form. Secondary sources such as biographies, published features, news reports and recollections of relevant interviewees will be utilised to provide additional insights into the socio-political context and creative influences on Phalke. Finally, a critical study of Phalke's surviving films will be undertaken in entirety (or in parts where only few scenes are available) to establish *rasa*-evoking elements and *rasa*-specific unity in their themes and presentation.

Image 2.1 Dhundiraj Govind Phalke (Photograph: NFAI)

Phalke's Context and Concerns

Phalke was a man of strong impulses and rigid convictions. He was not used to being dictated to and frequently abandoned many a prosperous project when his ideas and attitude towards the project clashed with those of his colleagues, financiers or co-entrepreneurs. 'His spirit always rebelled against being anyone's slave; he was an artist and artists needed their freedom' (Phalke Summanwar 2012: 50). In that ability to frequently let go and start afresh, he followed the principles of a *karmayogi* as discussed in the *Bhagavad Gita*: '…of a selfless doer, who carries on without worrying about the fruits of labour'[6], ascribing the consequences to the will of the almighty.[7] Dadasaheb Phalke's great-grandniece Sharayu Phalke Summanwar in her biography of Phalke, *The Silent Film* (2012), traces this attitude to his childhood grooming in a tradition of orthodox Brahmins from the Chitpavan community of Maharashtra, for whom an 'uncompromised righteous living' inspired by the Hindu scriptures defined the way of life. His father, Dajishastri Phalke, was an equally inflexible man of principles. She writes:

> Daji was a renowned Sanskrit scholar. He was a *puranik*, a Vedasampana shastri. And it was because of this that Dhundiraj and his brother Bapu knew the *Ramayana*, the *Mahabharata*, the *Bhagavad Gita* and the Vedas by heart; a fact that surprised his friends in later years. But for the Phalkes it was commonplace; their family performed all the Hindu rites except those connected with death… The lullabies that Dhundiraj's mother and grandmother sang to him were in fact musical narrations of the great Hindu epics. It was no wonder that by the age of seven he could recite good parts of them by heart, in Sanskrit. At some level he seemed to interpret life itself through these epics; a fact that is almost incomprehensible to most people today. Shri Ram and Shri Krishna were not mere household names but dominant influences in Dhundiraj's life. They were to greatly impact his work in later years (Summanwar 2012: 22).

According to Phalke, the desire to make movies first arose in him after a chance viewing of *The Life of Christ* (in the Christmas of 1910), post which he became obsessed with the idea of pioneering an Indian film industry. He writes:

> While the *Life of Christ* was rolling fast before my physical eyes, I was mentally visualising the Gods, Shri Krishna, Shri Ramachandra, their Gokul and Ayodhya. I was gripped by a strange spell… I felt my imagination taking shape on the screen. Could this really happen? Could we, the sons of India, ever be able to see Indian images on the screen? (*Kesari* 1913)

This urge to see and show Indian images on the screen that was to soon consume Phalke as a life obsession was no isolated articulation but a product of the Indian identity-seeking, tumultuous spirit of his times. He had seen films before, but there was something different stirring in the mood of his nation, an unstated atmosphere of assertion. Professionally, Phalke had just quit a job and hence was more inclined to take risks in a new career. Personally, he already had become a convert to, and a foot soldier of, Bal Gangadhar Tilak's concept of cultural nationalism. The end of the first decade of the 20th century heralded some assertive political times in India. Tilak in the western part of the Indian subcontinent along with Bipin Chandra Pal in the east and Lala Lajpat Rai in the north, had cast aside the Indian National Congress' moderate attitude of seeking governing rights within the British Empire for the more aggressive demand of complete *swaraj* or self-rule. Termed by British authorities as the 'father of the Indian unrest', Tilak was anointed by his countrymen as *Lokmanya* or accepted by the people (as their leader). A Sanskrit scholar, teacher, reformist and journalist, Tilak's idea of *swaraj* was not limited to political freedom alone. It was conjoined to an overall revival of everything *swadeshi* in every sphere of life—economic, social, religious and cultural—starting with the transformation of the household Ganesha festival into a *Sarvajanik Ganeshotsav* (public Ganesh festival) and the reconstruction and revival of Shivaji as a symbol of Maratha pride in popular imagination.

To this end his clarion calls were as much for young patriots as for young entrepreneurs in all walks of life. It was this climate of an all-inclusive *swadeshi* movement that inspired Phalke to make 'films on Indian subjects by the Indians, for the Indians', as he reflects:

> This was the period of the *Swadeshi* movement and there was profuse talking and lecturing on the subject. For me, personally, it led to the resignation of my comfortable government job and taking to an independent profession. I took this opportunity to explain my ideas about cinema to my friends and to the leaders of the *Swadeshi* movement (Phalke 1917).

Filmmaker and author of *Tracking Phalke*, Kamal Swaroop, traces a thought process in the above-mentioned reaction that was actively working towards countering the onslaught of Western images. He says:

> So, if they have Jesus, we will have Krishna… And then when Phalke realises that our mythological images could be infused with some sort of political messages and contemporised, the villain in *Keechaka Vadham* (The Killing of Keechaka) becomes a guy like Lord Curzon or Bhakta Vidur (Saint Vidur) looks like Gandhiji [w.r.f. to shared imageries]. Phalke is aware of these possibilities as he is constantly following Tilak, who was the first to use these images as political weapons in mass gatherings working on the collective consciousness (2013).

Phalke's mythological films also helped stir submerged feelings of national pride and identity by reminding Indians of their glorious heritage. Tilak's weekly paper *Kesari* in a review of *Raja Harishchandra*, published three days after the film's release on 6 May 1913, celebrated Phalke's arrival as a pioneer in Indian cinema, declaring:

> Most of the films shown in the cinematographs in Bombay were foreign and they had foreign images in them. But Mr. Phalke has changed all this in making his films. The images in his films are Indian and are drawn from the *Puranas* and are thus familiar to us all (1913).

This was followed by a long interview with Phalke in *Kesari* (Poona ed.) that introduced its subject stating: '...for the last 2 months, the shows of "Swadeshi" moving pictures made by Mr. Phalke are being arranged in Bombay and it is learnt that people are liking them very much' (*Kesari* 1913). *Swadeshi* was not just a sentiment or state of perception and being; it was an attractive advertisement and tagline for those intending to claim additional popularity in the local imagination.

Phalke, who never shied away from highlighting his status as 'the Father of Indian cinema' in the credits of his films, shares interesting anecdotes about fellow filmmakers, one of whom to prove himself more *swadeshi* than Phalke had advertised his film as 'being more *swadeshi* as its camera was made locally' (unlike Phalke who had imported his machines) (Phalke 1918). Another had advertised his film as being completely *swadeshi* as it had been 'made by a person who has not gone abroad' (Phalke 1918). Phalke indulgently acknowledges the competition stating:

> This phrase filled my heart with admiration for that man. I never dared to do that. I had been abroad thrice... in a way, the phrase 'made without going abroad' is serving the national cause. We, the lowly traders outside Poona have to be proud of the fact that India has been made ready for Home Rule by this sentence and will have to get inspired by it! Oh Mr. Montague! Why didn't you learn Marathi language and see for yourself the fire that lies in our press advertisements?

The pre-independence era film critic and script writer K. A. Abbas, argues:

> It is more than a historical coincidence that *Raja Harishchandra* was produced at about the same time that the Indian National Congress was beginning to voice the national aspirations of the Indian people (Garga 2012: 50).

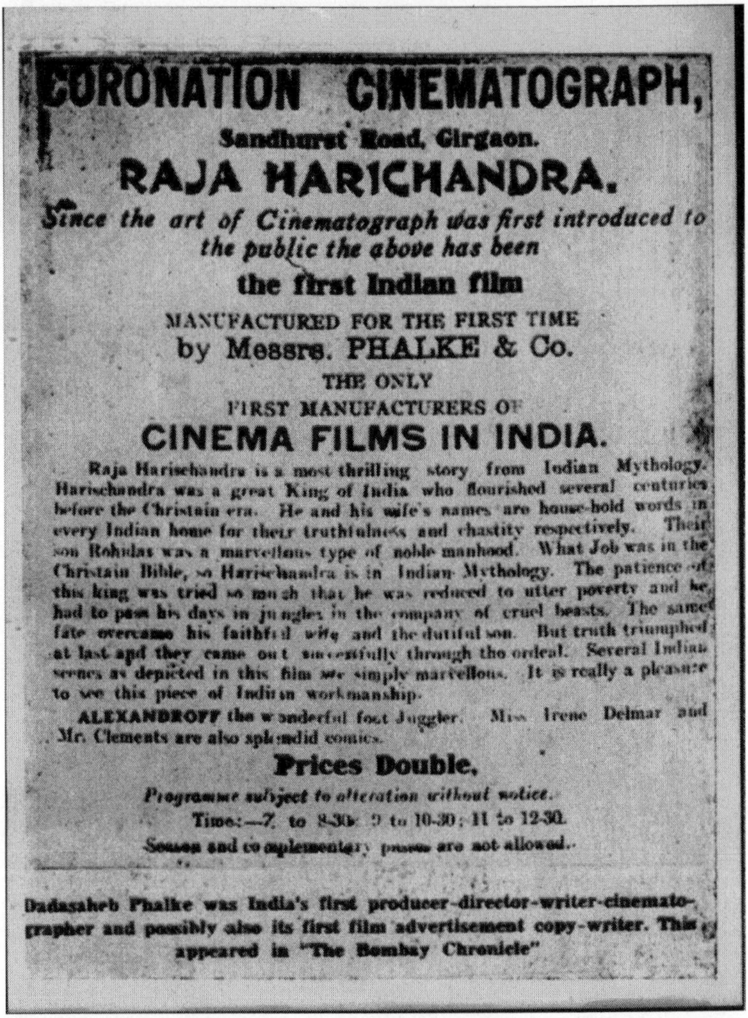

Image 2.2 An Advertisement in the *Bombay Chronicle* Calling Audiences to the First Screening of *Raja Harishchandra*, Advertising the Pioneering Role of D. G. Phalke in the 'Birth of Indian Cinema' (Photograph: NFAI)

Tilak further invited Phalke to use the Indian National Congress platform at its Poona session in 1917 to raise funds for his fledgling enterprise. Tilak, unlike Gandhi, who headed the *swadeshi* movement after him, was not isolated or insulated from the influence of the entertaining arts, especially cinema. He had discovered and christened

Marathi singer–actor Narayan Shripad Rajhans as Bal Gandharva, the greatest star-performer of early 20th century Marathi theatre. That endorsement had boosted the career prospects and cult status of Bal Gandharva in comparison to his other talented contemporaries. When Phalke went through a crisis of resources and lack of funds in his filmmaking career during World War I, Tilak's paper, *Kesari*, supported his pleas for public funding and the need for his continuance for the survival of *swadeshi* cinema, through liberal reviews, interviews and printing of fund-raising advertisements. For Phalke, Tilak, who was elder to him by 14 years, remained a life-long mentor, supporter, respected guide and trusted critic of his films and plays. For Tilak, Phalke was an Indian entrepreneur to be encouraged and enlisted. Phalke was invited by leaders of the Home Rule League to become a member with the assurance that when India got Home Rule (after World War I, as many of its then members believed), there would be no problem in raising capital for him. When Phalke launched a crowd-sourced funding scheme to generate capital, one of his fans wrote an article in the *Daily Sandesh* appealing to the 1500 heroes of Home Rule to donate five rupees each to get the *swadeshi* film industry going.[8] After Tilak's death, in the later years of World War I, the subsequent leadership of the *swadeshi* movement and its Home Rule counterparts (before they merged in 1921) reacted with mere lip service to Phalke's desperate pleas for funding. In despair, he lamented, 'Let us admit with regret that India is still unfit to claim Home Rule', adding in retrospect that 'If my Indian enterprise had died, it would have been a permanent disgrace for the *Swadeshi* Movement in the eyes of the people in London' (Phalke 1917). The comparative London reference was specifically made to highlight his refusal of lucrative offers by London-based producers to work in the UK, which followed the enthusiastic reception of his first set of films during his second visit to London in 1917. He had instead opted to struggle with an unpredictable career at home, attempting to nurture and establish what he saw as a still fledgling *swadeshi* film industry. Perhaps it was this determination to equate *swadeshi* with Indian-only stories and storytelling styles that caused Phalke's choice of feature film subjects to never go beyond *puranic*, epic and Sanskrit drama sources, even when popular taste had started veering towards other themes and genres like the Parsi-theatre-inspired fantasies or family socials and comedies inspired by Shakespearean dramas and European films. Phalke never made fantasy film adaptations of popular Parsi theatre themes like *Arabian Nights* and *Alif Laila* (products of an Islamicate cultural influence) or any Shakespearean drama. This was despite the fact that he had played a few minor Shakespearean characters in his theatre days at Baroda. Also, given the unavailability of female actors agreeing to act on screen, Phalke preferred to cast young Indian boys in women's parts (as was prevalent in many local Indian dance and theatre traditions), instead of casting British, Anglo-Indian or Western actresses with an Indian screen name, as was common in Indian films of the Silent Era. Phalke's motivations went far beyond the personal. He saw the establishment of the *swadeshi* film industry as a pioneer's responsibility, even if it came at the cost of his survival, sanity and financial security. He was driven by a firm *swadeshi* spirited 'conviction that the Indian people would get an occasion to see Indian images on the screen and people abroad would get a true picture of India' (Phalke 1917).

The Phalke Film *Shastra*

Phalke's idea of *swadeshi* was not limited merely to telling Indian stories with an Indian cast and crew. It was also about reintroducing his creative fraternity and successors to the traditional Indian style of storytelling and performance and its appreciation as postulated in the *Natyashastra*. Despite a decline in public performance of Sanskrit language dramas in the late medieval centuries (13th–18th century) critics and commentators consistently engaged with the *Natyashastra* as a dramatic treatise. In addition, performing Brahmin *kirtankars* like Phalke's father Dajishastri used it to educate and entertain audiences in temples and private functions through song narrations from the epics and the *puranas*. Phalke's exhaustive oeuvre of more than 100 films also sourced its stories from the *puranas*, the Ramayana, the Mahabharata and Sanskrit drama. Of the 138 silent films that were issued censor certificates for release in the first decade of Indian cinema (1913–1922),

95 were mythologicals, 14 devotionals, 14 socials (starting in 1920), eight historicals (starting in 1915), five classical or Sanskrit drama adaptations (starting 1920) and only one documentary (1918) and one fantasy film (1922). Among these, 25 mythological films and four devotional films were made by Phalke, first under his debut Phalke & Company Ltd. and subsequently under the Hindustan Cinema Film Company. Phalke's pioneering role was thus not only in initiating the film industry in India but in setting the agenda for its narrative choices, style and identity, especially in its first formative decade. It is worth noting that of the 138 films made in the first decade of Indian cinema, there was only one fantasy film, a favourite genre of Parsi theatre.

The direction that Phalke's filmography gave to Indian cinema in its early years could in fact challenge a tendency in existing film scholarship to credit the signature narrative attributes of Indian cinema like stylised acting as a bequest of its immediately preceding urban Parsi theatre. However, attributes such as ornamental dialogue, song and dance structure, grandiose mise en scène and larger-than-life characters had significantly gained currency in popular narratives by the end of the second decade of Indian cinema, after the arrival of talkie films in 1931 with Ardheshir Irani's *Alam Ara* (Ornament of the World, 1931). This was the phase when Parsi theatre influences made their presence felt in the films made by some of the Bombay based studios, while the other major Indian moviemaking centres like Calcutta, Madras, Lahore and Pune/Kolhapur were inspired by respective local folk theatre forms. These included the *jatra*, company theatre, Marathi *sangeet natak* performances and other *desi* (local/folk/regional) theatre variations of the *maargi* (classical) source traditions of Sanskrit drama.[9] Their performance conventions were not entirely outside of the *Natyashastra*'s rules and guidelines on dramatic representations. For instance, all the above-mentioned performance characteristics of the Parsi theatre echoed the *Natyadharmi* performance style prescribed by the *Natyashastra,* a play in which speech is artificial and exaggerated with elaborate sentences using ornate language, forceful actions, graceful gestures, emotive characters and costumes not from common use. Phalke's dramatisation, contrary to the Parsi theatre style, also had a reference in the Sanskrit dramatic treatise in the *Lokadharmi* style of storytelling.

The *Natyashastra* discusses two very distinct styles of storytelling: the *Natyadharmi* and the *Lokadharmi*. The latter is a play in which the characters look common and normal and behave, act and speak naturally, without any change in gestures or stylised limb postures in themes of social significance (Rangacharya 2010: 115, 351). Phalke, who frequently highlighted cinema's differences from theatre, opted for the *Lokadharmi* style in his dramatisation, which could be argued to be more cinema-friendly in its preference for capturing reality as it is. Unlike Parsi and other folk-theatre-inspired films, especially those of the late Silent and early Talkie Era that often were direct recorded reproductions of staged plays, Phalke's mise en scène exchanged the proscenium and its ornate, artificial indoors for real architectural monuments and natural locations. His actors were ordinary people who dressed and behaved like common Maharashtrian folk, and even his divine characters were shorn of heavy make-up or ostentatious costumes. The entire supporting cast in both *Raja Harishchandra* and *Kaliya Mardan* (The Taming of Snake Kaliya, 1919) are dressed in the daily wear of ordinary 20th century Maharashtrians, contrary to the narrative's North Indian backdrop. They engage with a relatively less expressive, *Lokadharmi* (natural) style of acting, aiming at maximisation of audience emotion through dramatic action.

Adya Rangacharya notes the bypassing of the equally important *Lokadharmi* style of performance in favour of the *Natyadharmi* style only. He locates this oversight in post-independence theatre specialists, who in their 'enthusiasm to revive and reinforce the impact of India's ancient dramatic traditions gave credence to the notion that all Indian dramas in the ancient Indian traditions *only* had music, dance and stylised acting as described in the *Natyadharmi* category in the *Natyashastra*' (Rangacharya 2010: 351). According to Rangacharya:

> The correct position is that there could have been all kinds of dramas, the chief among which were *Lokadharmi* with natural acting and *Natyadharmi* with stylised acting (Rangacharya 2010: 351).

An erudite scholar of Sanskrit drama and the theory of *rasa*, Phalke had the critical acumen to distil the timeless aesthetic achievement guidelines of the *Natyashastra*, relevant to a new and evolving art form, in order to compliment the inherent character of the film medium. He was aware that the 'screenplay was a play for the eyes, contrary to the stage play which was for the ears' (Phalke 1917). Phalke's mythologicals therefore tend to contest notions that link the lack of cinematic realism in Indian cinema to its theatre traditions and explain its experimentations with naturalism as a later day Euro-American import. In his available films one can actually trace the birth of the first wave of Indian parallel cinema.

However, as the craft of filmmaking matured and technology enhanced the scope and possibilities for cinematic imagination, the subtle *Lokadharmi* approach to celluloid storytelling began transforming into the *Natyadharmi* style. A case in point is the dramatisation and presentation of the oldest surviving Indian talkie, V. Shantaram's *Ayodhyecha Raja* (The King of Ayodhya, 1932), which was also based on the legend of Raja Harishchandra. According to Paresh Mokashi, director of *Harishchandrachi Factory* (Harishchandra's Factory, 2009), a film on the making of Phalke's *Raja Harishchandra* (1913):

> Phalke's *Raja Harishchandra* tough low on scale was high on natural and realistic acting; *Ayodhyecha Raja* while being mounted on a grand scale is much more stylised in its acting (2014).

Phalke critiqued this trend in his deposition before the Indian Cinematograph Enquiry Committee (1927–1928), denouncing most of his contemporary film productions as lacking in technique and artistic merit and suffering from bad acting and worst-class photography by people who knew nothing about art (Rangoonwalla 1970: 72). Based on genres, a breakdown of the 133 films released in 1929 indicates a shift in trend from the previous 1913–1922 figures. Mythologicals overwhelmingly led the tally earlier, but by 1929, socials and fantasy/costume actioners were leading the list, with more than 40 releases in each category, followed by 14 historicals, 12 mythologicals, three devotionals and five classical dramas. Speaking at an address to the

Madras Chamber of Commerce in 1940 on what a film should be, Phalke reiterated:

> As films were essentially photo-plays, dialogue should be kept to a minimum. A movie should not be too long… Films should reflect India's cultural reality [and] stars must not be overpaid and addictions amongst them must be strictly discouraged (Summanwar 2012: 229).

Incidentally, this was no prescription for the films of the Silent Era only, as it was delivered nearly a decade after the dawn of the Talkie Era in Indian cinema. In retrospect, Phalke was actually stating concerns subsequently raised by the Indian New Wave directors of the 1970s and their post-2000 independent cinema counterparts in their championing of the cause of cinematic realism.

If the maturity in a maker's craft is to be mapped through choices made towards the culminating phase of one's career, once again Sanskrit drama influences seem to dominate Phalke. 1929 saw him make four Sanskrit drama adaptations: *Vasantsena, Malvikagnimitra, Malati Madhav* and *Kacha Devyani.* None of these films survive today, but his four elaborate essays on the art and craft of cinema leave little doubt about the greatest influence on the Phalke school of filmmaking. He extensively read the likes of *Bioscope* and other Western-cinema-shaping journals on filmmaking, but when it came to setting standards for his *swadeshi* film industry, his guidebook was the *Natyashastra.* For instance, while discussing his ideas about ideal actors and casting, Phalke states:

> The cinema demands a kind of real 'beauty' (which is the source of the happiness derived by looking at a person with a beautiful, healthy form) which gives rise to faultless visuals (Phalke 1918).

Phalke's obsession with beauty and employing handsome actors for lead parts is a concern directly derived from the *Natyashastra*'s chapter on actors. Again, when trying to convince ladies from cultured families to act in films, Phalke falls back on the *Natyashastra* to lend respectability to the medium, stating, 'In fact even in Sanskrit poetry, drama and dramaturgy support this view'[10]. According to Swaroop:

> Phalke's essays on actors and his experiences with casting, and the section on his expectations of the looks, talents, make-up, expressions, etc. of actors… can be directly sourced to *Natyashastra* postulates (2013).

The screen test scene for potential actors in Mokashi's *Harishchandrachi Factory*, a film depicting the making of *Raja Harishchandra*, reinforces the *Natyashastra's* influence as the guiding text in Dadasaheb Phalke's film factory at Nashik. Regarding his propriety parameters and purpose of good cinema, he states, 'The structure of a good film having a good, human, emotional, interesting and moral story leads us along the path of the Good!' (Phalke 1918). Phalke reaffirms his expectation of enlightenment through entertainment, a stance born of the intense ethos of religiosity inherent to the performance of all traditional Indian arts as recommended by the proponents of the *Natyashastra* and endorsed by its commentators down the ages. It is to be noted here that Phalke was reengaging with what he thought to be the ever-relevant ideas on good aesthetic achievement as enshrined in the *Natyashastra*. This was in contrast to the literal bringing of Sanskrit or other theatres to cinema, which was the method of many of his non-cinema-trained contemporaries and successors who just copied theatre on to cinema. Phalke's farewell message to the Indian film industry at its silver jubilee celebrations draws a symbolic, dramatic closure to his career. He compared the film industry to Shakuntala, and himself to her forgotten ascetic father, Kanva *muni*, incantation and instruction included. As with Bharata *muni*'s constant self-referencing in the original *Natyashastra*, he drew parallels between his life's ironies with that of a character from one of the greatest Sanskrit dramas[11].

A *Rasaeur* of *Adbhuta*

The *rasa* theory 'places the suggestion of emotion as the highest form of suggestion, higher than the suggestion of a fact or idea and the suggestion of a figure or image… Art suggests emotion. Emotion is suggested meaning' (Rayan 1965: 250). According to Jain and Daljit:

> For Bharata, 'mere narration' or 'bare utility' weren't art... That which afforded useful information, or created utility, could be arts of secondary type... Arts were [higher] arts only when they excited the senses and aroused emotions, and created '*rasa*', in which the mind perpetually rejoiced (Jain and Daljit 2005: 5).

Hence, it can be interpreted that in an artwork's most dominant sentiment resides its most important suggestion/meaning or its creator's intention. This test of greatness, or an artwork's ability to evoke only one *rasa* as predominant and others as subordinate, the *Natyashastra* observes to be normally achieved by one who is 'mature and expert enough' (Schwartz 2004: 13), i.e., an evolved master of the form *only*. In films, this can be interpreted to define a great director as one who, while evoking the nine principal *rasas* in their film, is able to unite them under one *rasa* that the audience eventually leaves with. This can be also read as an argument in favour of a director being a film's most important/decisive meaning provider, which is a founding 'auteur theory'[12] postulate. This is because the single *rasa* that they would choose as the lasting impression of their work from the pool of nine *rasas* is a clearly individual choice. In the context of *rasa* evoking cinema, such a great director I have termed a '*rasaeur*'.[13] He, like his great director counterpart in Western film theory—the auteur—is not only opting for a consistent cinematic *dhvani* (meaning) that 'defines his body of work internally and distinguishes it outwardly from others' (Nowell-Smith 1967: 137) but is also challenging and refashioning the conventions of his work system in the process.

Phalke debuted on stage playing bit parts in Shakespearean theatre, but his first direction was a college production in Sanskrit called *Veni Sanhara* (The Binding of the Braid). He honed his cinema skills on a diet of *Bioscope*, but for his suggestions on filmmaking he referenced and contextualised the *Natyashastra*. He learnt his craft from the Western film but used it to express Indian themes and impulses. He let himself be shaped in the interaction of the West and the East, but the values he sought to establish were of classical Sanskrit theatre. Of these values, the highest and most universally desired, as discussed in the first chapter, has always been the evocation of *rasa*. *Rasa* evocation was the primary goal in the films of Phalke, not least because of their skew towards the *Lokadharmi* style of dramatisation, which like every prescribed performative style in the *Natyashastra* had to evoke *rasa*. This will be evidenced in an episodic study of Phalke's only completely available film *Kaliya Mardan,* along with references to *Raja Harishchandra* and other available film clips.

Image 2.3 Mandakini Phalke, the Child Protagonist of *Kaliya Mardan* Playing Little Krishna, Portrays the Raudra Bhava (Photograph: NFAI)

The above is a glimpse of one of the nine *bhavas* that Mandakini portrays prior to the beginning of the film's narrative that are showcased as a study in facial expressions by a little girl of seven.

Kaliya Mardan depicts some of the childhood adventures of Lord Krishna and begins with a prelude sequence, equivalent to a 'director-as-*sutradhar*/narrator' masterclass on *bhavas* or facial expressions, which Phalke reviews as 'one of the two major means [the other being a good physique] of attracting spectator interest for an actor of the film play' (Phalke 1918). Before the film's actual adventure story commences, we see a close-up of the lead protagonist performing a series of expressions introduced by a title card declaring 'study in facial expressions by a little girl of seven'.

The narrative then proceeds towards working out the corresponding *rasa*-evoking events through a series of different action scenarios. The film's drama highlight of the taming of snake Kaliya occurs towards its fourth quarter, with the rest of the film proceeding through a series of specific *rasa*-evoking docudrama-like vignettes from a mischievous but kind-hearted kid's daily life.

The film's first episode is themed around the sentiments of hurt and revenge. The setting is Brindavan by the river Yamuna, where a *gopi* (village maiden) is shown to be indulgent towards little Krishna. However, she is rude to Krishna's friends in his absence. Krishna plots a tit-for-tat for the *gopi* using his *makhan chor* (butter thief) exploits. The episode ends with Krishna's insulted friends having a hearty laugh as the rude *gopi* is wrongly accused of having stolen cream, which had actually been stolen by them. The narrative then depicts two different episodes of Krishna's *karuna* (compassion) for the poor and the weak as he shares his gifts with the former and gets his friends to help the latter. The evocation of this *rasa* is hinted in the film's title cards, which state that these little acts of kindness were preliminary hints for the greater acts of universal good that he was destined to perform later in the film. The third episode depicts little Krishna as a prankster playing a practical joke on a sleeping couple. He ties the beard of the husband with the plait of his wife. The comic *rasa* is the theme of this episode that cuts to several *gopis* and the harassed couple complaining to Krishna's parents about his mischief. On being reprimanded, Krishna sulks, but following elaborate cajoling and apologising by the *gopis*, he wins their hearts with his melodic flute play. As they get into a dance trance, Krishna quietly escapes to the banks of the Yamuna, where the film's title plot of the defeat of the snake Kaliya begins. A fight ensues between the brave little kid and the giant snake, celebrating the heroic *rasa* 'composed' as a dramatic action evoking awe. In the fusion of these different episodes, Phalke endorses the *rasa* theory postulate that a good work of drama should try to provide its audience with an eclectic spectrum of *rasa* experiences. The climax of *Kaliya Mardan* has a five-headed snake emerging out of the river with Little Krishna dancing on its head to evoke awe or *adbhuta*, the lasting *rasa* in this cinematic experience.

Image 2.4 An Example of Dadasaheb Phalke's Use of Special Effects in the Climax of *Kaliya Mardan*; Daughter Mandakini (Centre) Plays Little Krishna (Photograph: NFAI)

Phalke's first film *Raja Harishchandra* also contains a trick-based scene; the king Harishchandra is conned into saving three vices being burnt in a *yagnakund* (sacred altar for sacrifice) by sage Vishwamitra. The vices are interestingly portrayed as three hyperactive girls who we see in the *yajna* flames from the waist upwards as the rest of their bodies are strategically covered by the sage's silhouette. The other 'trick of camera' that can be seen in the salvaged remnants of the film is the sudden appearance and disappearance of Lord Shiva in the film's climax. When Indian cinema's first auteur took his films abroad for an international showcase, all of this made the contemporary foreign press in London note that 'from a technical point of view, Phalke's films are excellent' (Rangoonwalla 1970: 74). These special effects may not seem awe-inspiring today, but for audiences in those days these tricks were the biggest attractions of a Phalke film. Early Indian cinema movie mogul, J.B.H. Wadia, in his experience of watching Phalke's first blockbuster *Lanka Dahan* (The Destruction of Lanka, 1917) recalls:

> *Lanka Dahan* was a minor masterpiece of its time. The spectacle of Hanuman's figure becoming progressively diminutive as he flew higher and higher in the clouds and the burning of the city of Lanka in table-top photography were simply awe-inspiring (Garga 2012: 55).

Thus, Phalke can also be argued to be the Méliès of Indian cinema. George Méliès, 'the father of special effects' in French cinema, had a studio and trained hands to realise his vision. Phalke just had himself and his imagination and yet the magician never tired from introducing 'new tricks', as cinematic special effects were called then, bettering their promise and scale of ambition with every subsequent film.

Phalke thus expressed his desired experience from his filmmaking journey: 'O God! May I remain a child forever! As I grow my beard and moustaches, let my inner heart always have the purity of a child!' (Phalke 1918). A childlike, curious wonder pervades the choice of subjects in Phalke's filmography—*Lanka Dahan, Kaliya Mardan, Jarasandha Baddha* (The Killing of Jarasandha, 1923), *A Quarrel Game of Narada* (1923), *Ram Ravan Yuddha* (The Battle between Rama and Ravana, 1924), *Dhanurbhanga* (The Breaking of the Bow, 1926), *Draupadi Vastrahan* (The Disrobing of Draupadi, 1927), etc.—in which often the attraction of a spectacle defines the climax or the core drama of the narrative. The story becomes a vehicle for creating the *rasa* of *adbhuta* or wonder. This is quite evident in the delineation of the drama in both his available films. Even in a tale of loss and deep pathos like *Raja Harishchandra*, the focus is on the possibilities for adventure or surprise in the journey of the protagonists. Phalke's filmmaking career was forever driven by an urge to create a bigger spectacle than before. His career's last two film projects—a sound film, *Setu Bandhan* (The Bridge on Sea, 1932) and his first talkie film, *Gangavataran* (The

Descent of Ganga, 1937)—both carved their drama around events of grand spectacle from the epics. They rode in on advertising that pitched them as a spectacle to beat all spectacles. *Adbhuta* remains the dominating *rasa* of *rasaeur* Dadasaheb Phalke's cinematic bequest of spectacular drama themes.

Conclusion

Phalke's first public engagement as a performer was as a *kirtankar* singer. He moved on to perform bit parts in Shakespearean plays but made his directorial debut on stage with a Sanskrit drama. Subsequently, he conducted magic shows, made films that abounded with tricks or special effects, took a break from filmmaking to script a mammoth seven-act play staged over two days and then returned to filmmaking, reaching the climax of his career with a spectacular talkie preceded by four adaptations based on some of the most acclaimed Sanskrit dramas. Theatre and film almost coexisted in his rather belatedly commenced career as a filmmaker in his 40s. Yet what Phalke chose to tell, and how he told it, set the bar, parameters and reference points for what a signature Indian narrative on celluloid was to be. In his tone of assertive prescription and inclination towards revelation and codification, it could well be argued that Phalke saw himself as the Bharata *muni* of Indian cinema. He was a figure who, in the context of filmmaking in India, almost assigned to himself the responsibility of recording a film *shastra* (a guiding text or book of codes) for his successors, akin to the *Natyashastra* in its prescriptive tone, and documenting examples illustrating the 'dos and don'ts' for anyone intending to contribute to filmcraft. His had a pioneer's impact and he went on to become the box-office leader in the first decade of Indian cinema, while influencing most of the genre, plot and performance style choices in the Silent Era. Most actors and technicians in the early years of Indian cinema were often discoveries or drop-outs from the Phalke Film Factory, as noted by Phalke in his deposition to the Indian Cinematograph Enquiry Committee of 1927–1928. The 'father of South Indian cinema, J. C. Daniel, had sought guidance and training at Phalke's Nasik-based studio before venturing to make *Vigathakumaran*

(The Lost Child, 1928), also the first Malayalam language film' (Kamal, 2013), just as Phalke had visited Cecil Hepworth's studio near London for his education in filmmaking.

Phalke's means were Western but the ends were uncompromisingly *swadeshi*. This was to be achieved, in Phalke's vision, by opting to reengage and reintroduce his countrymen and fellow filmmakers to India's eternal aesthetic traditions enshrined in the *Natyashastra*. He unpacked its ideas on performance, purpose and appreciation, previously limited to elite discourse, through his extensive commentaries in press and public lectures. Simultaneously, he trained an entire generation of actors, technicians and filmmakers to be mindful of 'entertainment with enlightenment', a tenet that would guide narrative concerns in popular Indian cinema. Most importantly, he brought into the domain of Indian filmmaking the concepts of *bhava* and *rasa*. He emphasised their relevance in acting, direction and the presentation of a film in sync with the limits and possibilities of the medium. In doing so, he set in motion certain signature performative and narrative styles of differentiation in most of Indian cinema that are still evident, creating a prodigious offspring that has managed to imaginatively mutate away from its foreign parent's DNA.

Note

1 Interview with Vikram Gokhale in New Delhi on 1 May, 2013. Gokhale is an actor and the great-grandson of the first female actor of Indian cinema, Durgabai Kamat, who acted in Dadasaheb Phalke's second film, *Mohini Bhasmasur* (1913). Gokhale's grandmother, Kamalabai Gokhale, debuted as a child artiste in the film.

2 Rangoonwalla 1970: 86 (Interview with Phalke from *Kesari*, Poona, of 19 August 1913)

3 It was the recording of a wrestling match in Mumbai.

4 'Any means of self-expression is an art and the message of self-expression is knowledge. When the purpose of the message creates agitation, that form of art is considered inferior. (Bad arts are used only to satiate the hunger of the body and the thirst of the eyes). When the message creates selfless love, truth and great character that art is considered to be sacred'

(Dwivedi 2012); See also *Natyashastra*: Ch. 1 (Translations by Ghosh 1950; Rangacharya 2010).

5 Brahmin scholars trained in Vedic traditions.

6 *Tasmad asaktah satatam karyam karma samacara, asakto hy acaran karma param apnoti purushah* (Therefore, without being attached to the fruits of activities, one should act as a matter of duty, for by working without attachment one attains the Supreme): Bhagavad Gita As It Is 3.19 (A.C. Bhaktivedanta Swami Prabhupada 1972).

7 'The lord deliberately kept me away from the Goddess of Riches during my period of education. Now, he feels that he has tested me enough. So he became kind and entered the hearts of other human beings and fondled me through them' (Phalke 1918).

8 Phalke 1917

9 Subrahmanyam 2010

10 Rangoonwala 1970: 102 (Ladies from cultured families for acting in films: Talk by D.G. Phalke)

11 'My dear children,

I have stepped into the 70th year of my life…

At this point I remember Shakuntala and her ascetic father Kanva Muni from the Mahabharata. Shakuntala was raised frugally by her poor father in a sage's ashram, on the fruits of the forest; she had to wear leaves for clothes.

The same is true of my own beloved daughter—the Indian cinema [Note this is very Hindu/Sanskrit association of equating art to a feminine deity]. When Shakuntala grew up to be talented and beautiful, she married a handsome prince and moved on to live in luxury in his royal abode. She was waited on hand and foot! How happy Kanva muni must have been to see his daughter thus. Just so is my happiness on seeing my precious daughter (the film industry) prosper.

I am here today to celebrate my daughter's 25th birthday. Which father wouldn't be thrilled to see his daughter's prosperity? But there is always a shadow under a light. So enchanted is my daughter with her newfound wealth, that alas, she has forgotten her own father. Her father has been cheated of even his meager possessions: the ashram is no more and the uprooted trees, bare of the leaves that long ago clothed her. But yet, she refuses to acknowledge her father.

I suppose, though, that finally his daughter will do what is right by him.'

(Phalke's 'Thank You' speech as read by director Gajanan Jahagirdar at the Silver Jubilee celebrations of the Indian film industry at Bombay in May 1939) (Phalke Summanwar 2012: 226).

12 According to the auteur theory, an auteur–director is one who either breaks the conventions of his work system or refashions and challenges its existing conventions, most importantly to create a signature cinematic worldview that 'defines his body of work internally and distinguishes it outwardly from another body of work' (Nowell-Smith 1967: 137).

13 I have used this term to define a director who not only manages to evoke each of the *navarasas* in their film but is also able to unite its meaning/suggestion under a single dominant *rasa*.

3

Rasa in Review: Exploring *Natyashastra* Legacies in the Birth of Odia Cinema

> Every rasa, even acting has to be of a certain optimum, for example, the 'look' in looking is different from that in staring. We should not give four doses of sringara where two is necessary, but how many are to be given depends on the creator. Sadly, what we see today is everything going beyond the optimum, exceeding its limits... The limitations have been fixed by the experienced in guides like the Natyashastra[1].
>
> K. Vishwanath, Dadasaheb Phalke award winner
> legendary director–actor

> Without melodrama there cannot be any drama. That is the faith in India. Universally too one cannot jump to the drama stage without some melodrama. In the beginning, melodrama was given importance in all theatre traditions of the world – sung sequences, dialogue duels, etc. are all elements of melodrama. Once melodrama comes in, lyrics follow, and once lyrics come, there will be music, tala[2] (span), laya (rhythm)... This has been given priority in India. We do not accept a drama that is devoid of music. It has been thus in the past, and continues to be so today. Our finer point in narrating something is poetic, and that's why it has happened in our films too[3].
>
> Sarat Pujari, actor–director and a doyen of Odia cinema

Introduction

In cinema's early, foundational years, the depiction of drama on-screen in every major film industry across the world has been scripted by their theatre traditions to varying degrees. Cinema's subsequent global evolution has coincided with an increasing experimental disassociation from its theatrical umbilical cord as it carves a medium-specific niche of its own. In India, the regional and state-specific language cinema industries have followed a similar trajectory. This is reflected in 'the adherence to drama and performance guidelines as suggested in the *Natyashastra* in the initial attempts and experiments at moviemaking by most regional cinemas including the Odia language cinema' (Pujari, 2013). Filmmaking practices in many of these industries continue to retain evidence of a conscious or subconscious engagement with *Natyashastra* postulates on the nature, purpose and appreciation of a cinematic creation. The previous chapter highlighted this foundational influence of the *Natyashastra* and its seminal theory of the *rasas* on the premier pioneer of Indian cinema, Dadasaheb Phalke and his craft. It also explored a possible correlation between his choice of plots and style of cinematic expression and his personal identification with a *swadeshi* ideology.

This chapter aims to contribute to the book's unifying argument for recognising the influence of *Natyashastra* guidelines on filmmaking practices across India and conducting a *rasa*-based criticism of Indian cinema with film evidences from the early Talkie Era, two decades after the commencement of the making of silent films. The evidence under study extends beyond the Centre-West origin space of Indian cinema to engage with the birth moment of the East Indian film industry of Odia language cinema. It will seek to prove the influence of the recommendations of Sanskrit theatre on song situations and dance segments in early Indian films and will engage with contemporary and retrospective reviews of the first and second Odia language films, *Sita Bibaha* (Sita's Marriage, 1936) and *Lalita* (1948), in order to examine the *rasa* theory's influence and continued shaping of film criticism discourses in the Odia cultural space and language media.

The Odia film industry is one of the oldest regional Indian language cinema industries. It is second to East India's most influential Bengali film industry in terms of the number of films released annually. The cinemas of West Bengal, Odisha, Assam (and Manipur in terms of critical acclaim) are collectively the source for over 95 per cent of the films released in East India. Its formative years were shaped by constant collaboration with filmmaking talents in technical help and directorial supervision from West Bengal, with the production capital, acting and music talent being sourced locally from Odisha. This was not only because of a shared cultural affinity between the neighbouring states of Bengal and Odisha 'but also the fact that until the 1970s, Bengali cinema courtesy its originality and evolved sensibility had emerged as a huge creative influence across India, including its national language cinema made in Hindi' (Nanda 2013). The first two Odia films were shot in (then) Calcutta-based studios, and most of the critically acclaimed films in the first half of the 'Golden Age of Odia cinema'[4], the 1960s, were either based on Bengali novels or 'directed by Bengali filmmakers from Kolkata or Bengali-speaking culturatti residing in Odisha like Nitai Palit' (Nanda 2013). Nurtured by Bengali filmmakers, writers and technicians in its infancy and influenced by the dramatic traditions of South Indian cinemas (especially Telegu and Tamil) in its post-1970s maturity, the narrative style of Odia cinema, especially in its early years, has constantly negotiated between the subtle and the theatrical, the realistic and the fantastical, fusing local Odia folk traditions of the *jatra, rasalila*[5] and *gitinatya* with the *Natyashastra*'s *rasa*-evoking prescriptions for an ideal dramatic achievement.

Most of the directors, writers, actors and musicians who were involved in the foundation and establishment of the filmmaking enterprise in Odisha hailed from two of its major drama-performing platforms existing in the early 20th century. The first of these was the touring *mukta mancha jatra* (open air theatres), with its *rasalila* troupes primarily enacting mythical tales and catering to the masses. These were performed in rural and open urban spaces like playgrounds and fields by artists for whom the performances were a means to earn their livelihood. The second were urban theatre groups who performed in a proscenium-like stage at a fixed venue with elaborate sets and lighting, featuring *adhunik* (modern social dramas mostly translated from their Bengali genre counterparts) plays with high acting standards directed primarily by *natyacharyas*[6]. These were normally nurtured by elite patrons and middle-class youth clubs and attracted educated talent from the middle and upper classes for whom theatre was a hobby, which they pursued along with other life-sustaining professions. *Sita Bibaha* and *Lalita* were made from a talent pool sourced from these two public performance platforms. Apart from being landmarks in the history of Odia cinema, they are also valuable representative films from

Indian cinema's Talkie Era. Both were co-production projects shot in Kolkata-based studios involving two of East India's largest language cinemas, Bengali and Odia, with cast and crew collaboration from both industries.

This chapter aims to evidence a revival and reconnect with Sanskrit drama traditions in filmmaking practices in the founding years of Odia cinema. The argument will be based on published print reviews and recorded recollections of audience response to *Sita Bibaha* (no negatives or copies of the film are available today) and an analysis of the presentation (mise en scène), characterisation and song-and-dance scenes in *Lalita* (the oldest available Odia film to view), with fresh insights culled from personal interviews with film archivist and critic Surya Deo, veteran Odia actor-filmmakers Gopal Ghosh and Sarat Pujari[7] and Odia cinema's most prolific filmmaker and commercially successful actor–director turned politician, Prashanta Nanda. The influence of the *rasa* theory in Odia film criticism will be validated through a critical evaluation of *Lalita*'s cinematic advancement on, and correction of, the causes of failure of the first Odia film *Sita Bibaha* as highlighted by its reviews. In this way, it will be established how the evocation of *rasa* was a major parameter of review from the early days of Indian cinema and how it remains an important criterion in a vernacular film criticism discourse.

Reviewing the Reviews of *Sita Bibaha* and *Lalita*

Sita Bibaha was released at the Laxmi Hall in Odisha's coastal temple town of Puri on 28 April 1936. This landmark moment in the history of Odia cinema had happened 27 days after the independent state of Odisha (then Orissa) was born on 1 April 1936, following the British Parliament's resolution in 1933 to reorganise states on the basis of linguistic identity. It was an ambitious venture because, unlike most Indian regional film industries, Odia cinema was bypassing the silent film phase to debut with a talkie. *Sita Bibaha* could have been an important cultural monument and moment in the myriad early-20th-century sociopolitical movements dedicated to the establishment of an independent Odia identity. Instead, 'it was unanimously rejected by both critics and viewers' (Pujari 2013). A review of *Sita Bibaha* by critic Atanu Patnaik, published in the Odia publication *Utkala Dipika* on 1 May, 1936 states:

> Is this film (*Sita Bibaha*) worthy of conveying any *bhavas*? I could say an emphatic 'no'! First of all, (the film's source) Kampala Mishra's play (1899) is inadequate from a modern perspective. Added to that, producer Mohan Goswami's unimaginative production has rendered it completely distorted, and completely devoid of any *rasa*. The result is an unusual product born from mixing *rasalila* and Kampala Mishra's narration. It is worthy neither of the classes nor the masses (Patnaik 1936). [Translation: mine]

The critique of *Sita Bibaha* is based on the absence of two significant aesthetic terms from the *Natyashastra*—*bhava* and *rasa*—from the film's viewing experience. What does the use of these terms, which are over two millennia old, in *Sita Bibaha*'s review tell us about the role and influence of the *Natyashastra* in the shaping of criticism debates within an emerging 20th-century art form? The research into their use is particularly pertinent given the broad consensus among historians and art critics that the *Natyashastra's* influence had almost disappeared by the turn of the 12th century in North India and the 14th century in the South, due to the evolving sociopolitical contours in the Indian subcontinent of the period. The most significant factors involved included a decline in the political fortunes of local Hindu patrons, the rising influence of Islamicate and European rulers and cultures with differing artistic and linguistic sensibilities, an overall fusion of cultural experiences and change in popular tastes[8]. The negligent use of Sanskrit in conversational usage, continuance of region-specific modern vernaculars and emergence of new and popular lingua franca, like Urdu, Hindi and later English, resulted in the rigorous *Maargi* (or classical theatre) giving way to a more flexible folk theatre. An aesthetic guide motif that had been continuing uninterrupted for over two millennia, however, could not disappear without trace. Sanskrit theatre continued to thrive in the private drama and temple spaces of Hindu kings, in the personal *baris* of *zamindars* (in Bengal), in *Bhagavata Tungis* in the villages of Odisha and in a few publicly performed theatre forms like Kerala's *Koodiyattam* (where the main characters spoke in Sanskrit, while the side characters like the *vidushaka* or jester spoke in vernacular languages like Malayalam and occasionally even Hindi) and Tamil Nadu's *Bhagavata Mela* tradition. Although not always practised in public as a dramatic form, in essence, the performance postulates of Sanskrit dramaturgy continued to influence and shape the many *desi* offspring of the ancient Indian theatre. These are being performed to date, for example the *Therukuttu* (Tamil Nadu), *Bhavai* (Gujarat), *Sangeet natak* (Maharashtra), *Katha* and *Ramleelas* (of Central and North India) and *Jatra* and *Rasalilas* (of Bengal and Odisha), among others. According to classical Bharatnatyam dancer, teacher, scholar and Indologist, Padma Subrahmanyam:

> The *Maargi* theorised by Bharata survived in snatches unconsciously in most of the regional traditions, proving the imperishable nature of what the *Natyashastra* prescribed and its ability to transcend strong and specific regional identities… Roving theatre groups must have had a mastery over Sanskrit, enabling communication across regions (Subrahmanyam 2010: 35, 43).

Though the performance of plays and songs became more frequent in the existent and emerging Prakrit languages, they were 'still being directed by *natyacharyas* well-versed in the *Natyashastra*' (Ghosh 2014), while many drama, poetry and dance pieces continued to be written in Sanskrit, like Jaideva's *Gita Govinda* (12th century CE) or Bhanudatta's *Rasamanjari* and *Rasatarangini* (early 16th century CE). Sanskrit also continued as the language of record for critical debates and new commentaries on the *Natyashastra*. The production of these remained consistent for Sanskrit scholars and *natyacharyas* across medieval India, peaking with Abhinavagupta in Kashmir in the 11th century CE. The performance of Jaideva's *Gita Govinda*, a dramatic lyrical poem in Sanskrit, was introduced as a *seva* (service) ritual by rulers of the Ganga dynasty in the Sri Mandir, or the Jagannath temple of Puri, in coastal Odisha in the 13th century CE. It continued to remain an influential and frequently performed dramatic work in Bengal and Odisha's religious folk theatre traditions of *rasalila* performances (performed only by boys up to the age of 14) and Radha–Krishna centric *prema rasalilas* (performed by adults portraying adult characters) (Khokar 2010). These commanded the highest respect amongst the variety of performing arts that defined the vibrant Odia dramatic space at the time of the release of *Sita Bibaha* in the 1930s.

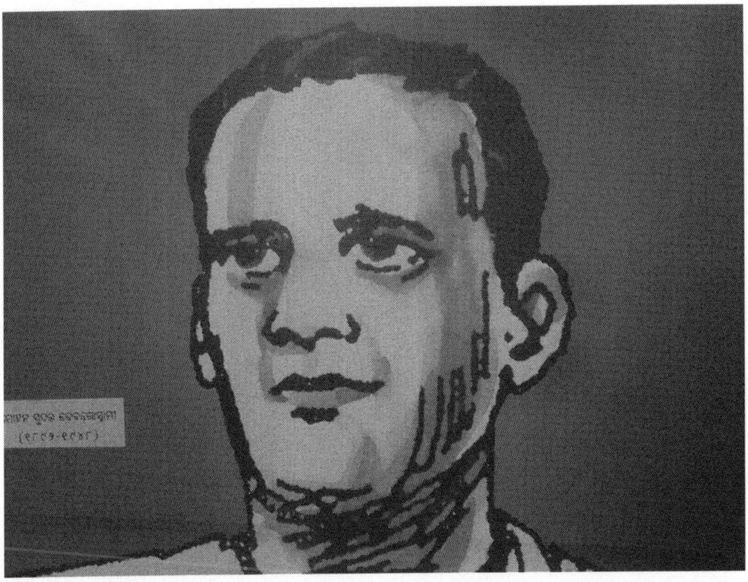

Image 3.1 Mohan Sundar Deb Goswami: A Portrait (Photograph: Piyush Roy)

Mohan Sundar Deb Goswami was chosen to direct the first Odia film as a measure to assure investor confidence. He had a patron-association with Odisha's then *rasalila* traditions, and his contribution to its popularisation had made him a cultural icon of East India. Before making his cinematic debut with *Sita Bibaha*, Goswami was an acknowledged writer, poet, actor and *bhajan-kirtan* singer 'who could play 27 different instruments and also served as a priest in the Puri temple' (Deo 2013). In 1918, he founded a touring *rasalila* group, the Sriradha Kunjabihari Rasa Party, which performed to critical acclaim both inside Odisha and in places like Calcutta, Madras and Bombay. It earned a steady fan following in the Odisha, Bengal and Assam drama circuit. Producer Priyanath Ganguli of Kali Films, who produced *Sita Bibaha*, was one such fan and he considered Goswami his guru.

Kalicharan Patnaik, the director of the second Odia film, started his performance career as the head of a local *rasalila* group, before founding the Orissa theatre, 'which was one of the three major urban theatre groups operating in coastal Odisha around the time of India's independence along with the Bharati and Annapurna theatres' (Ghosh 2014). He spent the last phase of his creative career in popularising and enriching the Odissi dance form by contributing to the research and dissemination of its historical connections with the *Natyashastra*. Patnaik's studied engagement with and referencing of the *Natyashastra* in theatrical practice was not unique to the Odia theatre space. The treatise was being engaged with as a revered guide and reference for many legends-to-be from the early years of most Indian language cinemas. Tamil cinema's first superstar, Sivaji Ganesan, in his *Autobiography of an Actor* (2007), narrates how he slept with the *Natyashastra* under his pillow as a trainee actor in Madras' company theatres, 'hoping for a subconscious slipping of its vast knowledge into his conscious mind while asleep' (Swamy 2007). Hindi cinema's first leading lady from the South, Vyjayanthimala Bali, 'whose success is credited with having made training in at least one classical Indian dance form an unstated essential for subsequent Hindi film heroine aspirants' (Khan 2015), has discussed in her autobiography *Bonding... A Memoir* (2007) how the *Natyashastra* was the only manual she referred to in her training as a Bharatanatyam dancer. She describes how that knowledge helped her sustain and enrich her long cinematic innings as a leading Hindi cinema dancer–actress in the 1950s and 1960s (Bali 2008: 48). Her dancing legacy successor in the 1970s, Hema Malini, says, 'Film acting came easy to me because of my training in classical dance, which is all about how to express *bhavas* and convey *rasas*' (2013). Odia cinema's first superstar Sarat Pujari states, 'Because I used to research a lot on *Natyashastra* guidelines, when not rehearsing, I could draw my own interpretations on how to emote differently for cinema while remaining true to its expectations from good acting' (2014).

In the previous chapter, I discussed how Dadasaheb Phalke's father, Dajishastri Phalke, was a tutor of Sanskrit, a priest and a *kirtankar* trained in the *Natyashastra*, who used to educate and entertain audiences in temples and private functions through song narrations from the epics and the *puranas*. Mohan Goswami himself was a popular *bhajan-kirtan* singer, actor and dramatist. He trained artists in his *rasalilas* and theatre groups in *rasa*-evoking performance.

Working within a pan-Indian creative context where the *Natyashastra* was an integral guide for actors, writers and directors, how did Goswami's cinematic debut, *Sita Bibaha*, become '*rasa sunya* or devoid of *rasa*' (Patnaik 1936), as it was unanimously condemned by its critics? Three broad reasons offered for the film's failing were: 'Goswami's ignorance of the film form'[9], the mid-way takeover of the film's direction and making by Kolkata-based technicians of Kali Films that overrode Goswami and the mid-way loss of interest of the film's producer due to production delays and frequent squabbles between the film's cast members from Odisha and Bengal. As a result, the film's producers just wanted to finish the project and move on. Actor–dramatist Kartik Kumar Ghosh, one of the few film crew members from Odisha, who collaborated on the Odia translation of the screenplay of *Sita Bibaha*, stated:

> The quality of the film suffered because of creative squabbles on the sets, indiscipline among cast members and the lack in authentic performance and delivery styles of most actors who were *rasalila* performers with no prior experience or training in acting for cinema (Ghosh 1985).

Though the credits of *Sita Bibaha* declare Goswami as the film's originator, conceptualiser, producer and director (*suchaka, ayojaka, prajojaka, nirdeshaka*), 'the film was produced by Bengali entrepreneur Priyanath Ganguli under the banner of Kali Films and directed by Prafulla Sarkar, a director employed with Ganguli's studio with assistance from cameraman Noni Sanyal' (Singh 2008: 39–42). The critic Surya Deo blames the film's failure on 'Goswami's complete dependence on the crew from the Bengali film industry, which was unaware of the regional aesthetic styles of Odisha and the expectations of the local Odia audience' (Deo 2013). The most significant contribution of the film's Odia team members was the music composed by Haricharan Mohanty, which was 'tuned to authentic Odia folk and traditional devotional singing styles based on songs written by Goswami and popular literary compositions like the '*Bitalaku alingana*' (Embracing the depths) *chanda* excerpted from Odia Kabi Samrat (King of Poets) Upendra Bhanja's popular medieval *kavya* (epic poem) '*Baidehi-sa-Bilasa*' (Sojourning with Sita)' (Deo 2013).

The severity of the indictment and commercial rejection of *Sita Bibaha* meant that it took almost 12 years for the second Odia film, *Lalita*, to get made. Gopal Ghosh, lead actor and a producing partner of the second in production, but third to be released Odia film *Sri Jagannath* (Lord Jagannath 1950) says:

> In India, unlike Hollywood, the dominant narrative themes in the early years of movie making for a long time followed the trend of Phalke's *Raja Harishchandra*, selecting tales from *itihasa* (history) and *kimbadanti* (local mythology and folk lore), before attempting social dramas. In Odisha too, we opted for a safe and well-known story from local lore on the making of its most revered shrine, the Sri Mandir at Puri, dedicated to *rashtra-debata* (state deity) Lord Jagannath. But given the disastrous performance of *Sita Bibaha*, generating funder confidence was a big challenge because of which we decided to launch a public limited company called Rupa Bharati Public Ltd. Co. (Ghosh 2014).

Before the public limited company could take off, a private limited company funded by the royal family of Dhenkanal (a central Odisha province) under the banner of Great Eastern Movietone started and released *Lalita*, which was based on a short, love-story-based subplot, also from the making of the Jagannath temple legend.

The Auteurship of a *Natyacharya*

Irrespective of who took the final creative decision, Goswami's was the official name on record responsible for the *Sita Bibaha* disaster. Gopal Ghosh stated that 'the film's poor quality reaffirmed the notion that Odia films would not work unless helmed by technical talents from Calcutta' (Ghosh 2014). He had seen the film during its initial release in 1936 at the age of 16. One of the criticisms of *Sita Bibaha*, published in a review in *Desha Katha* (5 April 1936), suggested that 'instead of searching for/employing Odisha's *natyakaars* and *natyacharyas*, and (better) plays in the Odia language, the producers, Kali Films, have opted for an easily available source. The result is not only a waste of money but also presents a distorted image of Odia art'. The critique can also be seen as articulating an elite bias that popular art forms are frequently subjected to on the basis of the class of their consumers or for their use of narrative conventions presumed to be simple and less intellectually stimulating. Goswami, having risen from a lesser and mass-consumed drama form like the *rasalila,* is thus supposed to be less qualified to work within a new dramatic form like cinema in comparison to a *natyacharya* like Kalicharan Patnaik, who had experience in a more evolved drama form like the urban theatre. According to Ghosh, 'To revive the lack in confidence of the Odia audience in the ability of Odia filmmakers it thus became necessary that the second film be directed by a *natyacharya*' (Ghosh 2014). Along with being one of the foremost authorities on the performing arts of Odisha, Patnaik was also popularly acknowledged as the Bharata *muni* of the modern Odia dance and drama space for his pioneering contribution towards the shaping of modern Odia theatre. He fused Western stagecraft techniques with performance styles of folk and Sanskrit theatre and helmed the revival and codification of the Odissi dance in the mid-20th century. The highlight of the need for a *natyacharya*, a theatre guru well-read and trained in the traditions of the *Natyashastra*, also indicates an endorsement of the relevance of Sanskrit theatre traditions in critical aesthetic debates around the time of the making of *Sita Bibaha.*

The making of *Lalita,* like *Sita Bibaha*, was outsourced to studios in Kolkata, where the film was made with help from Bengali technicians like Gaur Goswami and Suren Pal (music directors), Banshi Chandragupta (art direction), Baidyanath Chatterjee (editing) and Kalyan Gupta (technical advisor), but attempts were made to not repeat the disconnect of Odia audiences with *Sita Bibaha*. It was hoped that this would be assured by entrusting greater autonomy in its direction to a *natyacharya* whose credentials are visibly highlighted in the film's opening credits as a valuable suffix to his name—Story, Dialogue, Direction: Kabichandra Kalicharan Patnaik Natyacharya—just as many subsequent Indian films would highlight the prowess of their technicians by frequently suffixing their names with their degrees in the credits. According to film historian Bhim Singh:

> With Kalicharan Patnaik oscillating back-and-forth between Calcutta and Odisha, the job of completing *Lalita* too, eventually fell on its technical consultant Kalyan Gupta (who was soon to court international acclaim as the production manager of Jean Renoir's *The River,* 1951), just like Prafulla Sarkar had directed *Sita Bibaha,* while the film's credits acknowledged Mohan Goswami as its director (Singh 2008: 66).

While he does not completely deny Singh's observations, Deo argues that Kalicharan Patnaik's involvement and impact on the making of *Lalita* was comparatively more than that of Goswami on *Sita Bibaha*, with Patnaik's directorial signature being distinctly visible in the film's song moments. This perhaps explains the abrupt oscillations in *Lalita*'s mise en scène between song-and-dance sequences shot on elaborate sets with changing screen backdrops retaining the Orissa theatre influence and actual outdoor shots that hint at emerging experiments with realism in Bengali moviemaking. *Lalita* does at times indicate an unimaginative replication of the *Natyashastra*'s theatre-specific dramaturgical prescriptions on emoting, production and set design aimed at just evoking a *rasa*, instead of an evolved approach to sustaining the *rasa* in accordance with the limits and possibilities offered by the cinematic medium. Deo says:

> Kalibabu definitely directed the song sequences, which are good compositions that became quite popular with the viewers, and remain a highlight of the film to date. But most of them appear like inserts interrupting the film's narrative continuity, especially the dance numbers that appear to have little connect with their preceding or following drama sequences (Deo 2014).

Lalita, however, is not completely devoid of attempts at authenticity and integration of elements from the local Odia culture. For example, the practice of the caste system is displayed in how a tribal family treats a Brahmin guest; social attitudes are highlighted through the concept of *atithi devo-bhava* (guest is god); scenes explore greater characterisation nuances, such as the depiction of Lalita's inner conflicts after the sudden disappearance of Vidyapati and a perceptible consideration for local sensitivities is shown in the depiction of mythological miracles integral to the story of the making of the first temple dedicated to Lord Jagannath in Puri.

Sita Bibaha vs. *Lalita*

In retrospect, *Lalita* may seem to be a quaint mixture of evolving cinematic sensibilities in Bengal and the *jatra* and *rasalila* form of acting in Odia theatre. The criticisms of *Lalita* notwithstanding, there can be no doubt that while *Sita Bibaha* was a flop, *Lalita*, though not a hit, recovered its making cost 'as acknowledged by its producer Gourendra Pratap Singh Dev' (Singh 2008: 67). It was only with the third Odia film *Sri Jagannath*—which was based on the same legend as *Lalita* but was shot with greater cinematic imagination (outdoor locations, flashback sequences, natural acting, etc.) and which released after *Lalita*—that Odia cinema got its first critical and commercial blockbuster. It also became a huge hit in neighbouring states like West Bengal and Andhra Pradesh, where it was dubbed and re-released in the Telegu language. Deo measures the achievements of these films on the *rasa* parameter, progressing from 'no *rasa* in *Sita Bibaha*, to first attempts at *rasa* realisation in *Lalita*, followed by maximum achievement of *rasa* in *Sri Jagannath* (1950)' (Deo 2014). He explains:

> *Sita Bibaha* was basically a static camera recording a play. It was like a recitation by actors with no *bhava* (in its performances) or relevant supporting facial expressions. In *Lalita*, there is greater focus on *bhangi* (gestural acting), than *bhava* (emotion expressing acting). We can at least see the character of Lalita articulating feelings of joy and despair in the presence and absence of Vidyapati. It marks a conscious effort towards engaging with some cinematic values. The fundamental difference between the two is that one can notice a conscious effort being made for the first time in *Lalita* to portray *bhavas* and evoke *rasa*. Those who have seen *Sita Bibaha* opine that no such efforts were tried in it. *Sita Bibaha* was primarily a *gitinatya*, *Lalita* at least had dialogue and conversations that contributed towards articulating character motivations. Kalibabu (Kalicharan Patnaik)

> was a great actor, dance teacher and theatre director but not technically sound with regards to the cinematic language. So, the cinematic quality of *Lalita* though better than *Sita Bibaha* was still of a middling standard, which was finally corrected in the third Odia film *Sri Jagannath,* in its competent merging of the cinematic medium's possibilities at conjuring a believable spectacle in the outdoor along with realistic performances by Odia actors that lent a regional flavour and authenticity to its narrative. For *rasa* to be felt by the Odia audience the subject and its telling had to be in sync with local culture, customs and modes of being and behaving. While the selection of a story based on the best known, most popular lore around the making of the temple of the state deity, Sri Jagannath, was a wise decision to address box-office concerns around attracting Odia audiences after their unanimous rejection of *Sita Bibaha*, *Lalita*'s limitations lay in its limited engagement with the possibilities of the cinematic medium and the casting of yet another incompatible lead pair [like *Sita Bibaha*] (Deo 2014).

According to actor Kartik Ghosh:

> Leaving aside lead actor Makhanlal Bannerjee, none of the performers in *Sita Bibaha* were able to strike a chord with the audience. The heroine looked elderly and healthier than the hero. There was also something unnatural about the way the spoken language sounded in the film, as it had been translated from Bengali to Odia (Ghosh 1985).

The actors in both *Sita Bibaha* and *Lalita* were regular theatre performers and had no previous knowledge or experience of acting for cinema. *Sri Jagannath*, however, had a mix of local Odia actors from traditional and new performing mediums; hence their acting and dialogue delivery was relatively more authentic and relatable to the Odia audience. Gopal Ghosh, who was initially approached to play the lead male role of Lalita's lover and husband, Vidyapati, in *Lalita*, says:

> *Lalita* was mostly shot indoors like a lavish stage play with painted screens in the background, some of which could be seen shaking in the final frames. The heroine Uma Bannerjee at that time was on a contract with Calcutta's Star theatre and could only shoot in the evenings because of which all her shots [except one brief running shot]

had to be shot indoors. Uma, who was the widow of Makhanlal Bannerjee, the hero of *Sita Bibaha*, was senior in age and experience to the film's debuting hero, and looked more like his *mausi* (aunt), if not mother. Her pronunciation of Odia was defective with a heavy Bengali accent. The hero played by Lokanath Mishra, who went onto become a member of Indian Parliament and governor of Assam, had joined the cast because of his interest in theatre, but he had no previous professional experience in acting. Their casting was a visual mismatch and the discomfort was too telling for the audiences to be convinced or feel any lasting *rasa* of *sringara* or romance in their on-screen love story (Ghosh 2014).

Sringara rasa in *Lalita*

I will now discuss what Deo suggests as some of the elements of 'blindly adhering' (Deo 2014) to the *Natyashastra* in *Lalita's* structure and characterisation that are representative of and common to filmmaking styles in India's early Talkie Era. This will be followed by a detailed analysis of the aesthetic achievements of the film—namely, the emotively performed, *bhava* rich lyrical music scenes—and discussion of how they enhance the evocation of the narrative's dominant *rasa* of *sringara*.

Narration and Characterisation

The characters in *Lalita* in their *angika* (physical), *vachika* (verbal), *aharya* (ornamental/costume) and *satvika* (emotional) *abhinaya* (acting)[10] literally embody the prescriptions for playing their type of parts, as recommended in the *Natyashastra*. All the tribal characters, including the protagonist Lalita, the daughter of tribal chief Biswabasu, speak in a comparatively higher decibel, in animated tones, and appear easily excited or moved to extremes of emotions. King Indradyumna and the head priest, on the contrary, speak in exalted intonations and appear in control of their emotions even in the face of disappointments and provocations. The Brahmin hero and army commander, Vidyapati, too shares their regal aptitude for a controlled display of emotions, though he speaks in a relatively normal, common man's Odia.

The narrative of *Lalita* is taken from a subplot in the popular Odia legend on the building of the Jagannath temple in Puri, which is also considered as one of the four holy destinations for Hindus. The original story has King Indradyumna and his queen Gundicha as its protagonists. Indradyumna organises a search for Lord Krishna's material remains at the end of the Dwapara Yuga[11]. The remains are discovered by his commander Vidyapati and brought to Puri, where the king then builds a grand temple to Lord Jagannath, who Vaishnavite Hindus believe to be the present-day manifestation of Krishna. It is primarily a devotional tale, as seen in two subsequent Odia blockbusters titled *Sri Jagannath* (in 1950 and 1979). The film *Lalita* retells the above legend as the love story of Lalita and Vidyapati, celebrating the *sringara rasa*. It inserts narrative novelties to enhance the *romantic* telling or the *sringara rasa* in its drama, through discernible plot inspirations, arguably from Kalidasa's *Abhijñānaśākuntalam*, featuring the separation and union of its lead pair of lovers. The film's preference for love songs over devotional songs, unlike other films on the same theme, can be interpreted as a deliberate distraction in the service of evoking its dominant theme *rasa* of *sringara*. However, under this uniting arch of *sringara*, the film tries to conform to the *rasa* theory postulate regarding the need of a good drama to serve a variety of *rasas*, while uniting them under one dominant *rasa*. Its narrative has subplots and supporting characters serving as triggers for conjuring the remaining *rasas* from the *navarasas*. These include the heroic as present in Vidyapati and Biswabasu's lady warriors, marvellous as represented by the sequence of events leading to the discovery of the cave of Nilamadhaba and most of the group dance sequences, *hasya* as evinced through the caricatured court priests' jealousy of the head priest, furious as illustrated by Biswabasu following Vidyapati's betrayal of his trust and fearfulness as present in Biswabasu's tribesmen over a rumoured attack by king Indradyumna's army. According to veteran Odia actor-filmmaker Prashanta Nanda:

> A film having characters embodying various *rasas* is a requirement here [in Odisha/India], and we are used to it. In all those entertainment forms that predated cinema in Odisha, like *jatra, pala, dashkathiya, gitinatya*, etc. the *navarasas* have been played. So, having all the *rasas*

> in their entertainment has become a requirement of our audience. If you do not give it to them in a drama or cinema, the audience feels that there is something missing somewhere. Even if you take just one *rasa* and make a film, the other eight have to be incorporated in different measures. You cannot just ignore them. Sometimes when we ignore the *navarasas*, people accept those films too, but those are exceptions not the rule (Nanda 2013).

Dance and Music

The dance and music scenes of *Lalita*, according to Deo, remain 'the only timeless elements in an otherwise dated film' (Deo 2014). They also identify and accentuate the directorial contribution of Kalicharan Patnaik, a dancer–actor and dance guru of repute. He says:

> Kalibabu was a believer of the Vaishnava cult and a performer of *rasalila*. He was a musician, who performed and critiqued the then existing Odia dance forms and had an understanding of how to use them with various forms of typical Odia *raga malikas* like *chanda, champu*, etc. This makes the song sequences of *Lalita* an authentic representation of then existing dance traditions of Odisha and a valuable cultural document for art historians. The dance sequences in the technically superior *Sri Jagannath*, which released after *Lalita*, too pale in comparison to the brilliance of *its* choreography and song compositions. The film also features the first ever on the screen portrayal of a dance form, the *Dakhini nacha*, which could be identified as the closest precursor of the *Odissi* dance form, which was subsequently recovered from the temples and codified into its modern form in the 1950s and 1960s (Deo 2014).

Released in 1948, at a time when the craft of filmmaking was already on the cusp of experimenting and interacting with 'emerging realism imperatives in world cinema'[12], *Lalita* opted to tell its tale in the stylised theatrical tradition of the early Indian talkies, when 'the advent of sound made Indian filmmakers revive the *Natyashastra* inspired popular Indian drama tradition of song-and-dance interspersed narratives almost with a vengeance' (Benegal 2015). Frequent musical breaks occur in *Lalita* to accommodate seven songs and three dance sequences in the 90-minute-long film. The first is a hymn to Lord Jagannath in the *Natyashastra* tradition of invoking a god such as Shiva, Ganesha or Indra before the start of a performance or play. The film uses documentary footage of the Jagannath temple to go with its opening hymns. It thus acknowledges the realism aspects of the cinematic medium, while retaining a narrative opening convention prescribed in the *Natyashastra*. It also moves beyond a pure recording of a play on stage or indoor sets (as in the case of *Sita Bibaha*) by cutting its action occasionally with real life, outdoor shots.

The film's three dance sequences come as pure dance events unaccompanied by any singing. This is in conformation with the idea of inserting dance as a means of embellishment or *alankara* in a *natyadharmi* play, which is aimed at evoking the *adbhuta rasa* in the audience as an element of joyous wonder. The film begins with an aesthetically choreographed dance sequence, a *chitra purvaranga* act, which seems to be performed in the *devaloka* (land of gods) as it ends with a dialogue between the god of love, Kamdev, and his wife, Rati, with the latter challenging Kamdev to prove the prowess of his flower arrows on Lalita. The next dance performance, a robust group dance by tribal characters with choreography similar to Western Odisha's Sambalpuri folk dance, is inserted prior to the film's first major confrontation sequence between the royal forces and Biswabasu's tribesmen. It is experienced from a perspective of curious wonder as two urban pundits snatch a glimpse of an exotic and tribal art form. The film's third and penultimate dance sequence is presented as a *devadasi* performance celebrating the consecration of the new temple of Lord Jagannath. Performed in the then prevalent *Dakhini nacha* (dance) style, the dance piece is now regarded as an influential predecessor of subsequent Odissi dance sequences on screen.

The abrupt nature of the appearance of the dance sequences in *Lalita* can be seen as evidence of Patnaik's comfort with, and control and continuance of, the theatrical style of storytelling, instead of a relatively linear and logical cinematic structure. Their afterthought-like insertion is not unnatural if placed in the context of an introductory precedence fable from the performance event of Bharat *muni*'s first drama in the *devaloka,* titled *Amrutamanthan* in the *Natyashastra.* The first chapter of the *Natyashastra* mentions how, after Bharata *muni* composed the first drama, dance sequences by *gandharvas* and *apsaras* (celestial musicians and nymphs) were inserted as an afterthought on Lord Brahma's suggestion to make the performance more entertaining, complete, beautiful and appealing to all.

The Love Songs of *Lalita*

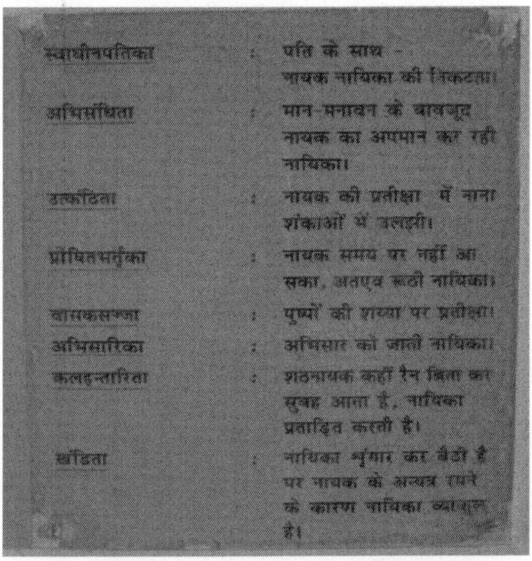

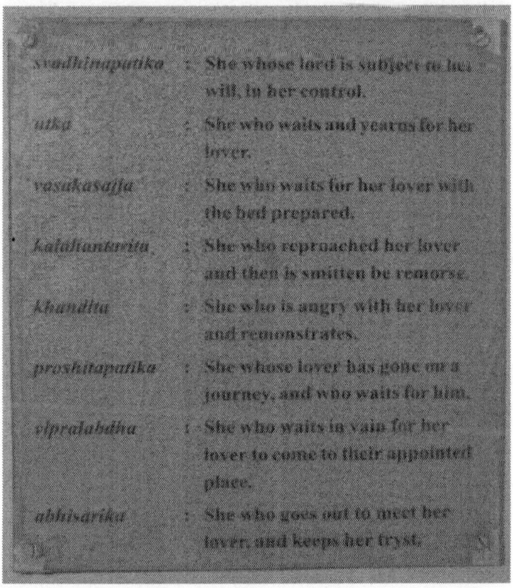

Image 3.2 Patna Museum Displays Explaining the Various *Ashta-Nayika* Moods (Photographs: V.P. Sahi)

The *rasa* achievement in *Lalita* is arguably the most pronounced in its songs, some of which, like character Lalita's introduction song '*Thare kiri basanta*' (Patnaik 1948)[13]/'Slowly o spring' (Roy 1993)[14], became popular with audiences and are the most remembered bequest of the forgotten film in popular imagination. These are conceived as lyrical scenes 'in the *Radha–Krishna premalila* tradition of performing the *Gita Govinda*' (Deo 2014). Like the verses of *Gita Govinda* 'where Radha is visualised in a series of [*ashta-nayika*] moods in Krishna's presence—angry, jealous and resentful of his dalliance with other *gopis* (village maidens), wilting in pangs of separation from Krishna, etc.—all dictated by the one basic emotion of love for Krishna called *rati*, which is the *sthayibhava*' (Subrahmanyam 2010: 50), the lyrics of the songs in *Lalita*, through similarly inspired situations and reactions, articulate the stated and unstated (in love) *bhavas* of its protagonist. This contributes to the film's overall impact as a dramatic work evoking the *sringara rasa*. Lalita is established as the ideal *Natyashastra* heroine in the film's songs. They become a vehicle for presenting most of the '*ashta-nayikas*' (NS 24.210–224), a collective name for the eight types of heroines, representing eight different mood states in relation to their heroes within the two extremities of the being-in-love mood state, *sambhoga* (the experiencing of a joyous state of love in union) and *vipralambha* (the experiencing of a sorrowful state born of love in separation).

Image 3.3 The Poster of the Film *Lalita*, Highlighting an On-Screen Shot from the *Thare Kari Basanta* Song Portraying the *Bhava* of a *Vasakasajja Nayika* Essayed by Actress Uma Bannerjee as Lalita (Photograph: Piyush Roy)

Lalita's introduction song presents her as a *vasakasajja nayika* (a heroine eager for union), ready, decorated and playful, in the full bloom of youth, expecting to meet a lover or fall in love. She sings, '*Thare kari basanta pheriona, phulamana kari chori...*' (Patnaik 1948)/'Slowly o spring look back; why have you stolen the heart of the wild flower' (Roy 1993).

She next meets Vidyapati, whom she falls in love with at first sight, as the god of love, Kamdev, plays cupid. The mood of the *vasakasajja nayika* continues into the next song, '*Ae dhani Jamuna ku jaye...*' (Patnaik 1948)/'The damsel goes to river Yamuna' (Roy 1993). This is a celebratory description of the adornments and decoration of a heroine in love in sweet anticipation of returning to her lover. The song is sung by Lalita's friends, as they discuss the radiance of her being and the beauty of her adornments, teasing her about her first experiences of love:

> [Song 2: Translated lyric excerpts from stanzas 2 and 3]
> The damsel goes to Yamuna, her beauty endless in blue attire
> The sounds of bells on her feet, tinkling.
> The pot on her shoulders makes her beauty endless...
> Her mind dances in love, the cupid has struck (Roy 1993).

The influence of *Gita Govinda* and the Radha–Krishna *prema-rasalila* is evident in the lyrics' reference to the Yamuna river, where Radha used to go with her water pots to furtively meet Krishna, though Lalita is going to the banks of the Mahanadi. According to Deo:

> The gestures, choreography and flirtatious interaction of Lalita with her friends are inspired by similarly performed *rasalila* songs, while the nature of their interactions and imageries used can be sourced to situations in the *Gita Govinda*, which thus also reaffirms the latter's influence on performed arts in Odisha (Deo 2014).

The Radha–Krishna reference returns in the next song, '*Banaphula Radhe Krishna bolo he*' (Patnaik 1948)/'O' wild flower sing Radhe Krishna' (Roy 1993), where Lalita's unstated emotions and pining for Vidyapati are heightened by comparing them to that of the mythical heroine Radha's longing for Krishna. The song is sung by a friend of Lalita, who articulates the heroine's moods of the *virahotkanthita nayika* (one distressed by separation):

> [Song 4: Translated lyric excerpts from stanzas 2 and 3]
> O wild flower sing Radhe Krishna, my lord is here
> What is it that makes the stranger your own?
> In the moonlit night, why don't I get sleep?
> Have I not cared for all your pining?
> My heart has heard all your beatings… (Roy 1993).

The choice of the Radha–Krishna *rasalila* imagery of anticipation and restlessness evoked in the song helps further accentuate the unstated onscreen mood state of the separated lovers, Lalita and Vidyapati.

The film's penultimate song, '*Pheri ana-a-na aau thare*' (Patnaik 1948)/'Why don't you look O' traveller at those left behind' (Roy 1993), is played after Vidyapati's uninformed abandoning of a sleeping Lalita to attend a call of duty to King Indradyumna. It is once again sung by a third person, a bystander, articulating Lalita's hurt and angst as a *vipralabdha* (a heroine deceived by her lover) and a *proshitabhartruka nayika* (a heroine missing her sojourning husband/lover, who is absent from home). Lalita is seen sitting distressed, with her hair hanging loose, in conformation with the *bhava* state's suggested description in the *Natyashastra* (NS 24.218). The song is performed by a sombre male voice in an empathetic state of visible distress. It conjures associations with and imagery of loss to further amplify the protagonist Lalita's state of heartbreak, thereby accentuating the audience's experience of the *rasa* of *sringara* in *vipralambha* (love in separation):

> [Song 5: Translated lyric excerpts from stanza 3]
> So many unspoken words
> Those moonlit-soaked half made garlands
> Those watery eyes of the wild deer
> Let they be left behind.
> If thoughts come to you in lonely nights
> Do not look back O' traveller
> Do not look back… (Roy 1993).

Between these song sequences, Lalita gets to embody the other *ashta-nayikas* in passing or in totality, including the '*abhisarika nayika*' (NS24.219)—a heroine driven by love or infatuation, who lets go of the limits of her modesty or the shyness expected of her gender and takes the initiative to meet her lover. Lalita initiates the love and courtship scenes depicted in the film, since Vidyapati is depicted to be of a shy nature. Subsequent to her marriage to Vidyapati, she is primarily seen in the role of the *svadhinabhartruka nayika*, that is, a heroine with a husband who, captivated by her beauty, is perpetually by her side in near-complete subjugation to her charms. In the framing of their romantic scenes, it is interesting to note how Lalita frequently assumes a position of higher perspective and an active role (e.g., initiating interaction) conventionally reserved for the male (for instance, Krishna initiating most action in the Radha–Krishna imagery).

Lalita, however, is never seen as a *kalahantarita* (an impatient heroine separated from her lover over a quarrel), or a *khandita nayika* (a heroine enraged with her lover for cheating on her), as the film's romantic plot and its allied tensions do not require any articulation of those role types.

The film, in its characterisation and the behaviour of its protagonist in both its song and drama situations, thus adheres to the acting guidelines prescribed in the *Natyashastra* when selecting and rejecting relevant *ashta-nayika* types suitable to its heroine. These eight archetypal emotional situations of the romantic heroine have been depicted and have inspired recurrent themes, images and character-inspirations in Indian paintings, sculptures, literature and classical dance.

They find a cinematic interpretation in protagonist Lalita's various *bhava* states in love, endorsing Deo's review of the film as a conscious attempt to evoke some element of *rasa* through complimenting lyrical and expressive acting, compared to the non-*rasa*-evoking performances in *Sita Bibaha*. The songs offer an eclectic mix of Odia *raga-sangeet*, rendered in the traditional singing style of devotional songs (*bhajans*), *chanda*, interactive *gitinatya* (musical dramas) and *nrityanatya* (dance dramas) style of conversational lyrics, along with mood-highlighting lyrical commentaries in the three-stanza poetry format of most Indian film songs.

The acting in the songs may seem emotive or theatrical in light of changing audience sensibilities, but the presentation of the songs in *Lalita* is not completely oblivious to the cinematic medium's possibility to distinguish between the diegetic and non-diegetic sound sources. In contrast to the early talkie films, where the characters, irrespective of whether they had a background in music or not, had to sing songs due to the unavailability of playback singing, in *Lalita*, the hero Vidyapati, in deference to the reserved nature of his character, never sings himself. For instance, in the song '*Pheri ana-a-na*' (Patnaik 1948), he has a wandering minstrel articulate his unstated emotions. These considerations for logic with regards to a singing source indicate an acknowledgement and use of evolving film music styles. This is in contrast to *Sita Bibaha*, which had a plethora of songs in traditional '*bhakti sangeet, chanda, kirtan, pala* and *gitinatya* formats' (Deo 2013), performed in the *rasalila* style, where everybody sang irrespective of the plausibility and possibility for singing in the context of their characters. *Lalita* therefore makes a conscious attempt to consistently adhere to the characterisation, acting, music and dance guidelines in the *Natyashastra*, while occasionally integrating some of the theatre-to-film transitions necessary for better cinematic impact. Nonetheless, it totally fails to achieve a consistent sustaining of the *rasa* impact by short-changing the relatively more true-to-life medium of cinema with some avoidable odd compromises. Prominent among these oddities, as already discussed, are its choice of an incompatible lead pair, the protagonist's speaking Odia with a Bengali accent and the shooting of most of the film's drama moments inside painted sets. These make *Lalita* more of a commendable theatre effort on celluloid rather than a pure product of cinematic achievement.

Conclusion

This chapter provides evidence and interview-based observations from a significant film industry in the eastern part of the Indian subcontinent. It argues that the advent of cinema in India, across regional movie industries, attracted pioneers who saw in filmmaking an opportunity to re-engage with the aesthetic values prescribed in the *Natyashastra* to achieve a moving and impactful storytelling experience. While the films under review happen to be the first and second releases in the history of Odia cinema, the integral involvement of Bengali technicians, writers and directors in studios based in Kolkata can also be considered as valuable evidence on filmmaking practices in the then Bengali cinema. It is no coincidence that *Sri Jagannath*, the third and most successful film in the foundation phase of Odia cinema (after insinuations of the first two films being ghost-directed by Bengali directors), was officially helmed by a Kolkata-based Bengali filmmaker, Chitaranjan Mitra, heralding the beginning of a glorious era of co-production in Odia cinema that featured talent from West Bengal and Odisha. This output, in retrospect, is reviewed as the beginning of the Golden Age of Odia Cinema. The chapter also finds adherence to *Natyashastra* postulates in the emotive nature and articulation of song and dance sequences in Indian cinemas. It uses *bhava* and *rasa* concepts to identify and appreciate the *ashta-nayika* mood states of a heroine in love, providing a valuable template to review the performance, music and lyric achievements in the music scenes often dismissed as melodramatic. These *ashta-nayika* mood states and their articulation in a gestural-lyrical form is a recurring motif in the song and dance sequences in romantic Indian films celebrating the *sringara rasa*. *Lalita*'s concluding dance piece is now acknowledged as a groundbreaking moment in Odisha's post-independence classical dance revival movements aimed at making Odissi—one of India's oldest classical dance forms—synonymous with Odia culture and tradition. This is the first time any Odissi-like dance form was recorded in cinema.

The evidence of this and the preceding chapters further aim to argue against research positions that tend to equate the unique narrative attributes of all early Indian cinemas to the Parsi theatre. It is worth noting that at the time of *Lalita*'s release, the Parsi theatre had already marked its influence on the Indian talkie film scene (starting with *Alam Ara*) and on the narrative styles of certain Hindustani (a mix of Hindi and Urdu) language cinemas made from India's most prolific film industry at the time, operating out of Bombay (now Mumbai) on India's Western coast. By then, the cinema from Bombay had already emerged as the dominant Indian national cinema post-independence. Yet *Lalita*, the second Odia film and a representative case study of filmmaking practices in East India, opted to seek box-office security and favourable critical response by telling a local legend in the trusted and admired dramatic template of the *Natyashastra.* The level of *rasa* evoked and the intensity of *rasa* achieved in the audience from the experience of viewing *Lalita* may be an issue of debate, but the achievement of *bhava* and *rasa* as integral elements of film appreciation do get reinforced in critic Surya Deo's analysis of *Sita Bibaha* and *Lalita.* They remain as relevant parameters for film criticism today as in the reviews of the early Odia films eight decades ago.

Note

1 Interview with K. Vishwanath in Hyderabad on 17 August 2015.

2 *Tala* 'is a unit of measurement for time and also for space, for it means, span' (Subrahmanyam 2010: 38).

3 Interview with Sarat Pujari in Bhubaneswar on 27 June 2013.

4 'The 1960s and 1970s are known as the two golden decades of Odia cinema' (Chakra 2013: 65).

5 This is different from North India's *ramleelas*, which will henceforth be differentiated as '*leela*' instead of '*lila*' as mentioned in the context of Odisha's folk theatre.

6 Drama and theatre directors, who sourced authority as the most important meaning-maker in a theatre set-up based on their researched knowledge and performed expertise of the *Natyashastra*, to train performers and direct plays in accord with its guidelines.

7 Both the interviewees passed away subsequently, thus making these interactions their last professionally recorded interviews.

8 Pujari 2013; Roy 2014; Subrahmanyam 2010: 21

9 Goswami had never witnessed a film on-screen before getting roped in to make one. This was because the only two places where films were screened in his hometown Puri were located in areas of bad reputation (infamous for prostitution and frequented by men of ill-repute or low caste and class), visiting which was unbecoming of a Brahmin and a recognisable cultural icon like Goswami.

10 The term *abhinaya*, according to the *Natyashastra*, is not merely about acting out a part; it 'connotes a carrying forward of ideas with involvement,

evoking as a consequence, an aesthetic experience in the audience' (Subrahmanyam 2010: 24).

11 The Dwapara Yuga is the third of the four *yugas* (ages) described in Hindu scriptures. It ended at the moment that Lord Krishna renounced his material body and returned to his eternal abode 36 years after the Mahabharata war.

12 1948 marked the height of the Italian neorealism movement that had started after World War II and influenced filmmaking across the world, including Hindi cinema.

13 Kabichandra ('a king among poets') Kalicharan Patnaik, along with directing *Lalita* (1948), also wrote its dialogue and songs, and played an integral part in the composing of its music. The 'integral involvement and contribution of a director in the creative aspects of a film's music, dance and songs, was quite common in the Talkie Era of Indian cinema' (Begum 2013). This also highlights the role and significance of those elements in a filmed narration. Kalicharan Patnaik will be cited for the Odia lyrics of all the songs discussed in this chapter.

14 The English translations of the songs of *Lalita* used in this chapter are based on the film's subtitles by Leela Roy of NFDC Bombay. She will be cited as 'Roy 1993' in accordance with the Censor Board of Film Certification's issue date of a fresh certificate as mentioned in the copy of the film accessed for study. The subtitles, as the film's digital copy indicates, were added at a later date after the film's original release.

4

Rasa in Adaptation: Analysing the Emotive Ingredients of a *Masala* Film

> Look at any big hit film in our cinema, and it will intentionally or unintentionally have the navarasas. A careful viewing of *Sholay* [Embers 1975] too will reveal the navarasas to you. As a filmmaker or a writer, whether you are aware of, or unaware of the rasas, whether you are intentionally or unintentionally adding, incorporating or triggering the rasas, the navarasas are bound to be evoked in every good film. Without them, a film cannot be successful[1].
>
> Salim Khan, actor–script writer

> Time and again if we see the few films that have worked beautifully commercially and got critical acclaim, whether it was *Sholay* [1975] or *Mr India* [1987] or *Dilwale Dulhaniya Le Jayenge* [1995] or now *The Dirty Picture* [2011], are the ones which have completely explored the navarasas[2].
>
> Vidya Balan, actress

The *Masala* Film

Sholay (Embers 1975), arguably 'one of the world's favourite movies' (Harris 2008), has been repeatedly reviewed by Hindi cinema fans and critics as the greatest Bollywood film ever[3]. Even four decades after its release, a 3D version of the film, released in January 2014, attracted media attention and fan interest equivalent to the release of a new film. Senior critic Subhash K. Jha compares *Sholay* with Hindi cinema's biggest hit of 2014, *Dhoom 3*:

> Undoubtedly, the current films that seem to make so much money seem to pale into flamboyant insignificance when weighed against the hefty impact of *Sholay*. As many as 38 years have passed since *Sholay* and its astonishing lines (Salim–Javed at their pithiest) created immediate and enduring history. With each viewing of *Sholay*, I come

away wiser and richer. Yes, this is what 'Bollywood' entertainment should always be but seldom is (Jha 2014).

To highlight the film's continuing impact on the Indian film industry, filmmaker Shekhar Kapur divided its history into two eras—one before *Sholay* and the other after *Sholay*. The film's characters today are part of India's culture lore, almost as popular as the protagonists of the great epics the Ramayana and the Mahabharata. They have been observed to enjoy a near-sacrosanct status among many of the film's fans to the extent that any tampering with the film tends to stoke tempers akin to blasphemy as evident from the reaction and reception to director Ram Gopal Varma's remake of the film as *Ram Gopal Varma Ki Aag* (Ram Gopal Varma's Fire) in 2007[4].

Amitabh Bachchan, one of the lead actors in the original *Sholay* and an Indian cinema legend at the time of the remake's release, was criticised for trying to reprise the role of *Sholay*'s celebrated villain, Gabbar Singh, in Ram Gopal Varma's *Aag*. *Sholay* continues to remain the final word and a textbook reference for generations of subsequent Indian filmmakers aspiring to make the perfect *masala* film[5]. The term *masala* entered the Indian cinema lexicon in the 1970s. Veteran film critic Ali Peter John argues that it gained credence among box-office analysts as film trade terminology coined in retrospect to identify films that tried to replicate *Sholay's* multi-genre-mixing and multi-emotion-evoking style of storytelling for similar success. According to him, 'Prior to *Sholay*, all mainstream films [successful or flop] were called entertainment films' (2014).

In a TV interview around the release of the 3D version of *Sholay*, its co-scriptwriter Javed Akhtar corroborated that *masala* is a post-*Sholay* term. Discussing the film's writing process, he said, 'We were just writing interesting characters that were fascinating us. We were not trying to make a *masala* film' (Akhtar 2014). In perhaps what can be regarded as an indulgent moment of self-review by *Sholay*'s writer duo Salim Khan and Javed Akhtar, they list some of its attractive ingredients and acknowledge the film's guaranteed emotive potential by having one of the heroes, Veeru, sum up his on-screen story mid-film to an audience of villagers declaring, 'Ye mat pucho chacha tumhare aansoo nikal aayenge… is mein emotion hai, drama hai, tragedy hai' ('Don't ask me the details uncle, you will start crying. In my story there is emotion, drama, tragedy'; Salim–Javed 1975)[6]. These narrative attributes are now considered essential for a *masala* film. Some critics also contend that the term *masala* film came to be associated with *Sholay* post its review as a 'curry western by film critics in the West [Europe/USA]' (Kabir 1999: 58). They did this as an observation on *Sholay*'s liberal borrowings of dramatic situations and confrontation moments from some landmark movies in the mid-1960s' Hollywood subgenre of Spaghetti Westerns[7]. *Sholay*, however, was also inspired by some popular dacoit-themed Hindi language films that preceded its release. Today, *masala* as an aesthetic term is broadly understood to be a cocktail of action, emotion, drama (or melodrama), song and dance, which 'the Indian filmmakers [making popular cinema] and the film-consuming public have embraced, as a rejection to realism that is seen as part of an arguably different Western aesthetics' (Subramani 2013). From a conservative, Western film criticism perspective, the *masala* film has occasionally been criticised, ridiculed and/or misunderstood as a lesser genre for putting 'the sacred and the profane into the same pot' (Subramani 2013) in its mixing of the signature and the inflexible (hence sacred) attributes of universally recognised Hollywood cinema genres, such as tragedy, comedy, romance, adventure, horror and others.

A Fresh Perspective

While not contesting the above interpretations, this chapter contributes towards a broader understanding of the term *masala* film. It postulates that this is a post-1970s' Indian film industry classification for any movie that, in accordance with the ideal dramatic achievement criteria of the *Natyashastra* discussed in the previous chapters, is able to evoke the *navarasas* in its narrative. It contends that instead of its commonly presumed attributes—song, dance and melodrama—the perfect *masala* film is the one that is able to cohesively present a diversity of *rasa*-embodying characters and *rasa*-evoking drama situations within one grand narrative. By engaging with the *rasa* principles of the Sanskrit drama, this chapter further aids the appreciation of the emotive achievements of a Hindi or an Indian film narrative; it engages with alternate parameters for film criticism that offer a fairer review of plots and characters often erroneously dismissed as melodramatic or stereotypical.

Sholay's retrospective labelling as the perfect *masala* film, one that generations of subsequent filmmakers continue to aspire to and are inspired by, was a post-release phenomenon. Myriad theories and arguments have been offered since to deconstruct the film's unparalleled success. *Sholay* ran for over five continuous years in Mumbai's Minerva theatre after its release on the Indian Independence Day in 1975. The film worked well because it was able to evoke and fuse each of the nine *rasas* to memorable effect. The argument for this is constructed as follows. First, a sequence-by-sequence analysis of the entire film is undertaken, looking at its evocation of all the prescribed primary *rasas*. This includes a discussion of the dominant projected *bhavas* of each of its memorable characters as evidence of the film's success in conceiving characters embodying each of the *rasas* as a mood state or a dominant character trait. How *Sholay* has come to be acknowledged by the Indian film industry as the perfect *masala* film has already been discussed. This chapter also examines whether *Sholay*'s continuing popularity among new viewers and existing fans can be attributed to the culmination of its visual experience in the *shanta rasa*. Finally, it will propose that in a narrative's ability to convincingly suggest and blend each of the *navarasas* into a unified emotional experience, as is the case with *Sholay*, there lies a potential recipe of how to make a successful Indian *masala* film. A detailed deconstruction of the film's plot structure, based on the dominant sentiments of each of its scenarios, further helps clarify that while the *masala* film is an important genre in popular Indian cinema, it is unfair to categorise every popular film as a *masala* film. Hindi film scriptwriter and secretary of (Bollywood's) Film Writer's Association, Kamlesh Pandey, argues:

> Not every film can have all the *rasas*, though no film can be without the *rasas*. It may have two, three or all the nine, but this depends on the requirements of the story (2013).

The previous chapters have demonstrated a conscious awareness and influence of the *Natyashastra* and the *rasa* theory in Indian filmmaking and reviewing processes with a sample of films from different regional film industries. This chapter considers the nature of the realisation of *rasa* in the practical aspects of plot construction and characterisation. Hence, detailed interviews have been referenced as empirical support for my theoretical argument that the need to evoke *rasa* shapes the *masala* film and differentiates the Indian film writing process from its Western counterparts. Interviewees include two of Hindi cinema's most successful post-1970 writing influences, Salim Khan and Javed Akhtar[8], who also are the story, script and dialogue writers of *Sholay*; contemporary screenplay writers like Kamlesh Pandey; one of post-2000 Hindi cinema's most feted and critically acclaimed actresses, Vidya Balan and directors known to also write their films, such as Nirad Mohapatra and Chandraprakash Dwivedi. Finally, two seminal scenes from *Sholay*, featuring the entry and exit of its most memorable character, Gabbar Singh, are compared, to establish how the *rasa*-evoking needs of an Indian *masala* film differentiate this Curry Western from its Spaghetti Western sources. These scenes were inspired by a landmark Spaghetti Western film *For a Few Dollars More* (1965), from Sergio Leone's Dollars Trilogy[9]. A selection of the film's dialogue is cited to discuss their evocation of *rasa* and impact on the overall film experience. Some of *Sholay*'s frequently repeated and remembered dialogues in their original Hindi language are engaged with, as an acknowledgement of their continuing popularity in Indian popular culture, along with their translations in English. The writers of *Sholay*, Salim Khan and Javed Akhtar, have been cited for the dialogues discussed in the chapter as SJ, an abbreviation of their popular on-screen name of Salim–Javed.

In the remainder of this book, starting with this chapter, methods have been proposed on how to use and extend the aesthetic appreciation templates offered by the *rasa* theory as a practical recognition and valuation guideline for ascertaining the creative merits of an Indian feature film, its performance achievements and different-from-the-norm narration priorities and the nature of pleasure sought and expected by its viewers. A detailed study of a diversity of influential genre- and region-representing Indian films provides the foundations for this. Ultimately, it indicates how to use a *rasa*-based criticism of a film for a fairer and better review of the profane, misunderstood or different attributes of popular Indian cinema. These attributes have been successfully entertaining nearly half of the global movie-going audience, while constantly challenging the 'sacrosanct' First-World codes for identifying a good film.

Table 4.1 Analysing *Sholay*'s Scenarios in Terms of their Dominant *Rasas*

Timeline	Description of Scenario	Character in Focus	Character *Bhavas* and *Rasas* Conveyed	Dominant *Rasa* Evoked
00:00–03:40	A jailor arrives at a deserted railway station and is received by an aide of Thakur Baldev Singh. As the credits roll, the audience is introduced to the topography of the scene of the drama, the village Ramgarh.	Ramgarh	An upbeat tune, evoking elements of energy, surprise and adventure, plays in the background.	Curiosity is kindled among the audience (evoking an element of the ***adbhuta*** *rasa*), for what will happen next.
03:41–06:01	Thakur Baldev Singh is introduced. The jailor talks to him with awe reserved for a much-admired senior. Thakur[10], instead of exchanging any pleasantries, immediately requests the jailor to help him in finding two petty thieves. Surprised by the request, the jailor dismisses them as good-for-nothing characters, full of vices. Thakur thinks otherwise and delves into a flashback to highlight their virtues.	First, Thakur Baldev Singh; then two courageous thieves, Jaidev and Veeru	Thakur is presented as a serious, matter-of-fact person, who does not betray any emotion. He nurtures a secret purpose and a rage within, which perpetuates the *rasa* of wonder around his unusual disposition.	An element of wonder (*adbhuta*) as curiosity is perpetuated, first in the Thakur's request being termed unusual, and then for Jaidev and Veeru, because of the two contrasting reviews about their worth, as shared by the jailor and Thakur.

Timeline	Description of Scenario	Character in Focus	Character *Bhavas* and *Rasas* Conveyed	Dominant *Rasa* Evoked
06:02–16:57	The flashback scene is a set-up for *Sholay*'s most spectacular action sequence (also a first in Indian cinema at the time of its release), featuring a gang of dacoits on horseback, chasing, ambushing and then trying to loot a goods train. Thakur, with the help of Jaidev and Veeru, whom he was taking to the jail in the train, foils the ambush. The ambush is preceded by a conversation amongst the trio, which highlights that each is a braveheart by choice, and that they share a common passion for playing with fire. This is the reason why Thakur, although owning enough land, opted to join the police force, and Jaidev and Veeru chose the life of outlaws, for the relentless adventure of the calling, pursuit and escape included.	Jaidev and Veeru	Veeru comes across as a talkative and humorous character. Jaidev is reticent and introspective (as if he does not give a damn), while Thakur shows attributes of a compassionate human being who is able to see through and trust the real worth of even his prisoners. Veeru boasts that together they could tackle at least 10–15 challengers. Thakur challenges them to prove their word when the dacoits suddenly attack. The duo's compassionate '*daya vira*'[11] side is revealed when, after defeating the bandits, they decide to take an injured Thakur to the hospital instead of using the opportunity to escape by letting him die.	Spectacular fight scenes and stunts perpetuate the sense of *adbhuta*/awe, but in service of the ***vira*** *rasa* that establishes the three as the film's 'hero' characters. The scene is presented as a ballad-like testimony to not only reveal the courage quotient of Jaidev and Veeru but also establish them as good human beings on the wrong side of law.

16:58–17:30	The flashback ends and the narration returns to the conversation between the jailor and Thakur, with the latter assessing the 'misunderstood' Jaidev and Veeru as natural *viras*, who are: 'mischievous, but brave, dangerous because they know how to fight and wrong, but humane' (SJ 1975).	Jaidev and Veeru	Other noble attributes of Jaidev and Veeru (e.g., *karuna* as compassion for a fellow human), beyond their already displayed bravery, are highlighted.	***Vira***
17:31–23:59	The film's first song scene—'Yeh dosti hum nahi todenge' (We will never break this friendship. Bakshi 1975)[12]—is an ode to Jai and Veeru's friendship. It is accompanied by some comic encounters of the duo on the road.	Jaidev and Veeru	The third-person perspective up until now towards Jaidev and Veeru changes to one of direct engagement as the audience is introduced to the platonic love, intimacy and the potential sacrifice in their bonding as they express a lifetime of togetherness and the putting of friendship before life through the lyrics of the song.	Though bromance is the focus of the song's lyrics, the events in the song introduce into the film its first humorous sequences aimed at evoking the ***hasya*** *rasa*.

Timeline	Description of Scenario	Character in Focus	Character *Bhavas* and *Rasas* Conveyed	Dominant *Rasa* Evoked
24:00–26:29	Introduction of Surma Bhopali, (played by 'comic actor'[13] Jagdeep), a lumberjack and acquaintance of Jaidev and Veeru, whom they co-opt into a plan whereby the former will hand them to the police and pocket the prize money (announced for their capture). The amount would then be shared by the trio after they escape from jail.	Surma Bhopali	Surma is introduced as a loud and exploitative trader, who speaks in a comical and exaggerated Hindi dialect. The mood is humorous. The non-exploitative side of Jaidev and Veeru is hinted at in their offer to share the prize money with Surma.	***Hasya***
26:30–29:18	Introduction of a jailer from the British era, played by Asrani, a supporting actor popular for his comic parts. His entry march is parodied to the tune of *He's a jolly good fellow* in the background. Jaidev and Veeru are entrusted into his custody.	A comical jailor hailing from the British era	Modelled on Charlie Chaplin's caricature of Hitler from *The Great Dictator* (1940), he too behaves in an exaggerated manner and fumbles with his orders, which make him an object of ridicule among his prisoners.	***Hasya***

29:19–30:48	Introduction of barber Hariram as the jailer's informer. Jaidev and Veeru start planning their escape by leaking misleading information to Hariram.	Hariram	Hariram is deliberately given a comical hue by the casting of popular comedian Keshto Mukherjee in the part.	***Hasya***
30:49–35:49	More humorous interactions of the comical jailer with prisoners of different shapes and sensibilities (from the menacing to the sexual) is followed by Jaidev and Veeru's trick escape with a fake pistol.	The jailor	The escape is planned as a con game, which lends it a comical mood instead of the thrilling mood typical to escape sequences.	***Hasya***
35:50–38:05	Jaidev and Veeru collect their share of the ransom money from Surma, after catching him off guard through one of his narrations of false bravado to naive listeners.	Surma Bhopali	Surma's embarrassment and caught-in-a-bind body language heighten the sequence's mirth metre.	***Hasya***
38:07–38:40	Before Jaidev and Veeru can escape, they are caught by the police and sent to the custody of the jailer seen in the film's opening sequence.	Jaidev and Veeru	There is an element of surprise as the conmen get 'conned' by their fate.	A fleeting feeling of ***adbhuta,*** underlined by *hasya*

Timeline	**Description of Scenario**	**Character in Focus**	**Character *Bhavas* and *Rasas* Conveyed**	**Dominant *Rasa* Evoked**
38:41–41:35	Thakur meets the duo on release and offers them a great deal of money to work for him. When asked about the nature of the work, he stokes their appetite for adventure, before striking a goal-driven, hard bargain, saying 'The payment will be whatever you quote, the work will be whatever I say' (SJ 1975). He then asks them to catch dacoit Gabbar Singh alive for him but refuses to reveal his motive.	Gabbar Singh is introduced as a 'wanted' criminal evading the law, who also happens to be shrewd and brave.	A fleeting sense of foreboding is evoked in Jaidev and Veeru, but their competence is assured when Thakur justifies his decision to choose them to catch Gabbar: 'Only an iron can cut iron' (SJ 1975). While the surprise around Thakur's quest for Jaidev and Veeru is finally quelled, fresh suspense is generated around his motive for wanting to capture Gabbar, apart from the character of Gabbar himself.	Though fleeting *rasas* of surprise, fear and repressed anger are evoked, ***vira*** remains the connecting *rasa* through the nature of a tough challenge (finally) thrown and promptly taken. The scene also marks a decisive turn in its brave but purposeless lead duo as they are presented for the first time as potential heroes.
41:36–46:37	Jaidev and Veeru arrive in Ramgarh and get introduced to a feisty, free-spirited and garrulous horse-cart driver, Basanti.	Basanti	While for Veeru it is love at first sight with Basanti, Jaidev reacts to Basanti's non-stop chatter with comic irritation.	Though there is an undercurrent of *hasya*, the triggering of ***sringara*** *rasa* is most perceptible in the scene.

46:38–49:37	Thakur receives the duo with a matter-of-fact reiteration of his demand, pays them their second post-arrival instalment and the audience is introduced to the only other family member in his huge mansion, his widowed daughter-in-law, Radha.	Thakur and his family	The mood of suspense returns, along with disgust over Veeru's suggestion to rob Thakur's unguarded safe. Jaidev and Veeru still seem to be tied to their petty thieving predispositions.	***Bibhatsa*** is the scene's trigger *rasa* for the film's potential heroes, who are still being driven by their unscrupulous urges.
49:38–51.45	Jaidev and Veeru are faced with a surprise attack by Thakur's men hiding in their room. They defeat all in a hand-to-hand combat as Thakur is assured that the vigour of his choices has not diminished with time.	Jaidev and Veeru	Having established the shooting skills of Jai and Veeru in the train robbery event, their combat abilities and other physical and mental attributes expected from a fighting hero are highlighted in the surprise fight.	***Vira***
51.46–53.44	Jaidev and Veeru plan to rob Thakur's vault at night but are caught by the young widow, Radha. She gives them the key and asks them to 'take everything and then leave', as that will give her father-in-law respite from misplaced hopes from rogue strangers (like them).	Radha	Disgust is the trigger *rasa* for Jaidev and Veeru's treacherous act, but Radha's unconventional reprimand (hinting sarcasm), shames them and awakens their humanity.	***Bibhatsa***

Timeline	Description of Scenario	Character in Focus	Character *Bhavas* and *Rasas* Conveyed	Dominant *Rasa* Evoked
53.45–54.32	The inherently nice but roguish duo are reformed, as Jaidev returns the key to Radha and assures her that no breach of trust will happen again.	Jaidev and Radha	A hero's word is given; Radha's doubts lessen for Jaidev, who is already shown to be intrigued by her. The beginning of a second love story is thus hinted.	***Sringara,*** inspired by respect and compassion for a fellow loner (in Jaidev)
54.33–55.36	Introduction to Basanti's family and her lone guardian, an elderly aunty, who is referred to as 'Mausi'[14] by all.	Mausi	Mausi's interaction with Basanti once again highlights how the latter's talkative nature unintentionally makes her an object of comedy.	***Hasya***
55.37–57.29	Introduction of an elderly and blind Muslim cleric, Imam sahib, and his son, Ahmed	Imam sahib	Basanti helps the blind Imam reach the masjid, as the latter talks about similar acts of compassion by fellow villagers.	***Karuna*** is further perpetuated in Ahmed's insistence on not leaving his blind father alone in the village to follow better career prospects.

57.30–1:00:56	Basanti meets Veeru in a mango orchard, where he tries to flirt with her more audaciously.	Basanti and Veeru	The so far one-sided Veeru–Basanti romance is hindered by unintended confusions that lend a comic flavour to their romance.	***Sringara*** is the dominant *rasa* as Veeru attempts to kindle feelings for him within Basanti.
1:00:57–1:02:37	Radha smiles for the first time over town-boy Jaidev's nascent attempts at shepherding.	Radha and Jaidev	A kindling of feelings between the silent Radha and a brooding Jaidev is hinted at.	A restrained manifestation of ***sringara***, in contrast to Basanti–Veeru's loud histrionics
1:02:38–1:06:37	The narrative cuts from individual/couple personal stories to a collage view of life in Ramgarh village, which is interrupted by three dacoits of Gabbar. As they terrorise the villagers, Thakur challenges them. Jaidev and Veeru defeat them in a gun battle as the villagers cheer their saviours.	Gabbar Singh's dacoits	The mood changes from helplessness and terror on the part of the villagers to fear among the bandits as they flee the village after being disarmed by Jaidev and Veeru.	***Bhayanaka*** is the dominant *rasa*, experienced first by the villagers and then by the dacoits. In the audience too, a foreboding is created for Gabbar's reaction.

Timeline	Description of Scenario	Character in Focus	Character *Bhavas* and *Rasas* Conveyed	Dominant *Rasa* Evoked
1:06:38–1:13:00	The much-discussed dacoit Gabbar Singh is finally introduced, first as a cold, dispassionate voice interrogating the three scared dacoits who fled Ramgarh, set to an ominous background score. Suddenly, he yells at his team for not staying on to fight Thakur's two aides (and we see him in entirety for the first time) and plays a game of Russian roulette, which the three bandits survive. But just as they burst out laughing at their narrow escape, he shoots them point blank and declares: 'Death to the cowards!' (SJ 1975). The fable of curiosity woven around Gabbar so far is thus shredded to reveal him as an agent of terror, prone to acting whimsically, like killing his own men to simply make a	Gabbar Singh	The fear of Gabbar is established through the unpredictability of his character. For example, after giving his men an assurance of forgiveness, he kills them in cold blood when they are least expecting it, and then pauses to survey the reactions of his remaining men before justifying his cruelty. According to *Sholay*'s co-scriptwriter Javed Akhtar, 'Gabbar is a strange man… There are eight or nine scenes in which Gabbar appears but in each of these scenes you are always on the edge, guessing what his next move will be' (Kabir 2006: 61). This lends to his fearsome character a sense of the *adbhuta*.	The *rasa* of ***bhaya*** permeates the scene, first evoked among Gabbar's three deserter bandits in anticipation of the quantum of punishment, and then in the audience for the villagers of Ramgarh, as the scene ends with Gabbar hinting at revenge on the Holi festival.

	statement. The act highlights his disregard for human life and reveals a psychotic character that revels in wanton spilling of blood. This is then reinforced in scene after scene, featuring his killing of weak, defenceless villagers, an adolescent lad and a little boy with no direct challenge or enmity.			
1:13:01–1:18:40	The film's second song sequence occurs as a festival dance number, where the villagers, led by Veeru and Basanti, celebrate the festival of colours, Holi [15]. But while the villagers are dancing to an assurance of freedom from Gabbar's terror, the audience is aware that it is only a temporary respite. The threat of Gabbar's revenge thus lends a feeling of fear to a seemingly joyous event.	Basanti–Veeru and Jaidev–Radha	The lyrics of the song 'Holi ke din dil mil jaate hain' (forget friends, even enemy hearts get united on the occasion of Holi, Bakshi 1975) articulate a progress in the relationships of Basanti–Veeru and Jaidev–Radha.	Though ***Sringara*** is articulated in the song featuring each of the film's emerging romantic pairs, a sense of *fear* keeps lurking in the background.

Timeline	Description of Scenario	Character in Focus	Character *Bhavas* and *Rasas* Conveyed	Dominant *Rasa* Evoked
1:18:41–1:28:32	Gabbar and his dacoits plunder and attack Ramgarh. Chaos reigns, and in spite of a fight where the odds are heavily against Jaidev and Veeru, they use strategy and, with timely help from Basanti, force Gabbar and his men to retreat. Thakur, who remains a mute spectator through the shootout, is unable to provide Veeru with any cover at a strategic moment of need, because of which he calls him a coward and threatens to exit the mission.	Gabbar, Jaidev, Veeru and Basanti	Gabbar's arrogance, self-obsession and cruelty are juxtaposed against the magnanimity of Jaidev and Veeru, who risk their lives willingly for a just cause like true *dharma-viras*. Thakur's inability to help at a strategic turn in the fight, when Gabbar is close to capturing Jaidev and Veeru, creates the curiosity for another back story and revelation.	***Vira*** *rasa* is in focus through the bravery of Jaidev and Veeru and of Basanti (for the first time). Its impact heightens in the context of their achieving an awe-inspiring victory by making Gabbar flee in spite of his superiority in numbers.
1:28:33–1:47:09	The film's second flashback reveals the story behind Thakur's obsession behind capturing Gabbar. Gabbar had massacred Thakur's entire family (two sons, daughter, elder daughter-in-law and grandson) in cold blood.	Thakur	Thakur's flashback has trigger elements for most of the *rasas*, from *vira* in his daring pursuit and capture of Gabbar Singh, to *bibhatsa* in the sadistic nature of the latter's revenge. *Karuna* is evoked among Jaidev–	***Raudra*** is the culminating *rasa* of the sequence as manifested in the Thakur's incensed visage at the end of the narration.

	Shaking with vengeance, when Thakur lands alone in Gabbar's hideout, the latter chops off his arms and condemns him to a life worse than death. It is at this juncture that Jaidev and Veeru are made aware of the reason of his inability to help them in the gun battle, and the film reaches its 'intermission' with a pre-climactic dramatic revelation.		Veeru for Thakur's tragedy. They now empathise with his righteous anger and in a subsequent scene offer to return his advance money and fight without compensation for a fair cause.	
1:47:10–1:48:10	*Sholay*'s second half begins with the police arriving in Ramgarh to investigate the dacoits' attack during the Holi festival. Thakur assures that Gabbar will be handed over to the police dead or alive.	Thakur	Subsequent to the pre-intermission revelation of his *only* weakness, Thakur, like a true *vira*, is once again back in command.	***Vira***

Timeline	Description of Scenario	Character in Focus	Character *Bhavas* and *Rasas* Conveyed	Dominant *Rasa* Evoked
1:48:11–1:50:02	Jaidev and Veeru offer to return Thakur's payment money, but he warns them that they only have to catch Gabbar and not kill him. He then directs them to the wandering Gabbar's next hideout and suggests that it is a good opportunity to capture him.	Jaidev and Veeru	With the second suspense element in the plot—i.e., Thakur's revenge against Gabbar—now explained, fresh suspense is built around his insistence on wanting him to be captured alive since he has now been revealed to be physically unable to punish him. *Adbhuta* as suspense returns as the support *rasa* to the film's emerging unifying *rasa* of *vira* revolving around an increasing band of brave men and women.	***Vira/Heroism*** continues as the driver *rasa*, as the film's triad of heroes prepare themselves for their first assault against the villain Gabbar. But while anger fuels Thakur's revenge, Jaidev and Veeru are driven more by compassion for the villagers and Thakur's loss.
1:50:03–1:54:01	The film's third song, an erotic dance number, 'Mehbooba o' mehbooba' (Darling o' darling, Bakshi 1975), filmed on a gypsy couple performing for Gabbar's pleasure, is shown as Jaidev and Veeru destroy his stock of arms and ammunition. Gabbar escapes the attack and Jaidev gets injured.	Gabbar Singh	*Sringara* is the theme of the gypsy couple's song, interspersed with moments of fear and heroism for Jaidev and Veeru's daring.	***Sringara***, though the nature of its manifestation in this situation is oriented towards lust, not love.

1:54:02–1:55:57	Radha, on seeing an injured Jaidev, breaks her widow's restraint and rushes out with her head uncovered, visibly distressed. This reveals to Thakur her growing feelings for Jaidev.	Radha and Jaidev	The so-far unarticulated love of Jaidev and Radha gets articulated as Jaidev's eyes and pensive notes on the mouthorgan seek Radha's attention. Compassion drives their unspoken love, just as mirth drives the Veeru–Basanti romance.	Though *sringara* drives character reactions, ***karuna*** is the dominant *rasa*. While *karuna* is manifested in Radha's concern for Jaidev's safety, in Thakur it is revealed in his compassion-driven understanding of his widowed daughter-in-law's need for a companion. This empathy makes him react to a possible scandal with calm and not anger or reprimand.
1:55:58–1:58:20	The narrative shifts to subplots featuring supporting villager characters like Imam sahib, his son Ahmed, Basanti and the village postman. The Imam tries to convince Ahmed to leave the village for better job prospects, but he insists again on not leaving his blind father alone.	The Imam and Ahmed	Another manifestation of the *karuna rasa* is shown, as affectionate concern between parents and children that naturally encourages them to make mutual sacrifices.	***Karuna***

Timeline	Description of Scenario	Character in Focus	Character *Bhavas* and *Rasas* Conveyed	Dominant *Rasa* Evoked
1:58:21–2:06:51	Veeru stages a marriage proposal to Basanti as a ruse, implying divine intervention, but is caught in the act. As an angry Basanti tries to leave, Veeru pursues her with a song, 'Koi haseena jab rooth jaati hai' (When a damsel gets angry, she looks even more beautiful, Bakshi 1975). He now directly articulates his love for Basanti, which is acknowledged and reciprocated by the latter by the end of the sequence.	Veeru and Basanti	Mirth (as romantic banter) is the conveyed emotion in the actions and reactions of Veeru and Basanti in tandem with the former's prankster nature and the latter's comic garrulousness. But its end purpose is to take their love story to the next stage of a reciprocated affair from its one-sided progress until then.	***Sringara***
2:06:52–2:17:05	Veeru asks Jaidev to argue his case for marriage with Basanti with her guardian aunt, Mausi. Continuing the narrative's comic mood from the previous sequence, Jaidev deliberately ruins his friend's cause by exaggerating his vices. Mausi	Mausi and Veeru	The sequence highlights the comical vein in Veeru's character, seen in flashes until now, to its full humour potential. His literal over-the-top drunken attempt at suicide is ably complemented by Jaidev's deadpan comedy,	***Hasya***

	naturally rejects Veeru, and the latter tries to change her decision by attempting public suicide in a drunken state from atop a village tank.		the villagers' confused interpretation of Veeru's threats and Mausi's dramatic rebuttal, to make it one of Hindi cinema's most reprised comic sequences.	
2:17:06–2:20:36	In the typical *masala* style of storytelling, the narrative once again switches from one extremely contrasting emotion to another in consecutive scenes, as the narrative cuts from a hilarious sequence to one of extreme barbarity as Gabbar captures and tortures Ahmed to death.	Ahmed	Ahmed's unusual defiance before Gabbar generates the *vira rasa*. Gabbar's act of torturing the teenager to death, instead of just shooting him, because he feels it would be less painful, generates both fear and disgust.	***Bibhatsa*** for the gruesome nature of Ahmed's death, which is indicated by Gabbar trying to render him blind before killing him

Timeline	Description of Scenario	Character in Focus	Character *Bhavas* and *Rasas* Conveyed	Dominant *Rasa* Evoked
2:20:37–2:28:17	Ahmed's dead body arrives in Ramgarh on his horse, with a note of warning from Gabbar that more killings of innocent villagers will follow if they do not hand over Jaidev and Veeru to Gabbar. The scared villagers want to turn in the duo, but the Imam pleads for calm and argues that in spite of losing his son, he would rather opt to die with dignity than live a life of fear and servitude. His exit plea that despite bearing the world's heaviest burden—'a father having to carry his son's bier' (SJ 1975)—he will oppose the surrendering of Jaidev and Veeru and ask God why He didn't give him more sons to sacrifice for a just cause establishes the Imam as both the hero and a restorer of the heroic sentiment in the sequence.	Imam sahib	The scene triggers a series of *rasas*, starting with pathos for the Imam's loss, disgust at some of the villager's fear-induced intention to turn in Jaidev and Veeru, to one of anger and revenge for Gabbar. The Imam's unusual calm in the face of a great personal loss highlights his compassion, strength of conviction and fearlessness.	***Shanta*** is the continuous *rasa* evoked in the Imam's ability to not only face the death of a loved one with contemplative calm but also make an example of it to return sanity to the villagers losing their courage and compassion to fear.

2:28:18–2:30:45	Jaidev and Veeru return Gabbar's challenge by killing four dacoits and sending a warning that henceforth they will kill four of his men for every villager felled. A furious Gabbar threatens a complete massacre of Ramgarh.	Gabbar Singh	The courageous streak in Gabbar is hinted at for the first time, when he reacts to the threat with a competitor's glee over the meeting of a worthy challenge—'ab aayega majaa' (now the real fun begins, SJ 1975)!	As bodies threaten to pile up on both sides, ***bhayanaka***, amplified by vengeful heroism is the scene's sign-off *rasa*.
2:30:46–2:31:31	A quick cut to Thakur's aide, Raamlal, readying a boot with nails, as Thakur looks on with a surety of will, approving the unusual nature of the footwear. An ominous background score similar to the one playing when Gabbar killed the Thakur's grandchild plays in the background.	Thakur	Suspense is generated by an unusual creation, which is heightened by an eerie complementing mood music.	***Adbhuta***

Timeline	Description of Scenario	Character in Focus	Character *Bhavas* and *Rasas* Conveyed	Dominant *Rasa* Evoked
2:31:32–2:37:22	The reticent Radha shares a laugh with Jaidev as he tries to sustain a conversation but does not speak. Raamlal remembers how she was once an extremely boisterous girl. The flashback continues into an evening sequence where Radha acknowledges and returns Jaidev's gaze, as he plays a pensive tune on his mouthorgan.	Radha	*Karuna* as pity is evoked in the contrast between the boisterous Radha of the past and her present silent-lady-in-white avatar. The poignancy of the emotion is heightened by her parting dialogue in the flashback sequence: 'Wouldn't the world be so dull, without these colours?' (SJ 1975).	***Karuna*** is manifested through its support emotions of pity (for Radha's fate in Raamlal) and compassion (in Jaidev). It is this compassion that builds empathy and encourages Jaidev to make the tough decision of proposing marriage to a widow, which would normally be frowned upon in a rural society.
2:37:23–2:42:00	Jaidev discusses his decision to marry Radha with Veeru; Thakur discusses the possibility of her remarriage with her father and Radha indicates her assent to the developments with a muted smile. Jaidev and Veeru discuss giving up their life-on-the-run to marry and settle in Ramgarh as farmers.	Radha	Compassion and genuine care motivate the Thakur to take a decision that challenges social norms, as indicated by the surprise of Radha's biological father. *Karuna* is an important support *rasa* in the scene, with flashes of *hasya* thrown in by Veeru's asides, albeit all united under an arch of *sringara*.	***Sringara*** is the driver *rasa* as the film's second love story inches towards a happy culmination, and the two heroes dream about the bliss of conjugal life.

2:42:01–2:56:48	Basanti is kidnapped by Gabbar's men. As Veeru follows to rescue her, he too is captured, and Basanti is forced to dance and entertain Gabbar and his bandits to save Veeru's life. Gabbar warns her that Veeru's life will last as long as her feet move, as she dances in scorching heat, singing '*Jab tak hai jaan, jaane jahaan main nachungi*' (I will dance to the last drop of my breath, Bakshi 1975).	Basanti	The scene begins with a thrilling cart-and-horse chase that highlights Basanti's grit and courage. She is not afraid of Gabbar but, out of love for Veeru, even dances on glass pieces thrown at her feet by Gabbar. The sequence provides yet another example of Gabbar's sadistic pleasure at inflicting torture (aimed to evoke disgust), while establishing Basanti as a *virangana* by disposition.	The *rasa* of ***sringara*** is highlighted and celebrated as the romance of Basanti and Veeru emerges triumphant in spite of difficult tests and unsavoury provocations.
2:56:49–3:01:30	Jaidev arrives just before Basanti is about to faint out of exhaustion and provides cover for her and Veeru to escape with some of Gabbar's ammunition. The dacoits chase the trio, and a gun battle ensues on a bridge, in which Jaidev is shot at and injured. Yet, he convinces an unwilling Veeru to go to the village for Basanti's safety and gather support and ammunition, as he offers to keep guard until his return.	Jaidev	Heroic skill in putting up a doughty fight in spite of the odds being heavily against them is displayed by both Jaidev and Veeru.	***Vira***

Timeline	Description of Scenario	Character in Focus	Character *Bhavas* and *Rasas* Conveyed	Dominant *Rasa* Evoked
3:01:31–3:11:32	Jaidev singlehandedly kills a few dacoits. But as his stock of bullets get over, in a near-suicidal attempt to hold the dacoits from further advance, he comes out of his protected cover behind the rocks to blow up a bridge separating him from the dacoits. He is grievously wounded and dies in the arms of his best friend, Veeru, as a sad version of their friendship song—'*yeh dosti*' (this friendship)—plays in the background to heighten the impact of his melancholy passing. Filled with the renewed energy of revenge, Veeru gallops towards Gabbar's hideout to finish the final climactic battle.	Jaidev	Jaidev dies with the sole regret that he widowed Radha for a second time. Veeru's sorrow is increased manifold when he realises that Jaidev deliberately played the loser to save his life in a tossing-of-a-coin-game to decide who between the two would stay back and fight the dacoits. Grief thus becomes the ammunition for his resolve for revenge as he declares: '*Ek ek ko chun chunke marunga*' (I will personally select and kill each one of them, SJ 1975).	***Karuna*** as pathos defines the impact of the actions and reactions in the sequence, be it the sacrifice, like death of Jaidev, the end of hope for Radha or the end of a lifelong friendship for Veeru. The impact is heightened further in the heroic nature of Jaidev's death, with the villagers turning up to mourn him and the playing of a poignant ode to his passing.

3:11:33–3:22:16	Veeru ravages Gabbar's den and singlehandedly neutralises his few remaining fellow dacoits. He then defeats Gabbar in a literal hand-to-hand combat. But before he can kill him, Thakur arrives to exact his revenge. Gabbar wonders how he can fight him without arms, to which the Thakur replies: 'Snakes are to be crushed by feet, not the hands' (SJ 1975). As Gabbar coils into a snakelike bind, the Thakur's nailed boots are revealed. He pins him to the ground and eventually kills him by pushing him onto a pointed nail on a pillar.	Thakur and Gabbar	Anger and revenge drive the unconventional heroism (both in a handicapped Thakur killing a seasoned dacoit and Veeru's singlehanded vanquishing of a few dacoits) on display in this sequence. Gabbar meets a gruesome death and Thakur experiences catharsis as he finally mourns the death of his loved ones (he is never shown grieving his loss until the climax). As Veeru drapes the shawl hiding Thakur's disability and shame, he weeps on his shoulder, and a new bond is forged.	Though *vira* is the most manifested *rasa* in terms of the stunts and fights on display, ***shanta*** is the lasting *rasa* as Gabbar's death allows both Thakur and Veeru to mourn their loss and achieve a sense of closure and calm (in which the *bhava* on Veeru's face is a manifestation of *shanta*), to be able to attempt a new life without any burden of the past.
3:22:13–3:23:13	Jaidev is given a hero's funeral by the villagers, as Radha watches from a distance and closes the window of her room. This can also be interpreted as a symbolic closure of any hope for change or the return of happiness, as she withdraws into the silent anonymity of the Thakur's mansion.	Radha	The mourning of the death of a hero and the death of any hope for a better life for Radha as she returns to her previous state as a lonely widow.	***Karuna***

Timeline	Description of Scenario	Character in Focus	Character *Bhavas* and *Rasas* Conveyed	Dominant *Rasa* Evoked
3:23:14–3:24:24	Veeru is united with Basanti, who is waiting for him on a train. He leaves Ramgarh with Basanti, as Thakur sees them off at the railway station. Thakur's parting words offer empathy, as he says: 'I cannot share your grief, but I can understand it' (SJ 1975). And the film's end credits roll.	Thakur and Veeru	A new beginning (for Veeru and Basanti), closure of past wounds (for Thakur) and the making of new bonds for life based on empathy (Thakur and Veeru) suggest a return to calm and stability in the tumultuous lives of the two survivors out of the film's three heroic protagonists.	***Shanta***

Sholay, offering a roller coaster of the eight *rasas* listed by Bharata *muni*, culminates in the *shanta rasa*, for both its on-screen characters and off-screen viewers. This is the preeminent mood state and the ultimate goal of a dramatic aesthetic experience as recommended by the *Natyashastra*. According to actor–filmmaker and Indian Film Censor Board member Chandraprakash Dwivedi:

> The purpose of all *rasas* is to finally create *shanta* (quietude), a state of tranquility and equanimity. The purpose of all arts is to finally take you to a level where you are one with the reality, so that you are *shant* (calm). All the *rasas* occur because you are not *shant*. You are angry because you are not *shant*, you are laughing because you are not *shant*... That's why we say '*om shanti, shanti, shanti*' at the end [e.g. of prayers and *yagna* offerings]. That is what is desired from life, and that is what is desired from all art forms (2013).

Each of *Sholay*'s independently popular subplot episodes have, in retrospect, achieved 'a throbbing autonomous life of their own' (Jha 2014) in public memory: the spectacular train robbery in the beginning (evoking *adbhuta*); comic encounters with the British-era jailor (*hasya*); Gabbar Singh's playing of Russian roulette in the ravine with his scared henchmen (*bhayanaka*); his massacre of the Thakur's family (*bibhatsa*); Veeru's suicide drama atop a water tower (*hasya*); the poignant death of the Imam's son (*karuna*); Radha's unspoken love (*sringara*); Jaidev's heroic sacrifice (*vira*) and Thakur's climactic killing of Gabbar without arms (*raudra*). However, after evoking every *rasa* sentiment individually, they are still able to subsume their varying emotive collage within an emotionless state of calm. Like the multiple colours of a rainbow revealed through the prism of a raindrop, they are subsequently returned to the singular white of the sunlight. This ability to evoke a true *shanta rasa* experience, which also is 'the culminating *rasa* sentiment of the Mahabharata, as an epic poem as reviewed by 9th CE philosopher, Anandavardhana' (Rao 2014: 257), makes *Sholay* arguably India's third most popular epic after the Ramayana and the Mahabharata. Indian national award-winning writer–filmmaker Nirad Mohapatra explains that to be able to conjure *shanta* as the ending emotion of an aesthetic experience is a rare and difficult cinematic achievement. The reason for *Sholay*'s lasting appeal as a story that has been able to enthral viewers across generations, unlike other equally successful *masala* films that have failed to retain a timeless appeal, can be attributed to this achievement. According to Mohapatra:

> To sum your narrative with the *shanta rasa* you do not end a film at a point where the emotion is very strong. You have to basically go a little further and beyond that event to neutralise its impact. A *shanta rasa* ending does not mean that the audience will sort of forget the film; it rather means that it has actually sunk in. The [vocal] emotions may get neutralised, but the subject stays in the mind... If you finish a story abruptly, where an emotional catharsis happens [for instance concluding *Sholay* at the point of the completion of Thakur's revenge], you do not carry its impact beyond the theatre. It is all over then and there. But to make it linger in your mind, you have to go beyond a cathartic moment. *Shanta rasa* is basically a tranquil state of mind where the audience is no longer agitated by any overwhelming emotion, which is achieved by taking the events in a story, a little after the [conventional/happy] end (interview, 2013).

Mohapatra has explained the working of the *shanta rasa* impact in the context of the ending of Yasujirō Ozu's *Tōkyō Monogatari* (Tokyo Story, 1953), which he argues to be a rare world classic achievement in the *shanta rasa*. According to him:

> The film's narrative does not end with the mother's death where everyone is crying and pathos is reigning supreme. It instead goes a little further to show how the father is coping up with his loss, how the children are reflecting on their disappointing lives, and other events built after the tragic moment of a death that help neutralise a powerful emotion to eventually sign off with a shot of a river with steamers moving on, almost in a tranquil (*shant*), life goes on kind of note (2013).

Sholay also opts for a similar resolution, offering glimpses into the lives of each of its four surviving lead characters (Thakur, Radha, Veeru and Basanti) following Jaidev's death, thereby portraying a carrying-on-with-life attitude instead of despair. A relevant example is Veeru's decision to leave Ramgarh. He had come to Ramgarh with Jaidev and though, earlier in the film, had wished to settle in the village, in the changed context the location would have also constantly reminded him of his loss. Therefore, for a new beginning and a calmer emotional state, he seeks a destination away from the village. Thakur's last words to Veeru, 'I cannot share your grief, but can understand it' (SJ 1975), delivered for the first time in a non-commanding tone and with empathy, also suggest the passing of turbulence and a possible return to the state of *shanta* in his life.

Overview of the Dominant *Bhavas* of *Sholay*'s Major Characters

Sholay does not merely achieve a harmonious blend of various *rasa*-evoking scenarios; each of its major characters also manifests the *sthayibhavas* of the various *rasas* as recognisable character traits. Dwivedi observes, 'Every character has a personality, and that personality also creates *rasa*' (Dwivedi 2013). Meticulously written introductory scenes for every character highlight this dimension of characterisation. These are 'typical to popular Hindi cinema narratives whereby the trait of a character is established at the very moment of his or her appearance'[16] through relevant dialogue and encounters that establish their nature. Table 4.2 presents an overview of the dominant *bhava* states and their supporting submoods from the introduction scene of each of *Sholay*'s major characters.

Table 4.2 The Dominant *Bhavas* of *Sholay*'s Major Characters

Sl. No.	Characters (By Order of Entry)	Dominant *Bhava* State	Dominant Rasa/Rasas Evoked
1.	Thakur	**Angry** *also* brooding and hurting (in a constant state of repressed anger, fuelled by an obsession with revenge)	*Raudra/Vira*

Sl. No.	Characters (By Order of Entry)	Dominant *Bhava* State	Dominant Rasa/Rasas Evoked
2.	Veeru	**Merry** *also,* funny, mischievous and courageous	*Hasya/Vira*
3.	Jaidev	**Courageous** *also,* compassionate, energetic and introspective	*Vira*
4.	Surma Bhopali	**Loud** *also* funny in a perpetually exaggerated state of being	*Hasya*
5.	The British-Era Jailor	**Hyperactive** *also,* loud and confused	*Hasya*
6.	Basanti	**Funny** *also,* romantic, courageous and high on energy	*Hasya/ Sringara*
7.	Radha	**Sadness** *also,* silent in terms of grieving loss and reflective	*Karuna*
8.	Mausi	**Funny** *also,* loud, chatty and curious	*Hasya*
9.	Imam Sahib	**Calm** *also,* determined, brave and composed	*Shanta*
10.	Gabbar Singh	**Ferocious** *also,* sadistic, unpredictable and full of surprise	*Bhayanaka/ Bibhatsa/ Adbhuta*

In this clarity and consistency in the dominant mood states of the characters, embellished with memorable complimentary mood dialogue and actions, perhaps lies an explanation as to why every character in *Sholay*, including those making a fleeting appearance, is still etched in the minds of its viewers. Akhtar locates their combined memorability in the contrasting emotional nature of their individual traits, stating:

> You have Thakur on one side, Gabbar on the other. Thakur is clean and impeccable. He is always clean shaven, his hair is made, he is crisp, and

> to the point. On the other side, Gabbar is dirty and gregarious. You have two friends, one is extremely boisterous, and another is sober and deep. You have two girls in the film, one is extremely talkative, and the other is totally silent. One is colourful, another is totally devoid of any colour in life, and quiet. These foils are perfect and because you have both the ends of the spectrum, the story covers almost all kinds of emotions (Akhtar 2014).

According to his co-writer Salim Khan:

> *Rasa* is evoked by even each of the smaller characters in *Sholay*. This subconsciously comes into our writing because those traits are within us. As a nation too we evoke the *rasas* in the way we live, and naturally they seep into our work. But if we start inserting it by proportion, it will not work because we do not have a formula for how much of which *rasa* should be inserted (2013).

In Khan's review, there can be found an endorsement of the argument that a good *masala* film will subconsciously factor in situations and characters that embody the various *rasas*. The entry scene of each of the major characters in *Sholay* (Table 4.2) establishes certain *bhava* states that the characters carry into their every subsequent appearance, including their positive or negative reactions to a situation, in accordance with the dominant mood trait of their character. For instance, the widow Radha remains reserved and silent throughout the film, when she develops attraction for Jaidev and even when she hears Thakur's decision on her remarriage to Jaidev. On the other hand, Basanti is perpetually in a state of high energy and constant chatter, be it during a comic banter with Veeru or while goading her horse to gallop faster when pursued by Gabbar's dacoits. According to Akhtar:

> Master plots are inspired from basic human instincts [i.e. the *sthayibhavas*], and so are made up of stories that represent one particular instinct: love, hate, curiosity or whatever. So, if your story relies heavily on one particular human instinct, the character will be obsessed with love or hate (Akhtar 1999: 33).

Image 4.1 A Poster of *Sholay* Depicting its Protagonists in their Most Recurring *Sthayibhavas* (Angry, Sad, Comic, Ferocious and Courageous Respectively) in the Film
(Clockwise from left to right—Thakur [Sanjeev Kumar], Radha [Jaya Bhaduri], Basanti [Hema Malini], Gabbar Singh [Amjad Khan], Jaidev [Amitabh Bachchan] and Veeru [Dharmendra]) (Photograph: NFAI)

Sholay's myriad characters and their stories encompass a range of human instincts. The success of this kind of an approach in conceiving a character is indicated by the fact that the actors are still remembered by their on-screen names. Filmmaker Tigmanshu Dhulia says:

> A character like Asrani's [playing the British era jailor], who probably had a screen time of less than ten minutes, is etched in people's minds

> forever. Or for that matter Samba (played by MacMohan) who barely has three lines. But ask anyone even today and they will tell you who Samba was and what his lines were (Dhulia 2012).

Most of these characters, as highlighted in Table 4.2, embody one or two complementary *sthayibhavas*[17] as character traits that they retain throughout. Yet it can be argued that the unusual popularity of one character—who, despite being the villain, ended up becoming one of the most popular characters in Indian cinematic history—Gabbar Singh, lay in his conceptualisation as a character embodying a mix of multiple positive and negative *bhavas.* These include anger, fear, disgust and daring, along with an aptitude to surprise and a sense of humour (albeit sadistic), that render him different from the stereotypical, pure evil villains that Hindi cinema viewers were used to until then. According to Akhtar:

> One thing you would notice in our villains whether in *Sholay, Mr. India* [1987], *Zanjeer* [Chains 1973] or in *Shaan* [Pride 1980], these villains are not lechers. Even when he [Gabbar] is looking at Basanti and asks her to dance there is no sexual innuendo in it – he just wants to torture her and Veeru. That's about all. He is not interested in her. They all also look powerful because they were not lechers. You cannot admire a lecher; you can admire an immoral person but that too should have a dignity. Our villains have always been very dignified, evil but dignified (Akhtar 2014).

If *Sholay* is a film with the perfect mix of *rasas*, Gabbar Singh is a character that attempts a merger of the distinguishing character attributes of the then hero and villain stereotypes. This was achieved with an imaginative blend of *bhava* traits that not only made the character larger than life but also won it an on-screen achievement worth repeating for its fans, despite its conception and actions not being entirely original. For instance, Gabbar's most brutal act of villainy, of a type seen for the first time on Indian cinema, features the point-blank shooting of a child—this was copied from a similar moment featuring Henry Fonda in *Once Upon a Time in the West* (Sergio Leone 1968). His psychotic nature and menacing laughter were also inspired by the lead villain of *For A Few Dollars More*. However, he courted an impact exclusive to debuting characters with never-before-seen attributes, because of his unexpected emotions in similar situations. For example, he treats women as objects of torture instead of lust and he guns down loyal but weak accomplices in order to make a statement on the uselessness of weak assistants. This novelty is the result of a different set of *rasa*-evoking considerations at play in the process of the adaptation.

Rasa in Adaptation

The writers of *Sholay*, Salim Khan and Javed Akhtar, have on record acknowledged being impressed and inspired by Sergio Leone's Spaghetti Westerns while conceiving their scenes. *Mera Gaon Mera Desh* (My Village My Country, Raj Khosla 1971), a hit film that released four years before *Sholay*, also had a similar plot featuring *Sholay*'s leading star Dharmendra (Veeru) playing a courageous thief who is hired by a retired soldier, a landowner, to kill a dacoit named Jabbar Singh. Senior critic Subhash K. Jha, however, still argues that *Sholay* remains as fresh a viewing experience today as it was at the time of its release, and Akhtar insists that 'there is yet to be another Hindi film since with as many memorable characters' (Jha 2014; Kabir 1999: 58). According to Salim Khan:

> *Sholay* was not based on any one particular film, but was inspired by many films. Being influenced is not a crime; plagiarising or copying is. We had made *Deewar* [The Wall, 1975] using sources from *Mother India* [1957] and *Ganga Jumna* [1961], but no scene in *Deewar* is like any scene from the other two films, because of which *Deewar* is considered as one of Indian cinema's most original screenplays. Plots have always been taken and shared across cinemas because (as they say) there are only about 14 basic plotlines in the world. [Akhtar contends to there being 10 master plots (Kabir 1999: 33)]. Hence overlaps are bound to happen as we tend to make films primarily on human relationships which are the same everywhere. Even *The Magnificent Seven* [1960] was inspired by *Seven Samurai* [1954], but what makes *Sholay* different is how we portrayed these

> relationships and the basic human emotions that shaped and defined them differently because of the different culture and approach to storytelling we hail from (Khan 2013).

In the above assertion can be seen the essence of the process of adaptation or of how a foreign plot source or character can be subjected to a reconstruction that highlights emotions by 'intelligent Indian script writers, who tend to transform a source idea into something so completely Indian culture specific and different' (Pandey 2013) that most of the resulting narratives have rarely been accused of copyright violations by their respective sources. Sam Joshi locates this differentiation between Hindi and Hollywood films' storytelling styles in the former's continuing adherence to the *Natyashastra*-prescribed need for prioritising affective (or emotional) realism over cognitive realism (Joshi 2004: 22). He argues that fans of cognitive realism expect their on-screen experience to mimic real life and hence the filmmaker tries to depict those events as logically as they could possibly unfold in real life. According to Joshi:

> Events flow in a cause-effect relationship and the film's mise-en-scène (stage setting) strives for maximum fidelity to real life... Under cognitive realism, the activity of the viewer is geared towards understanding situations, predicting likely outcomes based on available information, and proposing solutions to certain enigmas... constantly asking questions like "What will happen next?" In contrast, the viewer of affective realism is not interested in what will happen next, but in how a particular on-screen event feels. To experience a depicted emotion in as much depth as possible is the reward for a viewer of Hindi cinema (Joshi 2004: 22).

Anu Gordon, a member of the audience at a film screening commemorating 40 years of *Sholay* in Edinburgh in 2014, while reflecting on her viewing experience, says:

> I was engaged, I cared, which is essential for me to really enjoy a film, i.e. to care. Actually, I cared very quickly, and as the film progressed, I was caring more and more. When Thakur was kicking Gabbar in the end, I was glad! (2014).

Her expectations are akin to that of an ideal *rasika* as defined in the *Natyashastra*—a viewer who relishes the *rasa* of a scene by savouring its corresponding *bhava*, which is generated by the actor/character on-screen and born of an experience of shared empathy, called *sadharanikarana*[18] (the universalisation of an emotion). She is a *sahrydaya*[19], a sensitive viewer, who achieves a similar mood state as that of a character whose on-screen journey she can empathetically connect with. For this to happen, the impediment of a doubting/questioning mind has to be kept aside, 'as often expressed in the patronising and unfair judgments of critics of popular Indian cinema, who suggest that one has to leave one's brains at the theatre door before stepping in to watch a Hindi film' (Vijayakar 2012; Kesavan 2012). This 'need for Indian cinema audiences [at least of the popular or *masala* form] wanting to be moved by their cinematic experience' (Mohapatra 2013) makes its creators insert additions to create intense emotions and subtract concerns about continuity or realism that could delay or diminish the emotional impact of on-screen action. According to Vidya Balan:

> We not only dramatise and fictionalise, but also emotionalise a film. Films that have managed to marry commercial and critical success in India have always served the *navarasas* because it's the recipe for a fulfilling [viewing] menu. You go into a cinema to be moved by all the emotions. It need not just be tears. It has to touch you in some way. For instance, I do not connect with action films because they are normally devoid of emotions. Different people connect to different things. A *navarasa* palette offers something for everyone to find a connection (2014).

They heighten the emotive impact of a scene irrespective of whether it is logical or believable. According to Akhtar, 'An Indian film writer is supposed to write a totally original script that has come before' (Kabir 1999: 34). This is done, as in the case of *Sholay,* by imbuing a familiar scene or character with a new set of emotions. Scenes are rewritten for a relatively greater generation of *rasa*. Salim Khan explains:

> Hollywood's definition of genres need not necessarily match ours. We do not always laugh at their jokes. Cinema reception is also a

> cultural thing. We are much more expressive people. Their films are much shorter compared to ours, since they are normally limited to a linear emotional track, whereas we have multiple tracks, songs, etc. Agar single track ki kahani ho to majaa nahi aata hamare audience ko (a story with a single emotion track does not excite our audience as much). Our films are like our dawaats (meals)—kisi ko bulate hain to hamare yahaan dus dishes banti hai, halanki aadmi khata ek ya do jo use pasand hai (if we invite anyone, we make 10 dishes though an individual eats only the few that he likes). Even a vegetarian *thali* has 10 *katoris*… It is our culture *ki ek hi cheez mein sabke sab dal do* (Putting as many options as possible into one thing is our cultural trait). Even our weddings and mourning are ceremonial in nature often running for three to four to six days (2013).

A relevant example is the unfolding of the massacre of Thakur's family in *Sholay*. This scene is based on a similar sequence in *Once Upon a Time in the West*. In the Hollywood film, Brett McBain and his three children are murdered in cold blood by the hired gun, Frank (Henry Fonda), of a railroad tycoon. They are shot to freeze frame falls, like the massacre of Thakur's family members. In both films, little boys are shot point blank, but while Frank shares the reason behind his gruesome act as that the boy had heard his name and hence could reveal his identity to the police, Gabbar's shooting of Thakur's grandson is left open to interpretation. It may have been to establish a new low in his character's sadism, or he may have killed the boy for his defiance and refusal to plead with Gabbar for his life, or it may have been to justify Thakur's emotional decision to attempt a futile and dangerous singlehanded revenge in the subsequent scene. Lending reason to Frank's brutality helps a viewer who is conditioned to look for cognitive realism to understand the motive behind an unusual act and be satisfied with a believable and logical justification. By not explaining the reason behind Gabbar's brutality to a viewer conditioned by the claims of affective realism, 'who is more concerned about how an event feels rather than why it happened or what will happen next' (Joshi 2004: 22), the feeling of disgust is heightened. Each viewer then has to decide for themselves the justification for Thakur's subsequent reckless and doomed attempt at revenge against Gabbar.

It is McBain's new wife and only surviving kin, Jill McBain, who discovers the massacre of the McBain family. This takes place nearly half an hour later, after a riveting action sequence in a tavern involving characters who are eventually revealed to be the film's two male protagonists. By the time Jill discovers the massacre, its shock impact has already been diluted for the audience by the intervening event with a different emotional import (*vira*). Later in the film, Jill is aided by two outlaws of similar characters to Jaidev and Veeru in exacting revenge on Frank. The McBain family massacre and its discovery take into account logical time and distance gaps between events and physical limitations of the wronged character.

Thakur's discovery of his family's massacre comes immediately after Gabbar's act, with the directorial aim of weaving a consistently heightened thread of complementary negative sentiments—from shock, to disgust, to anger. Craving vengeance, Thakur immediately takes off alone to kill Gabbar. This is a conscious suicidal act. Jill does not react in the same manner but rather prepares for the moment when she will have the edge and ability to exact revenge. Predictably, Thakur is captured, and Gabbar chops off his arms. Thakur's reaction is justified as an emotional response to a grave personal provocation. By putting these scenes of action and reaction immediately after one another, the *rasa* of *raudra* as vengeance is, for an emotionally attuned *sahrydaya* viewer, effected to an intense degree. It is supported by disgust and sadness to create an emotionally integrated standalone tale of revenge that makes for a keen cinematic memory. Aware of her limitations as a lone woman in a tough terrain, Jill McBain's restrained and delayed attempt at revenge is a believable and logical resolution to an unfair challenge, but it lacks *Sholay*'s emotional impact. For instance, Jill's discovery of the dead bodies of the McBain family is much less dramatic compared to that of Thakur's of his dead kin. The dead are revealed to Jill immediately on arrival, as her expression changes from surprise, to shock, to sorrow, to a final lament of 'Dear God' when she sees the corpse of the youngest McBain. Villagers offer their condolences as a mellow, poignant soundtrack plays in the background, and she tries to get on with the business of justifying her presence.

Thakur, on the other hand, does not see the faces of his dead family members at first sight. He just sees a line of bodies wrapped in white sheets from head to toe. As he approaches against the background of an ominous soundtrack, the same music that was played earlier at the moment of Gabbar's killing of Thakur's family[20], a gust of wind reveals the identity of the bodies one after another, and Thakur's shock changes to anger. He eventually reaches a mood state of maddening rage—which is retained throughout the film—as he pulls off the sheet covering his dead grandchild, which incidentally does not get blown away like the others. The body of the dead child is not shown, unlike its equivalent scene in *Once Upon a Time in the West*. Instead, the effect of its revelation plays out in a series of close-ups of the changing intense emotion on Thakur's face; what he sees is left to the viewer's imagination. His facial expressions, ranging from extreme grief to uncontrollable rage, are necessary to justify his subsequent decision to singlehandedly pursue and punish Gabbar. The tears that he holds back at that moment feed, sustain and justify his raging persona throughout the film. He mourns his dead only after exacting his revenge by killing Gabbar in the end. The continuity in his character's anger is thus maintained throughout, from his stern entry through his no-nonsense negotiations with Jaidev and Veeru and his raging attempt at revenge, to a violent combat with Gabbar at the end. It is in this retention of the relevant *rasa* throughout a film, beyond concerns of logical development and other cognitive realism imperatives, that make an Indianised (or *rasa*-ised) Curry Western diverge from its Spaghetti Western sources in similar drama moments to offer a totally different, signature and novel viewing experience. According to Salim Khan, 'Having too many emotional tracks is a more difficult script to write than a single-track story' (Khan 2013). In Pandey's opinion, 'Perhaps the only thing that Bollywood filmmakers take while adapting a Hollywood film is the plot. But the rest of it you have to make acceptable to the Indian audience' (Pandey 2013).

I will now discuss this process of adaptation with reference to the entry and exit sequences of *Sholay*'s most memorable character, Gabbar Singh, which were inspired by similar scenes in *For a Few Dollars More*.

The Introduction of Gabbar Singh

Indian cinema archivist, biographer and documentary maker Nasreen Munni Kabir has declared Gabbar Singh's introduction scene in *Sholay* as 'the last word in how to introduce a character to the audience… The location, different shot compositions, music, dialogue and [actor] Amjad Khan's performance all combine to make this a flawless scene' (Kabir 2013: 32). The scene begins with a top-down shot from a hillock summit to the accompaniment of the threatening sounds of a gong. As the camera pans down, we see a pair of boots restlessly pacing up and down the rocks to the background score mixing a beat of eerie menace with boot stomps. A belt dangling loose from the subject's hand grazes bare rocks. This scene takes place nearly an hour into the film. The audience's curiosity about the personality of the pacing character has been roused by various references and discussions through which he is revealed as either a fierce opponent (by the Thakur) or a scary dacoit and oppressor (by the villagers). Initially only the character's voice is heard, starting with a reflective 'Hunn…' as he asks:

> Gabbar: Kitne aadmi the? (How many people were there?)
> Dacoit: Sardar do aadmi… (Boss… only two)
> Gabbar: Hunn…Do aadmi… SUAR KE BACCHON!!![21] (Two people… SONS OF SWINES!!!) (SJ 1975).

As he yells a curse at his three runaway bandits, the camera reveals the face of Gabbar for the first time, reflecting palpable rage. He resumes the interrogation in his deadpan voice:

> Gabbar: Wo do the aur tum teen, phir bhi wapas aa gaye? Khaali haath? Kya samajh kar aaye the ke Sardar bahut khush hoga? Shabashi dega, kyun? DHIKKAR HAI!!! (They were two and you were three. Yet you have come back empty handed. What were you thinking... Boss will congratulate you? SHAME ON YOU!!!) (SJ 1975).

The scene proceeds in the form of a monologue, with Gabbar oscillating between a deadpan voice and sudden angry yells. This establishes both a sense of dread and of awe, highlighting the unpredictable nature of his character. In the film's subsequent engagements with Gabbar, this attribute recurs as he frequently thwarts the conventional expectations formed by the behaviour of on-screen dacoits in the predecessors of the genre, such as *Mera Gaon Mera Desh*. This unpredictable behaviour lends Gabbar's evil acts a sense of wonder, raising the question 'how next?' (as opposed to 'what next?'). This results in a relishing of the *adbhuta rasa* by the audience, even when his actions range from fearful to disgusting. Gabbar cultivates the aura of fear around himself when he asks one of his henchmen, Samba, about the prize money on offer for his capture. When Samba declares the amount to be ₹50,000, Gabbar explains, 'And this high price money is because in every village within 50 miles radius from here, whenever a child cries at night, the mother says, "Go to sleep my child, or Gabbar will come"' (SJ 1975). Akhtar highlights Gabbar's unique style of self-reference as a deliberate writing strategy used to intensify his fear factor through a fear fable. He explains:

> When I was writing it, I thought it was below Gabbar's dignity to have to say himself, 'I have a 50,000 rupees reward on my head'. A man with his kind of arrogance and conceit would more likely ask a subordinate – or rather order him – to boast his worth (Akhtar 1999: 59).

A dacoit works in the business of fear. Gabbar embodies that fear, but it is compromised by his henchmen running away from their confrontation with Jaidev and Veeru in Ramgarh. Fear has to be re-established in the rebellious villagers, but before that his men have to be taught that cowardice, even among his loyalists, will not be forgiven. He stages an unpredictable game of the absurd. He borrows a revolver with six bullets, lets off three random shots in the air, rotates the bullet cylinder and starts to shoot his three men, one after the other. Interestingly, all his first three hits are blank shots. The music turns to one of gradual dread as Gabbar's voice drops to a tone of conciliation, but for the audience it is just a temporary lull before another storm. Gabbar expresses surprise and starts laughing uncontrollably, declaring, 'What a miracle, all the three bastards have been saved!' (SJ 1975). The other dacoits follow the leader and as their communal laughter reaches a crescendo, the three dacoits realise that they have been saved by an unusual stroke of luck. They start with unbelieving fits and bursts and soon join the roar, laughing heartily. Just when the tension seems to have been relieved with laughter all around, Gabbar turns on his unsuspecting targets and shoots them down with the three remaining bullets, one after the other, with a cold-blooded precision that barely allows them any moment to react. The sound of the gunshots abruptly silences everyone in a shockingly memorable scene, which in its unpredictable unfolding leaves the audience with an everlasting awe. Gabbar then justifies the punishment in a deadpan, emotionless voice, devoid of any regret, declaring, 'Jo dar gaya, samjho mar gaya' (Death to the cowards! SJ 1975).

That quick felling of the three goons can be sourced to a similar moment featuring Clint Eastwood's 'Man with No Name' character in *For a Few Dollars More*. Gabbar's menacing laughter and streak of unpredictability has been sourced from another character from the film, an opportunistic and similarly psychotic gangster, El Indio, played by Gian Maria Volonté.

In Indio's introductory scene in the film, he is rescued from a prison cell by his accomplices after a long shoot-out sequence in which all but one policeman is killed. Indio leaves only one policeman alive to tell the tale of his exploits to feed the cult of fear around him in the area. He says, 'I am leaving you so that you can tell everybody what takes place here…' (Vincenzoni 1965)[22] and utters a menacing laugh. The scene then cuts to a poster advertisement announcing a hefty reward of $10,000 for Indio's capture, and two bounty hunters are shown pondering over the dare. Indio does not know about it. The sum is noticed by the bounty hunters for whom it is an attraction, rather than by the outlaw as with Gabbar, who discusses his reward money just for effect. The ₹ 50,000 reward on Gabbar is never reiterated as an inducement for Jaidev and Veeru. After the film's interval, they become true righteous heroes (*dharma-viras*) and want to capture him for the larger social good and not for personal gains. In *For a Few Dollars More*, Indio then proceeds to exact his revenge on the person responsible for his arrest and kills his entire family, just as Gabbar kills Thakur's family for sending him to jail.

Gabbar instils fear first among his own men by killing his three defeated dacoits. Next, he exports that fear to the villagers through a severe act of revenge. He however does not act on it immediately and waits instead for the festival of Holi, when the villagers will be least suspecting. The narrative then cuts to a colourful Holi song, where the villagers celebrate their newfound freedom and get drunk and Veeru and Basanti sing a song to articulate their budding romance. As the defences and preparedness of the villagers start crumbling, the engagement of the pre-warned audience with the joyous sequence is defined by the emotion of dread, as they anticipate Gabbar's approaching attack. The irony of the attack is further heightened by its occurrence immediately after a celebration.

In *For a Few Dollars More*, Indio's retributions are planned, justified by a motive (however sinister) and acted out in a logical manner that makes their occurrence look fairly plausible. For instance, his rescue from jail is made possible with the help of his men. It is never a one-man show of bravado, allaying any concerns of plausibility from the more questioning viewers. The focus in Indio's gun battles is on the success of a strategy; unlike Gabbar's introduction, where the scene of the killing of his men focuses more on chance, drama and applause-eliciting dialogue, as explained by Akhtar while discussing the scene featuring Samba. Both Indio and Gabbar are stylised villains, but Gabbar's undulating style of delivery—from subtle, to loud, to deadpan—contributes as much to his character as his acts, while Indio's evocation of dread is developed primarily by his actions.

The creators of Gabbar Singh and actor Amjad Khan use all the four recommended performance aids for a character as outlined in the *Natyashastra*—the *angika, vachika, aharya* and *sattvika* varieties—to highlight his unconventional appeal. His gestural (*angika*) behaviour conveys his unpredictability, as Gabbar constantly moves throughout his introduction scene. He first surveys his three men from a distance, sits down and chats with them, then gets up and runs to a colleague for a revolver, before returning to circle them as if scrutinising a potential prey. He then walks some distance away, but not too far to be able to shoot from close range. His verbal (*vachika*) performance is set at a complementing pitch; he speaks through memorable one-liners that are delivered in oscillating decibels, almost as a performance for the benefit of the other dacoits in his group. He talks throughout the scene, pausing only rarely to react or allow them a reply. His costume (*aharya*) too is contrary to the landscape and the context he inhabits. While all of the dacoits in the film are dressed in *dhoti–kurta* like the traditional dacoits of Chambal, Gabbar is made to stand out in pants and a shirt to accommodate the film's producer G.P. Sippy's fascination with Fidel Castro. Finally, Gabbar's emotions (*sattvika*) are articulated through a riot of expressions, starting with shock, turning to anger, surprise and mirth, which is actually a screen for sarcasm. His final expression is one of disgust, in order to justify his brutal killing of his men for their cowardice.

Gabbar is an agent of fear, but unlike Indio, he practices his sadism with a hint of the unexpected. This enables his character's dominant *bhava* of dread and disgust to also become the triggers for a pleasurable *rasa* like *adbhuta*, which perhaps explains his character's tremendous post-release popularity amongst all age groups, including children. According to Akhtar:

> So often people ask, here was Gabbar who is totally unscrupulous, ruthless and sadistic [yet] why he became so popular, and why he became so popular among children? [Because] you admire unrestricted power; you admire people who are a law onto themselves. That's why you admire Robin Hood or any underworld character like Al Capone. You see that complete absence of any conscience is somewhere admirable, like how when you look at a python or a shark, you are fascinated! (Akhtar 2014)

If *Sholay*'s attraction was its potent mix of contrasting counter-emotional characters that both complement and contribute, Gabbar becomes the most impacting of them all in his ability to have some of those contrasts reside within his personality. He is a sadist who performs some disgusting actions, but he also has a sense of humour. His acts are aimed at nurturing a reign of terror, but he delivers them with such unpredictability that he also makes the audience curious about how he will plan his next move. For instance, in the scene where he captures Basanti, the hitherto conventional behaviour of a villain in an Indian film would dictate the outraging of the heroine's modesty. However, Gabbar just asks her to dance and entertain his men in a cinematically unconventional manoeuvre. Yet, as he further stipulates that her lover will only be allowed to live as long as she continues to dance, the evil in his nature is manifested. Subsequently, when he makes a tired Basanti dance on shattered glass in order to break her spirit, the sadistic streak in his nature comes to the fore. The audience meanwhile wonders how this unusual scene of torture will resolve itself. According to Anil Zankar:

> Gabbar Singh's black sense of humour is extremely sadistic. He is merciless in his anger. In fact, he is the towering personality dictating the course of the story. The heroes have to measure up to him and his henchmen. From here on, Hindi cinema saw the emergence of the seemingly omnipotent oppressor as the villain. Significantly, he is the one who sets up the context and action of the story (Zankar 2003: 365).

For an audience for whom the 'how' of an action is the prime attraction over the 'why' and 'what' of it, Gabbar thus emerges as an unusual entertainer. He actually makes the audience derive pleasure from seemingly unpleasant *rasas* like *bhaya* and *bibhatsa*, which thus make him all the more memorable.

Image 4.2 Amjad Khan as Gabbar Singh Achieves a Compelling Portrait of a Dacoit Working in the Business of Fear (Photograph: NFAI)

The Death of Gabbar

The sequence begins with Thakur walking towards Gabbar, who, already battered by Veeru and just released from his murderous grip, lies curled up on the ground like a snake. He gets up to face the new challenge. The spiked nails under Thakur's boots have been deliberately revealed to the audience but remain unknown to Gabbar, who now seems to be contemplating an easy escape. The drama is once again built around how the armless Thakur will exact his revenge on Gabbar after he asks the physically more able Veeru to leave. To Gabbar's sarcastic quip about how he will fight without arms, Thakur retorts, 'A snake is crushed with feet not hands Gabbar; for you my feet are enough' (SJ 1975). He then leaps from his high vantage position on a rock to fell Gabbar with a kick to the chest with his thorn-laced shoes. He next crushes his left arm, repeating the very same words that Gabbar had said before amputating his arms, 'There is a lot of life in these hands' (SJ 1975). Closure is reached, both in action and emotion, through a repetition of dialogue. The final triumph is achieved when Thakur mutilates Gabbar's right hand, shouting, 'Gabbar ye haath mujhe de de…' (Give me your hands Gabbar, SJ 1975) to the latter's painful yell of 'No'. His victim is now thoroughly mangled like a snake, as was warned in the beginning. Thakur completes the task by strategically pushing Gabbar onto a pointed nail, which is protruding from a pillar the latter unknowingly tries to recline against. It is a five-minute long sequence and Thakur too falls and receives a few hits before recovering to finally kill Gabbar.

The turn of events is counter intuitive. The very nature of such a mismatched fight sequence between an able-bodied rogue and an aging, disabled man leads us to logically expect a different conclusion. In a realistic scenario, Thakur would have let Veeru complete the revenge on his behalf (like Jill McBain). However, that would have cheated the audience of the pleasure gained from witnessing the 'how' of Thakur's resolution of the mismatched duel, one that had been promised from the early moments of the film.

A comparison with the resolution of a three-man climax depicting the death of Indio in *For a Few Dollars More* further elucidates the contrast. The film has a bounty hunter, Colonel Douglas Mortimer (Lee Van Cleef), join cause with a rival 'Man with No Name' (Clint Eastwood) to track and kill El Indio. Indio has a musical pocket watch in which he plays music before engaging in gun duels. Flashbacks reveal that he had stolen the watch from a young woman after killing her lover/husband and raping her. She later committed suicide. In the climax, Mortimer and Indio face each other, as the 'Man with No Name' sits down to watch their face off. 'Now we start,' (Vincenzoni 1965) he says with a chuckle, sitting like a referee to ensure a fair fight. It was Mortimer's personal desire to engage with Indio alone, like Thakur wanting to fight Gabbar alone. The watch plays again. During the standoff, 'Man with No Name' looks into Mortimer's pocket watch and sees the same photo as in Indio's watch. The music ends and Mortimer guns down Indio in one quick shot, and the latter dies without much ado. He then takes away the pocket watch. There is no close-up of the pain or suffering of the crouched Indio, no prolonged fight sequence, no dramatic outpouring of grief from Mortimer on the fulfilment of an urge for revenge harboured throughout the film. Mortimer's motive for killing Indio is casually revealed as he parts with a goodbye, instead of any cathartic outpouring. When the 'Man with No Name' gives him back Indio's other watch and remarks on Mortimer's resemblance with the girl's photo in it, he candidly answers without any emotion, 'Naturally, between brother and sister' (Vincenzoni 1965). His revenge complete, Mortimer refuses any share in the reward money and they part.

The climax of *Sholay*, which also is about one man exacting his revenge for the murder of innocent family members, nonetheless offers an entirely different intensity of music, drama and dialogue-driven emotional catharsis. There is enough time for elaborate conversations between Thakur and Veeru—'The remembering of a dead comrade and a passionate discussion over who gets to kill Gabbar'[23]—as the object of their hate listens confused, wondering about his fate. Akhtar says:

> Our cinema is still heavily influenced by traditional theatre, and so cinema relies heavily on the spoken word. For us, it is an audio-visual medium and the 'a' is a very, very capital (Akhtar 1999: 57).

The quiet of the Spaghetti Western is thus exchanged for verbosity in its Curry/*masala* counterpart. In *For a Few Dollars More*, the link between one of its protagonist's backstory and his motive for revenge is only casually hinted at, because the attraction of a Spaghetti Western is in its action, not emotion. In *Sholay*, the backstory is revealed in an elaborate pre-climactic intermission; it remains in the foreground throughout to make a subsequent spectacular display of heroism on-screen seem plausible to its audience, who want to be 'moved' by their cinematic experience. Hence, the story of the personal loss is developed and built through strategic revelations with varying emotional impacts, which a viewer predisposed in favour of cognitive realism might denounce as melodrama. This heightened emotional effect not only lends a sentimental justification to the unusual bravado and sacrifice of its heroes but also makes them *feel* believable and possessed of their own logic.

The tactical narrative style of the Spaghetti Western is exchanged for a riot of emotions in the climax of the Curry Western. Accordingly, the aged Thakur does some gravity-defying jumps to singlehandedly kill Gabbar, while Veeru just disappears, when he should have been present like the 'Man with No Name' to ensure a fair fight. But asking these questions—instead of being moved by the overwhelming emotion of the climax—will deprive the logic-seeking viewer of any chance at relishing the surfeit of *rasa* on-screen. The desire for *rasa* demands for Gabbar's prolonged pain and death in the end. Shot with detailed blows and blood-soaked close-ups, his demise is portrayed as fit justice for the blood of the many innocent people that he has spilt until then. This is necessary in order for *rasa*-seeking audiences to leave their three-and-a-half-hour long *Sholay* experience feeling 'good, as in emotionally fulfilled or satiated' (Pattanaik 2015).

After killing Gabbar, Thakur breaks down in tears in Veeru's arms, as the latter suddenly reappears on the scene. The music transforms the creaking tune of revenge into a melancholic chorus as both men lament their loss, while comforting each other. According to viewer Anu Gordon:

> Thakur's catharsis in the end—since he had not mourned the loss of his family at all—was one of the things that for me made the film

> superior to any Western I have ever seen. It was that the men were weeping, they were showing their feelings, whereas in the American Westerns they are always stone faced. That difference and humanness for me made *Sholay* a richer film (Gordon 2014).

Thus, in the successful catharsis of a character, the relishing of *rasa* by a *sahrydaya* audience is maximised, so that the movie maintains its impact long after it has been witnessed in the cinema. As Gordon says, 'When Thakur was kicking Gabbar in the end, I was glad. Now, I can watch *Sholay* all over again' (Gordon 2014). Offering insight into how the concern of evoking *rasa* in the audience guides the writing process of a Hindi film script or a dialogue writer re-fashioning a story, Pandey says:

> I consider theatre and film as a gym for emotions. We [the Indian/ Hindi cinema audience] go to the cinema to exercise our emotions. We live the lives of the characters in the film vicariously—we laugh, cry, feel angry—and we come out of the theatres feeling much lighter, fresher and even stronger without realising. So tomorrow even if I face a tragedy in real life like the movie, I am better prepared because I have lived through somebody else's tragedy in the theatre. That is why the story is so important. We cannot do without a good story. And a good story cannot happen without evoking the *rasas* (Pandey 2013).

Conclusion

Sholay has plot motivations and a few lead characterisations similar to Spaghetti Westerns, a genre that stylised action in international cinema. However, it is ultimately a distinctly Indian, *navarasa*-evoking film. Spectacular action and stylised characterisation are indeed part of the film, but they are always secondary, supporting elements next to its primary emotive core. Every major scene in the film can also be interpreted as part of a pairing, or face-off, between sets of complimentary or contrasting emotions. These foreground a variety of human bonds, including sacrificial love between two friends, romantic love between two couples, compassion between single guardians and their wards, courage in three heroic figures fighting evil and hate between a police officer and a dacoit. The impact of these emotions lies in their being articulated by characters representing the universally recognised *sthayibhavas*. Such characterisation may make some of the characters look stereotypical, but they are sharply personalised and contextualised within the space of an event or the span of a scenario. This ensures that they convincingly evoke the various dramatic *rasas*, imprinting them indelibly in the minds of their audiences, from the illiterate to the intelligent. After making its audience laugh, feel angry, disgusted, surprised, grieved, charmed by romance and awed by some spectacular display of physical bravado, *Sholay* is able to leave that same audience in the desired aesthetic state of the *shanta rasa*, as recommended by the *Natyashastra*. In this fulfilling blending of the *navarasas* lies the most plausible formula for the making of the perfect Indian *masala* film, as testified by the still enduring best-in-Bollywood legacy of *Sholay*, decades after its making.

Notes

1 Interview with Salim Khan in Mumbai on 6 September 2013.

2 Interview with Vidya Balan in Mumbai on 11 June 2014.

3 *Sholay* was declared the 'Film of the Millennium' by a BBC India poll in 1999, topped the British Film Institute's 'Top 10 Indian Films' of all time poll in 2002 and was awarded a special 'Best Film in 50 Years' honour at the 50th Filmfare Awards, 2005. In a March poll in 2015 by Time Out featuring critics, curators and film academics from the UK, USA and India (voting together for the first time), *Sholay* was voted the 'Best Bollywood Film of All Time'.

4 User reviews and ratings for Ram Gopal Varma Ki Aag (imdb.com, 2016)

5 '*Sholay* really changed the way filmmakers made movies and will always be remembered as a classic. Be it the sharp and witty dialogue by Salim-Javed or the iconic characters of the movie, everything about *Sholay* stands out. In fact, when I was making *Paan Singh Tomar*, the dacoit scenes were inspired by *Sholay*. What makes a film iconic? Script? Characters? Performances? *Sholay* scores on all these counts and on some more as well. It is a memorable film and is deeply rooted in our culture and traditions. Over the years a lot of our movies and directors have been inspired by *Sholay* which is a testament to the movie's brilliance' (Dhulia 2012).

6 Though actor Dharmendra speaks the lines in the film, the original creators and the writers of *Sholay*, Salim Khan and Javed Akhtar, are credited for the dialogue.

7 'There are direct references to *Once Upon A Time In The West* and *One-Eyed Jacks*, and the spirit of *Butch Cassidy*, *The Magnificent Seven* and *The Searchers* runs throughout *Sholay*' (Harris 2008).

8 Javed Akhtar's quotes have been accessed from secondary print and online resources.

9 The Dollars Trilogy is a series of three films directed by Sergio Leone—*A Fistful of Dollars* (1964), *For a Few Dollars More* (1965) and *The Good, the Bad and the Ugly* (1966)—that established the Spaghetti Western genre (also known as Italian Western and/or European Western in contrast to the American Western).

10 Though 'Thakur' is normally used as a designation of address, in this chapter it will be used as a proper noun to refer to Baldev Singh's character.

11 A vira or a hero, depending on the nature of the motivation leading to his act of heroism, is categorised *as a daya-vira* (one driven by compassion for a cause, protection of weaker human beings, etc., like Lord Rama), *dana-vira* (driven by acts of charity like Raja Harishchandra or King Harshavardhana) and *dharma-vira* (who fights for the establishment of dharma, law, righteousness and other noble values, like Arjuna in the Mahabharata or Thakur in Sholay).

12 Anand Bakshi is the lyricist of all the songs of Sh*olay*.

13 Actors who have been successful in certain characterisations, especially those working within the popular cinema star system, have frequently been limited to repeatedly playing a recognised stereotype through their careers. So, a popular on-screen villain like Pran is continually assigned to play challenging negative roles, while comedians like Jagdeep, Asrani and Keshto Mukherjee (all starring in Sholay) have reprised many comic characters. As a result, so strong is their association with an acted emotion that the mere sighting of them in a scene is often used by writers and filmmakers to deliberately give a hint to regular audiences about an upcoming funny sequence.

14 Though 'mausi' is a Hindi term for one's maternal aunt, as in the case of Thakur, the term is used by all inhabitants of Ramgarh as a proper noun to address Basanti's aunt.

15 Such abrupt changes in mood between scenes (e.g., from a cold-blooded triple killing to one of song and dance), though not unnatural for audiences

looking for a rasa-driven emotional roller coaster in their film-viewing experience, often tend to draw criticism from viewers and critics used to a linear development or a gradual transition between emotions.

16 'Characters [in Hindi films] are not good or bad because of their personal idiosyncrasies, but rather due to their traits. Usually, the particular quality of a character is established at the very moment of his or her appearance. Being dutiful makes for a positive character. So does being religious. Being kind and forgiving is again being 'good'. This has an interesting obverse. Dereliction of duties on the part of same characters immediately portrays the 'evil' or negative side... evil expresses itself in many ways. A member in the family who causes strife and unhappiness in an essentially happy family is evil. In a love story, parents can be despotic... oppressive social beliefs and practices sometimes substitute the obvious villain, as in Bimal Roy's *Sujata*' (Zankar 2003: 356).

17 Veeru and Basanti, as opposed to most of *Sholay*'s positive characters that primarily embody a singular mood state (see Table 4.2), equally trigger the double sentiments of comedy and romance, which is in tandem with the *Natyashastra*'s recognition of *hasya* as *sringara*'s most complimenting *rasa*.

18 The concept of '*Sadharanikarana*—universalization or departicularization further illuminates the ways in which an aesthetic object achieves its effects. For example, a viewer watching a play about Joan of Arc feels sad when Joan of Arc is awaiting execution. What is the source of this emotion? The experience does not purely arise in the viewer, as the viewer has not been through the same experience as Joan of Arc. The actress may not be the source, as she is merely going through the motions. The writer may not be the source either, because she might well be describing something dispassionately. As for the character Joan of Arc—nobody can tell with certainty what emotion she was experiencing. And yet, the viewer is pervaded with the experience of grief. How has this come to be? The answer is that this experience occurs in a way independent of purely the character, writer, actor, or viewer in a general, de-particularized, de-individualized way. This process is *sadharanikarana*. In this way, aesthetic experience allows the viewer to feel intense emotion, but in a detached way that allows him to transcend his specific self, to be free of individuality... This detachment allows the viewer to experience an aesthetic "pleasure" even while watching films that espouse *rasas* like *Bhayanaka* or *Bibhatsa* which would never evoke enjoyment in real life' (Joshi 2004: 24).

19 'When we taste, say, a sweet and spicy drink, we immediately delight in the taste. This process bypasses intellectual and complicated cognitive processes. We do not speculate on the ingredients of the drink, their relative proportion, the recipe, and then arrive at an estimation of the drink's taste before we render the judgment that the drink tastes good. Our enjoyment of the drink is instead spontaneous and instant; it does not require a time period of reflection because it occurs simultaneously with the act of tasting. Aesthetic enjoyment is of a similar nature; we do not meditate on the number of a painting's pigments before we find that we are enthralled by the painting. Similarly, in viewing a film, our emotional response is instantaneously evoked by the combination of *vibhaavas, vyabhichaaribhaavas,* and *anubhaavas*. The mind contains the "seeds" of *rasa*. These seeds are present in the mind due to past emotional experience, in current or previous lifetimes. Upon receiving the stimulus of *bhava,* they mature into *rasa*… But in order for this to occur, we must be open to emotional suggestion, taking on the role of a *sahrdaya*—the refined and sensitive viewer, whose mind ignites with *rasa* upon receiving a stimulus just like a piece of wood that catches fire as soon as it is set alight. Being open to affective experience means having to put ordinary cognition on the backburner. In the song, "You did not think of me" [from *Kuch Kuch Hota Hai,* 1998] a dejected Anjali Sr. is shown walking through a dark tunnel in a ruined castle. This visual aims at delineating her emotional state. A viewer who asks questions like "Well, Anjali was on the college campus a minute ago, why is she in a castle? Is there a castle near the campus? This castle was seen in the dream-song earlier, so is Anjali awake or dreaming? The castle looks Scottish—but isn't the film set in India?" will miss the point. Such a viewer is not a *sahrdaya* and will deprive herself of *rasa*' (Joshi 2004: 24).

20 The eerie soundtrack is replayed when Thakur exacts his revenge by killing Gabbar to thus maintain an emotive continuity of a vengeful-mood-extolling music through the most dramatic events of *Sholay* involving Thakur and Gabbar Singh.

21 The upper and lower case is to distinguish the varying decibel levels in Gabbar Singh's dialogue delivery.

22 Luciano Vincenzoni is the dialogue writer of *For a Few Dollars More* (Leone 1965). One of Italy's most successful and prolific screenwriters, he was internationally best known for his two Spaghetti Western collaborations, *For a Few Dollars More* (1965) and *The Good, The Bad and The Ugly* (1966).

23 Thakur: Veeru Gabbar ko mere hawale kardo (Veeru hand over Gabbar to me).
Veeru: Nahi Thakur, main ise zinda nahi chodunga (No Thakur, I won't leave him alive).
Thakur: Wada mat bhulo (Don't forget your promise).
Veeru: Mujhe sirf itna yaad hai ki is kamine ki aadmiyon ne mere Jai ki jaan li hai... (I only remember that this rogues' men had killed my friend Jai).
Thakur: Tumhe usi Jai ke vaade ka waasta hai (SJ 1975).

5

Rasa in Characterisation: Reviewing Gender and Character Stereotypes as *Rasa* Achievements in *Mayabazar* and *Madam X*

> The Indian play demands of an actor total submission to a particular emotion. If you are sad you are really sad… we are very vocal that way. We are not inhibited in expressing ourselves and our feelings[1].
>
> Vijaya Mehta, theatre director–actor

> We definitely knew that one of the characters was Rama, and the other Ravana in Madam X[2].
>
> Deepak Shivdasani, filmmaker

Introduction

Appreciating melodramatic acting and stereotypical characterisation has been the Achilles' heel of Indian film criticism, especially with regard to performances in popular Indian cinema. The first Indian feature film, *Raja Harishchandra*, told the tale of an ideal husband and wife who upheld truth and righteousness at the cost of tremendous personal sacrifice. Harishchandra was an ancestor of Rama, the hero of the oldest Indian epic the Ramayana, and 'a consistent influence on the idea of ideal hero characterisations in Indian stories' (Kapoor 2013), irrespective of whether the stories were being told in literature, dance, drama or cinema. His wife, Sita, across film genres, 'remains one of the most enduring heroines in Indian culture' (Somaaya, Kothari and Madangarli 2012: 16). The biggest obstacle in their love story, Ravana, is acknowledged as a defining reference for on-screen villainy. Negative heroes and heroines have always been an aberration and never the norm in Indian cinema (Zankar 2012: 357). Vijay Mishra locates the pre-eminent association of on-screen lead characters with *dharma*/righteousness as a key legacy of the Ramayana and the Mahabharata (Mishra 2012: 5), epics that are recognised across India. He also attributes some signature aspects of Indian film narration, such as epic genealogy and the persistence of *dharmik* codes, to the same source. Since their creation, these epics have commanded a vibrant cultural presence in the Indian aesthetic imagination and retained a continuing influence in the daily life and moral consciousness of Indian civilisation. The necessity for memorable characterisations in Indian cinema to be supported by impactful dialogue is almost as integral to a stylised performance as ornaments on a bride. Scriptwriters credit this to the still-continuing tradition of an oral transmission and consumption of the epics in both public and private spaces (Khan 2013; Pandey 2013). According to Kishore Namit Kapoor, founder–teacher of the Mumbai-based KNK Acting (Lab) Institute, whose alumni include many post-2000 Bollywood stars, 'While the *Ramayana*'s influence can be seen in most of our films portraying the hero, heroine and villain as Rama, Sita and Ravana, like white and black characters, the *Mahabharata* provided the template for the multi-starrers featuring multiple or complex heroes, heroines or villains' (2013). Empirical evidence testifies to the recurrent depiction of the characters from the epics in every Indian storytelling tradition, be it art, literature, dance, drama or cinema. Over 90 per cent of the films made in the first decade of Indian cinema were based on stories from these two epics. This contributed to the establishment of a distinct Indian film genre, the mythological, as already discussed in Chapter 2[3]. Film writers and reviewers explain that the preference for adapting epic heroes—or conceiving contemporary characters with attributes akin to the epic heroes—arises from their ability to embody and evoke universally recognised *rasas*. This makes them identifiable and hence capable of establishing a connection with a diverse and primarily illiterate audience. According to actor–script writer Salim Khan, '*Mahabharata* is one of the greatest screenplays ever written and *Ramayana* is the greatest story ever told. Both have exerted tremendous influence on our cinema, our story telling, our story writing, and personally on me a great deal' (2014). 'The characters are not good or bad because of their personal idiosyncrasies, but rather due to their traits or *bhava* attributes that create a dominant *rasa* about and around them' (Zankar 2012: 357). The traits of the eight kinds of heroines in love (*ashta-nayikas*) have already been discussed in Chapter 3. The *Natyashastra* also lists seven graces[4] that naturally apply to ideal women characters—*sobha* (beauty as a radiant/glowing state of being post the experiencing of love), *kanti* (a beauteous state of being in expectation of love), *dipti* (heightened *kanti*), *madhurya* (moderation), *dhairya* (serenity), *praglabhya* (maturity) and *audarya* (a sense of civility or respect in all situations)[5]. Eight kinds of acting emotions for the ideal hero/man too have been enumerated. These are *sobha* (skill/brilliance), *vilasa* (graceful bearing), *madhurya* (self-possession), *sthairya* (steadiness), *gambhirya* (serenity), *lalita* (sportiveness), *audarya* (nobility) and *tejas* (spirit)[6]. A female or male character who behaves in a manner contrary to the above attributes, as manifested by their dominant *bhava*-guided traits, by default embodies a negative female (e.g., a vamp) or a negative male (a villain) character. These attributes are normally established in a character's introduction scene, as discussed in Chapter 4 in the context of *Sholay*'s significant characters.

The Four Types of *Abhinaya*

After discussing the influence of the *rasa* theory in plot construction, this chapter explores how the knowledge of the *rasa* theory and its guidelines on portraying the ideal hero, heroine or villain can help us appreciate the consistency of *bhava*. This knowledge can also aid our recognition of the continuity and unity achieved by the evocation of the *rasas* in a seemingly stereotypical or 'expressive'[7] dramatic performance that is often dismissed as loud or theatrical. According to Devdutt Pattanaik:

> Not every hyper realism film works, and not every melodramatic film works [with the audience]. So clearly it is not melodrama that works,

> there is a vocabulary and a language in the melodrama that some people are better at than others (2015).

This chapter explores how to identify and appreciate the working of that vocabulary in an actor's craft. Two sets of on-screen performances are discussed in order to understand how the maintenance of their character's *bhavas* is a necessary *abhinaya* achievement for actors to generate and realise specific *rasas* in the audience.

Bhavas are artistic expressions achieved by actors through varying combinations of the four types of equally important *abhinaya*(s) or performances[8]—*angika* (bodily gestures/physical), *vachika* (speech/verbal), *aharya* (costumes/ornamental) and *satvika* (emotions/emotional)[9]. They lend feeling to a conveyed thought or performed action to create a corresponding lasting emotional sentiment or *rasa* in the audience. The intertwined working of the above elements towards the cognition of an acted feeling is succinctly described in the following *sutra*: '*Yato hastasto-tatoh drishtih-yato drishtih tatoh manah-yato manas-tatoh bhavah-yato bhava-statoh rasah*' (The eyes follow the movement of the hands; where the eyes go, mind follows; where the mind goes, feelings follow; and where the feelings go, sentiments follow!)[10]. According to Rangacharya:

> When the emotion is impressively expressed, it (*samanya abhinaya*) is of a high kind; when it just equals i.e. is not dissonant with words and gestures, it is middling; and when it fails to register it is inferior (NS.24.1–2). The word *abhinaya* is usually translated as 'acting'; but that, according to Bharata, is not correct. *Abhinaya*, from *ni* 'to carry', with prefix *abhi*—towards means that which carries (the meaning of the play) towards (the audience). So, words (*vachika*) with physical gestures (*angika*) to suit the emotion '*sattva*', as well as make up and costumes (*aharya*) constitute *abhinaya* (Rangacharya 2010: 185).

This not only creates the ability to generate a feeling, or make the audience feel an important aspect of the Indian way of acting, but also highlights the need for complimenting dialogue, gestures and costumes to enhance that impact. Kapoor observes:

> That so much importance is given to dialogue writers in our cinema is yet another indicator of the fact that a lot of our ideas/notions around film acting have come down from the *Natyashastra*, whether an actor has studied it or not, or a director is consciously following it or not… (2013).

This chapter evidences the adherence of *rasa* postulates in on-screen acting using a diverse sample of performances from two distinct genres of Indian cinema. It will feature films from two different eras, regions and genres of filmmaking: *Mayabazar* (Market of Illusions, K.V. Reddy, 1957), an influential classic from South India's film industry, and *Madam X* (Shivdasani 1994), a Hindi cinema thriller representative of the star-driven Bollywood *masala* films of the 1980s and 1990s. It also considers using the theory to understand some of the dominant and recurrent stereotypes around characterisation in popular Indian cinema, especially in an actor's portrayal of characters with discernible performance binaries—for example, the male and the female or the good and evil. Just as the *Natyashastra* broadly categorises the *rasas* to be evoked in a performance as pleasurable and non-pleasurable, Indian cinema too has traditionally categorised characters and character attributes within stereotypical binaries of the positive and the negative or the masculine and the feminine. This chapter argues that the ideal or expected formulaic *bhava* traits for the on-screen characterisation of heroes and heroines, or for the differentiation of heroes from villains, can be better appreciated by adapting the extent of *rasa* achievement and *bhava* consistency in their performance as a lens for review.

Mayabazar and the Indian Mythological Film

The *Natyashastra*'s continuing influence on Indian cinema's narrative and performance aesthetics is most evident in films belonging to the mythological genre. Here, the *rasa*-achieving performance imperatives have gone beyond notional continuity to absolute adherence in the structuring of the emotional grammar and graph of a narrative and the presentation, disposition and categorisation of characters and their acts. A significant early Indian cinema genre, the mythological film has often been dismissed as inferior cinema because of its overt adherence to the *Natyashastra* guidelines and region-specific folk theatre indulgences. The latter include fantastical mise en scène, dialogue-driven drama, epic story lines and extravagant production values. Unimaginative filmmakers have often made these elements and the films belonging to this genre look like photographed plays. The acting, following the theatrical grammar of maximisation of emotions through representative character types, further prioritises melodrama over realism. It gives precedence to heightened *rasa* realisation over relatable acting. If you are sad, you are crestfallen; if you are angry, you are raging mad and if you are happy, you are bursting at the seams! The goal of a performance should be to epitomise the *bhava* and personify a *rasa* through the enactment of its most identifiable and representative behaviour, mood and disposition.

Of all Indian language cinema, nowhere has the mythological film survived the longest as in the cinemas of South India, especially the Telegu cinema, where it was a dominant genre right up to the 1970s, starting from its early-20th-century inception. In this context, writer–director K.V. Reddy's 1957 bilingual *Mayabazar* (Telegu–Tamil), which was 'based on a popular play with multiple on-screen adaptations'[11], and featured some of the legendary star-actors of South Indian cinema, including Akkineni Nageshwar Rao, N.T. Rama Rao, Savithri and S.V. Ranga Rao, continues to remain a path-breaking production. This film brought about a welcome change to the mythological template through its humanisation of gods and portrayal of extraordinary characters as ordinary human beings for the first time. The film was voted the greatest Indian film ever[12] in a 2013 online poll commemorating 100 years of Indian cinema that encompassed all Indian language cinemas. Technically, *Mayabazar* has been acknowledged for being a pioneer influence in terms of highlighting the significance of the screenplay over the story, scripting an influential turn in the genre's evolution in the film industries of South India, especially in the Telegu, Tamil and Kannada language cinemas.

The success of its structure has since been abundantly repeated, making it an influential landmark in the genre. According to S.S. Rajamouli, director of the blockbuster *Bahubali* (2015/17) film series and an influential 21st-first century filmmaker from Telegu cinema:

> *Mayabazar* is the greatest classic and absolute influence of all times, not only on me and my generation of filmmakers, but the entire Telegu film industry. Many of the super hit films of today cannot even come close to the magical screenplay of K.V. Reddy written in the 1950s, where each and every bit of the film, tells you so much story (2012).

The film further offers a sumptuous *rasa swadana* (a relishing of all the *navarasas*), skewed in favour of the pleasurable *rasas* of *sringara, hasya, vira* and *adbhuta*, to be reviewed and received as a complete *masala* entertainer. The film depicts a magical love story from the Mahabharata. Its highlight, in terms of drama and performance, comes in the form of its heroine Sasirekha's dual personality premise and the interpretation of this by actress Savithri. An interesting plot twist has her character replaced by a male illusionist demon Ghatotkacha. This means that Savithri has to oscillate between two diverse personas, one that of a bashful and young princess in love, and the other that of a demonic (Ghatotkacha-as-Sasirekha) princess in a comic, destructive mode.

The chapter explores specific *bhavas* (expressions) from the nine prescribed *sthayibhavas,* or primary human emotions, which Indian actors select and reject in their achievement of ideal *Natyashastra*-prescribed notions of masculine and feminine performance. The vehicle for this is a critical study of heroine Savithri's choice of different *rasa*-enhancing *bhavas* in her double-act, depending on the gender of her character: how she distinguishes, personifies and defines, in three similar situations, a 'woman-as-woman' Sasirekha, in contrast to a 'man-as-woman' Sasirekha, in a love story revolving around courtship, rebellion and marriage. A freeze frame analysis of her diverse *bhavas* on display is utilised. Henceforth, the real female Sasirekha will be referred to as just 'Sasirekha', while the male Ghatotkacha-impersonating Sasirekha will be referred to as 'the male Sasirekha'.

Sasirekha, the daughter of Balarama, the king of Dwaraka, and his wife Revathi, is betrothed to Abhimanyu, the son of Subhadra and the third Pandava prince Arjuna. This happens in the presence of Sasirekha's paternal uncle, Krishna, an avatar of Lord Vishnu, when she and Abhimanyu are children. They grow up nurturing their love for each other. When misfortune strikes the Pandavas and they lose their kingdom in a game of dice to the Kauravas, their jealous cousin brothers, Revathi is no longer keen to honour the commitment of marrying her daughter to the progeny of wandering foresters. She rejects Subhadra's request to marry their now-adult children in love, when the latter comes to Dwaraka with Abhimanyu to stay with her brothers. Balarama, meanwhile, in a parallel plot twist, is conned by the eldest Kaurava, Duryodhana, and his crafty uncle Shakuni into agreeing to marry Sasirekha to Duryodhana's son, Lakshman Kumar. It is then that Krishna steps in with a secret plan to unite the pining lovers, aided by Abhimanyu's cousin, Ghatotkacha. The son of the second Pandava prince Bheema and his *asura* queen Hidimba, Ghatotkacha is a demon king with mastery in creating illusions. The *mayavi* (magician) Ghatotkacha takes the place of the real Sasirekha in the disguise of the princess, while his talented assistants construct an illusory palace to hold the groom's party at bay. The Kauravas' real intentions are exposed through a comedy of errors involving mistaken identities, along with liberal doses of magical mayhem unleashed by Ghatotkacha and his partners-in-magic under Krishna's all-knowing direction. Eventually, the lovers are united, and the family is reconciled.

Mayabazar: Different Genders, Different *Bhavas*

Sasirekha in Courtship

As a romantic story revolving around the separation and union of star-crossed lovers from childhood, *Mayabazar* features elaborate courtship and romantic sequences that progress through four song sequences or lyrical scenes. Here I compare and contrast the first meeting sequence between an adult Abhimanyu and Sasirekha with that of the male Sasirekha and her second suitor Lakshman Kumar. Both scenes begin with a song sequence articulating the love-struck excitement of the two men at their first sighting of the gorgeous princess in a palace garden.

Abhimanyu and Lakshman Kumar indulge in a liberal wooing of Sasirekha. However, while for Abhimanyu the female is an object of indulgent, subtle affection, Kumar's overtures border on aggressive displays of affection and possessiveness. With both suitors, Sasirekha plays difficult to get; however, while she enjoys Abhimanyu's attention, she mocks and rejects the unwanted affections of Lakshman Kumar.

Given Sasirekha's delicate disposition and her stock reactions of anxiety, apprehension and helplessness (*vyabhicaris* of *rati bhava*) in adverse situations, Kumar's aggression would ideally have had her cowering or fleeing the scene, evincing the *rasas* of fear and disgust. Ghatotkacha-as-Sasirekha however, stands his/her ground like a natural *vira*, fending for himself/herself, returning Kumar's aggression with stern, mocking rebuttals.

In Abhimanyu's company, Sasirekha is bashful; she sings and prances around in joyous abandon as he sings 'You are as beautiful as I had imagined' (PNR 1957)[13]. He humours her playful shyness as they re-visit their mutual comfort from childhood that has blossomed into love in adulthood. The lovers reappear in two more songs, enjoying a boat ride in one and pining for the absence of the other in *vipralambha* (love in separation) mode in the second.

The *bhavas* used to differentiate their interpersonal relationships in these scenes of togetherness highlight the diverse set of expressions in use for members of different genders or differently gendered dispositions. In her equation with Abhimanyu, Sasirekha is a passive recipient—be it in her explorative waking up to wondrous love in their first meeting, expression of joyous love (indicated through their increasing intense expressions of love in stolen moments of physical intimacy in *hasya-sringara*) in the second song or suffering from painful love (love-in-longing) while portraying *shoka* (sadness/helplessness) in the third, evoking the *karuna rasa*. In all these three sequences, Sasirekha is the receiver of affection, who needs to be pampered in the first interaction, appreciated and cared for in the second and protected in the third sequence. In each scene, the male sets the tone of interaction with the female, who is always placed on a lower pedestal, in the role of a receiver. Most importantly, she always looks up to her man for love, care or comfort. Though in a state of joy, she still remains in essence a receiver, never driving or initiating any act of romance. The dynamics change drastically when Abhimanyu meets the male Sasirekha for the first time. She not only talks back and mock reprimands him as an equal but also maintains direct eye contact, to the former's evident surprise. The change in body language, she eventually explains to Abhimanyu's visible relief and joyous acceptance, is because 'she essentially is a he; his brother' (PNR 1957). Thus, as the character of Sasirekha switches genders, their temperaments and roles in courtship change from being an object of desire (as the female) to becoming a desiring object (as the male).

The male's role to initiate and lead all interaction in courtship is retained in a repeat of the sequence between Lakshman Kumar and the male Sasirekha. It is interesting to note that while Abhimanyu is represented as the heroic male in their first interaction (which perhaps explains the oddity of his arriving with a bow and arrows to a meeting with his lover), Lakshman Kumar, in his first meeting, is not only shorn of any weapons of masculine significance but is deliberately presented as a character with effeminate mannerisms. He mocks, sulks and hurts easily and is dressed in a garish costume with a sari-like drape. Moreover, in deference to the male Sasirekha's inherent stronger masculinity, Lakshman Kumar assumes the receiver role of the female. The superior male, Ghatotkacha the demon, gets to set the terms and tone of the courtship game, as Abhimanyu does with Sasirekha. Ghatotkacha opts for derision, complemented by an aggressive set of emotions bordering on anger, disgust and ridicule, allowed only to the male Sasirekha. Even when expressing joy, Sasirekha never goes beyond an appropriate *smita hasya* (modest smile), whereas the male Sasirekha exalts in an entire gamut of laughs from *upahasya* (ridicule) to *atahasya* (boisterous laughter)[14].

Image 5.1 The Diverse Nature of the Two Sasirekhas is Best Expressed in the Contrasting Body Language and Expressions in their Lone Face-off Scene in the Film. While the Female Sasirekha (Left) Stands in Passive Expectancy, Head Bowed, an Apprehensive Image of Delicate Feminity, the Male Sasirekha's (Right) Posture is One of Confidence and Aggressive Masculinity, Head Held Up, Ready to Lead From the Front, Matching Attitude and Energy with Her Male Compatriot. (Photograph: Roy 2016)

Sasirekha in Protest

In romantic tales, rebellion is a predictable reaction of young lovers to any censorship by adults. Despite *Mayabazar* being a mythical story presented with modern sensibilities, its protagonists never transgress the expected ideal of gendered behaviour in their responses to reprimand. When the romance between Abhimanyu and Sasirekha is censured, Abhimanyu's first reaction is akin to that of a character steeped in the *vira rasa* as he takes recourse to righteous anger. Abhimanyu challenges his elders to a duel before being calmed by his uncle Krishna. Sasirekha, on the contrary, resigns herself to her fate after a meek protest, for which she is slapped by her mother. Sulking, she opts for the muted, *viraha* route of release, becoming a picture of self-pity, embodying the *karuna rasa*. She sings sad songs of pining, awaiting rescue by her lover. Being a female character, her rebellion is limited to awaiting her lover's act of resolution, instead of taking any concrete action to undo the wrong.

The male Sasirekha, however, reacts like Abhimanyu, with righteous anger fuelled by a feeling to punish the wrongdoers. She takes upon herself the onus of finding a way out of the predicament by playing a difficult suitor. Her masculine spirit naturally allows her to echo the just anger of Abhimanyu. However, she channels it into a challenge that is permitted by her gender cover; she makes her suitor an object of mockery in perfect synchrony with Ghatotkacha's nature as a hot-headed braveheart with a comic disposition. She constantly mocks and teases Lakshman Kumar, forcing him into uncomfortable situations.

If Sasirekha's response to her resignation to her status quo is fear, courage is the reaction of the male Sasirekha. Yet, Sasirekha's censure is stricter; it involves physical restraint, given her weaker gender. Ghatotkacha's indiscretions, on the other hand, are met with gentle reprimands by Krishna and shocked pleading by her confidante, her maid—two characters most sympathetic to her cause. The male Sasirekha is admonished for transgressing the subtle body language expected of her female cover when she gets carried away by her inherent masculine nature.

Ghatotkacha's prompt corrections in behaviour, as she goes from boisterous to docile restraint in order to continue the charade without drawing suspicion, though amusingly contrite, reinforce the boundaries of the emoting repertoire available for the ideal woman. They cannot transgress the subtle *rasas*. The ideal heroine, as the upholder of the ideal female character on-screen, even in the company of other not-so-ideal women, has to operate within the subtle *bhava* stock of coyness, blushing and awe; it is only the excuse of a different gender that allows her to portray more aggressive emotions without looking inappropriate.

Sasirekha in Marriage

The union of its lead pair of star-crossed lovers is the narrative's driver dramatic goal, and their marriage the film's climactic event. Both the Sasirekhas go through their marriage ceremonies, one as a desired culmination and the other as the final set-up act for exiting a charade. Sasirekha goes through the ceremony as an image of restrained joy. Though content and elated within, her disposition remains demure. Keeping her head bowed, she rarely looks at the groom Abhimanyu, who sits in a regal posture, lording over the ceremony with an articulated excitement assumed natural to his gender. Her reactions maintain her character's mood of being in a perpetual gender-conforming state of passive reception.

The marriage ceremony of the male Sasirekha and Lakshman Kumar, in contrast, has a more equal participation of both the female and male characters. Unlike Sasirekha, the male Sasirekha does not mute her excitement. She meets Lakshman Kumar's gaze and returns it with more than equal confidence, which has him frequently cowering and occasionally backing off. While the script wants Ghatotkacha-as-Sasirekha to trigger unpleasant (or rather un-ladylike) actions to change the course of the ceremony, for the audience it is the knowledge of her superior gender that makes her dominant presence look natural. To scare Lakshman Kumar away, the male Sasirekha conjures three illusions every time he attempts to tie the *mangalsutra* (wedding necklace) around her neck. She appears as a monkey, a tiger and a demon, triggering corresponding feelings of laughter, fear and disgust respectively in Lakshman Kumar respectively.

Different Characters, Different *Bhavas*

This section discusses how certain *sthayibhavas* in the personality of characters are similarly selected and rejected to differentiate the heroic from the villainous, or the good from the evil, using the 1990s' film, *Madam X*, as a case study. According to its director Deepak Shivdasani, the film's makers, writers and lead actor Rekha were aware from its conception that its counter-protagonists would be reflective of Rama and Ravana, the ideal hero and villain characters from Ramayana. This is evidenced and analysed through a study of the film's lead actor Rekha's choice of a distinct set of contrasting *bhavas* presented as personality-specific mood states to distinguish the evil Madam X[15] from her good double.

Madam X, released 37 years after *Mayabazar*, is a film in popular Indian cinema's action/thriller genre, inspired by a 1970s' crime thriller, *Don* (Chandra Barot, 1978). The continuing popularity of the film's theme saw it being remade a decade after *Madam X*, as a modern 21st century action thriller *Don: The Chase Begins Again* (Farhan Akhtar, 2006). Based on genre attributes, *Mayabazar* and *Madam X* may appear to belong to categories with contrasting expectations and pleasures. Yet, their core drama is driven by two roles with opposite character motivations essayed by a single actor.

Madam X revolves around a fictitious Mumbai-based lady don who is ruthless, greedy and outside the reach of the law. Her protection from state prosecution is ensured by a high-ranking public servant, a mysterious character 'X', who is her partner in profit. Into this comfortably operating scenario enters an honest police officer, Inspector Vijay, who intends to end Madam X's mafia empire and expose her mentor 'X'. He captures her in a covert combat operation and trains and sends her lookalike, a smart street performer Shalu, to lord over her businesses and reveal her illegal wealth and secret hideouts to the police. By the time Shalu becomes aware of X's identity, the real Madam X, with the help of her Man Friday, Champak Lal, escapes Vijay's detention and captures Shalu and her siblings. In a protracted climactic combat with myriad twists and a physical fight between the fake and the real Madam X, good triumphs over evil, in the signature narrative resolution style of a melodrama. Madam X succumbs to her injuries, albeit in triumphant arrogance, mouthing her oft-repeated signature line, '*Hum hain Maut ki woh express, duniya jise kehti hai Madam X!*' (I am that death heralding express, which the world knows as Madam X) (AK 1994)[16]. The film thus begins, revolves and ends around Madam X who, according to director Shivdasani, was deliberately conceived as a 'character driven character' (Shivdasani 2014), of a type that the audience had never seen before. Her novelty and attraction 'like in the traditional stories was that she was conceived as a pure black character. There is no grey in her, like there is no grey in Ravana' (Shivdasani 2014). Coupled with her unique and elaborate wardrobe, another first for any character in Hindi cinema, negative or positive, this combined shock with wonder (like another unique and memorable Hindi film villain, Gabbar Singh from *Sholay*, discussed in the previous chapter), to create a character that is remembered even after two decades.

The Costumes and Dialogue of *Madam X*

Along with the casting of Rekha, a leading star-actress with a 'fashionista's sensibilities'[17], in the title role, the detailed attention paid to the costumes and dialogue, or the *aharya* and *vachika* aspects of *abhinaya*, has also contributed to the film's retrospective recall. In a review published 18 years after the film's release, journalist Shikha Kumar states:

> Painstaking attention has been given to Madam X's lifestyle. She has a witch-like cackle, goes horse-riding on the beach, smokes cigarettes and wears boots that are brought to her in a tray by her beloved Zaka. Fashion-wise Rekha takes this film to a whole new level. She dons blinding outfits, ranging from mink coats, spiked gloves, capes and long matching boots, with over-the-top headgear. There's a blue outfit to go with a sequinned silver headgear that would put Lady Gaga to shame (Kumar 2012).

While an actor's emotive identification with a character is universally privileged[18], the *Natyashastra* places equal importance on all four aspects/areas of acting in order for an actor to be able to best convey the sentiments of a character. According to Bharata *muni* (or the *Natyashastra* perspective on good performance), 'Acting is nothing but a process of creating sentiments in a discernible enough manner to be realised by the audience' (Mishra 2010: 102–103). Therefore, an actor's identification with the emotion/*sattvika* attributes of a character is as important as its visual presentation and the content and style of its speech. This becomes even more essential when a larger-than-life portrayal like that of Gabbar Singh (*Sholay* 1975) or Madam X needs to engage an uninitiated (into popular Hindi cinema) audience expecting logic or some assurance of cognitive realism[19] in their viewing experience. These are characters whose actions are unreal, emotions are loudly expressed, costumes are kitschy and unnatural and manner of speaking is exaggerated. But to fans of affective realism, who want to feel or get awed by the uniqueness and the impact of a character, these are what makes a character like Madam X an all-round, consummate achievement. They are able to offer something never seen before and unique in every aspect of their characterisation. According to the director of *Madam X*, Deepak Shivdasani:

> My dominant emotion expectation from Madam X was one of rarity, surprise, larger-than-life… It's not a normal run-of-the-mill character. Imagine how you would react if somebody says 'I will be a Madam X'. You will wonder 'what'? You never know what that one person in a crowd of 500 or 1000 gets fascinated by? It could be Madam X's personality [based on her dominant *sattvika*/emotion attributes], her wardrobe [the *aharya*], looks, mannerisms [*angik*/ gestural expressions], anything… But I was sure the character would get eyeballs. You cannot see a Madam X walking on the road or a next-door neighbour looking like her. Neither would you want or like to see your wife dressed as Madam X. It's a rare species, a thing out of the orbit. Hence it was created with all these add-ons like she would have a reply to any given situation, and that she would talk in similes and metaphors [speech elements accentuating the impact of *vachika abhinaya*]. That was the brief given to the dialogue writer. So, we created all those unbelievable things into her, and that is how we made her, and that is why you are talking to me about her because she was not one of those regular things. You are asking about her because she is rare, she is someone you have not come across. You may laugh at her, but you cannot forget her (2014).

Hence, it is no coincidence that Madam X dresses in a uniquely fused fashion 'never seen before on Indian cinema' (Shivdasani 2014) and refers to herself in the third person or in the plural 'hum' instead of the singular 'main' or 'apun' (the colloquial versions of 'I' as used by her ordinary/street-smart doppelganger, Shalu). According to scriptwriter Salim Khan:

> In Hollywood there are no separate credits for dialogue writers. There, the dialogue come within the screenplay. It is only in our [Indian] cinema that we have separate credits for dialogue writers in film titles (2013).

Kamlesh Pandey, secretary of the Film Writers' Association (Mumbai), defines this need for having good or clap-worthy dialogue as an expectation unique to Indian cinema audiences. He sees it as resulting from the many continuing traditions of oral transmission in practice in the nation's numerous sociocultural spaces, such as in the performed narration of stories from the epics at festivals, the chanting of holy mantras during rituals and the communal singing of devotional songs. According to Pandey:

> Good dialogue in Indian films is a tradition dating back to the *puranas*, epics and the Upanishads, which are endowed with meaningful statements, dramatic statements, classic and eternal ideas. We enjoy listening to good words as part of our tradition of oral culture of listening to recitations and readings of the Gita, the epics, the *puranas*, the poetry of the saints, etc. Hence dialogue is an integral part of our narratives and so are the lyrics of the film songs. The appreciation for movie songs can be argued as an extension of the public patronage of Bhakti/Sufi poetry traditions. People went to see a film like *Saudagar* [Subhash Ghai, 1991] because of the relentless banter [between its opposing lead characters played by Dilip Kumar and Raaj Kumar in the traditional theatrical mode]. But now we are moving to a more colloquial everyday speech, which cannot be dramatic all the time (2013).

In the above observation lies a possible reason for the unspectacular box-office performance[20] of *Madam X*. By the time of the release of the three-years-in-making film, the sensibilities that desired a *Saudagar* esque action film, with legendary superstars delivering verbose dialogue in exalted speech, had given way to a preference for crossover romances in conversational speech, led by a triumvirate of rising young stars-to-be such as Aamir Khan, Salman Khan and Shah Rukh Khan by the 1990s. *Madam X* thus remains one of the last Hindi films in the action genre to use rhyming, poetic dialogue with abstract metaphors in a Hindustani (Hindi–Urdu mixed) lexicon. Hindi cinema, incidentally, 'had started to abandon this kind of classical or theatrical dialogue template by the middle of the 1990s' (Shivdasani 2014). The similes, choice of language (Hindustani) and rhyming of dialogue in Madam X's introductory monologue establish her character's penchant for verbosity as a distinct personality attribute, which is maintained throughout the film:

> Madam X: Jis tarah Yamraj ko sirf yamlok hi dekh sakta hai,
> usi tarah Madam X ki shaqal bhi sirf uska samrajya hi dekh sakta hai.

> Jo bhi hamari jhalak dekhne ki zurrat karta hai,
> wo jalkar aise dhuan ho jaata hai,
> ki na zameen ko uski khaakh milti hai, aur na hawaon ko uski raakh! (AK 1994).
> (Just as only hell can witness the god of death, similarly only the empire of Madam X can see her in person. Any outsider attempting that dare will be burnt in a way that neither the earth gets their debris nor the wind their ashes).

This, is 'the vocabulary and the language in the melodrama' (Pattanaik 2015), which calls for an alternative and exclusively emotion-appreciating prism of review, like the *rasa* theory, a theory beyond those that are trained to prioritise and appreciate only adherence to realism, or *cinéma vérité* storytelling. Using as reference a sample of the speech, costume, behaviour and dominant emotion traits incorporated into the characterisation of Madam X, I now explore how the protagonist actress of *Madam X*, Rekha, uses these as effective differentiators to establish and distinguish her villain from her heroic doppelganger. The analysis is done in the context of three significant plot moments, by looking at the specific *bhava* reactions of either character to similar situational and people provocations. Furthermore, I have retained Madam X's original lines delivered in Hindustani, especially in the context of her longer dialogue and monologues, to convey the flavour in the phrase, the imaginative choice of words and the play with images that are as much a character in themselves as the protagonist's unusual range and choice of costumes.

The Introduction Scenes of Madam X and Shalu

The introductory scene of Madam X is arguably one of the longest for a titular character in Indian cinema. It starts with an anecdotal interaction, highlighting the character's aptitude for ruthless vengeance. She kills an agent who tries to double cross her by trying to secretly capture her image while striking a deal over the sale of a smuggled antique piece. She then triggers a massive explosion that decimates an entire police force that had gathered to capture her. A declaration of her signature line dialogue follows, on her being 'an agent of death' who the world dreads as Madam X. The line is repeated at strategic drama moments throughout the film.

The film's opening credits now roll, accompanied by a song in English, which goes as follows: 'She is mysterious, she is wanted, she is coming...' (Jaipuri 1994)[21]. This then changes to a Hinglish title track that articulates the nature and attributes of Madam X through a 4.10-minute-long song sequence, which is shot at 15 different locations, is picturised through 98 editing cuts and features 10 elaborate costume changes. The name Madam X is uttered 36 times like a chorus chant in the background score. The lyrics of the song further feed her 'agent of death' imagery:

> Jab jab saamne aati hai, ek qayamat chaati hai
> dasti hai vo logon ko, jab naagin ban jati hai...
> hai rang uske hazaron, us ne jo aafat macha di
> logon ki neendein uda de, vo hosh sabke mita de (Jaipuri 1994).
> (Her every vision is like a judgement day encounter; she stings people like a snake; a persona of myriad colours, she has been creating havoc; she gives many a sleepless night, while her mere sighting can strike others to numbness).

These attributes are revealed as clues to the puzzle that Madam X is presented to be. They are an answer to a repeating question that is articulated as a parable: 'No one knows her; nobody has seen her; none can capture her... [So] who is, who is, who is… Madam X?' (Jaipuri 1994). This metaphorical referencing of Madam X in the song, following her simile laden self-introduction, achieves a consistency in the twin elements of song and dialogue as an effective *vachika abhinaya* (high on dialogue) performance.

Madam X conducts her routine, functional conversations with other characters in similes and metaphors, be it a pompous declaration of her skills ('The art of treading carefully, Madam X has learnt from the tigress on a hunt in a jungle'); a rare generous appraisal of the talent of a loyal assistant ('Champak Lal is no lame horse, but a winning aide like the race horses'); a threat to an enemy ('Rai Bahadur, enmity with Madam X is like getting stuck with the sting of a poisonous scorpion that will neither let you die nor relieve you from perpetual pain'); a casual observation ('Those who view with the eyes of the mind rarely use the eyes on their face') or a callous mocking of the personal loss of an honest officer ('Inspector Vijay, your girlfriend was not born to take wedding vows around the sacred fire with you, but be the fire of the funeral pyre, that I could use to light my cigarette with!')[22]. These lines provide a glimpse into how the transitory mood states (*vyabhicaribhavas*) of Madam X are negative. She expresses arrogance, cruelty and vengeance, thus consistently contributing to her overall persona as a singularly black character sans nuance. The lines also indicate the detail that has gone into bringing out the sadism and ruthlessness in her villainy. Minute aspects of her characterisation are considered, so that even a dialogue delivered in passing is in accord with the dominant evil or negative *sattva*/emotion of her persona. This ensures that the *rasas* of fear and disgust are continuously evoked by Madam X. The film's dialogue, their relative verbosity and the manner of their delivery, however, vary from character to character. The dialogues of the real Madam X further accentuate the opposing traits of the two characters when compared to the straightforward speech of Shalu as Madam X. She uses no similes—'It is you, who got fooled into not being able to recognise me Mathur, not me' and only sparsely uses metaphor—'*Zamana badal sakta hai Mathur, lekin Madam X nahin*'/'The world may change Mathur, not Madam X!' (AK 1994).

In terms of fashion choices, when she is first introduced to us, Madam X is dressed in masculine pant-and-shirt outfits, with matching colour-coordinated crowns in dark shades like red, dark blue, purple, dark green and black. Incidentally, red, dark blue and black are the recommended colours for unpleasant or negative *rasas* like anger, disgust and fear respectively (NS.6.42–43). The film's opening sequence with the double agent is shot in the dark of night, lit only in a dark-blue hue in which Madam X appears chaperoned by shadow-like aides dressed in black.

The only time Madam X is seen wearing something light or of the colour of a pleasant *rasa*, like the white outfit (the colour for *hasya* or comedy) in her introduction song sequence, the white colour of the outfit is overshadowed by dominant black stripes, or she is shown grinning in pride or laughing loudly in bouts of *upahasya* (ridiculing laughter), *apahasya* (vulgar or obscene laughter showing grinning teeth) and *atahasya* (excessively loud laughter). While white is the colour that complements the comic *rasa*, according to the *Natyashastra*, the types of laughter Madam X is seen expressing are listed as identifiers of lower or demonic characters and unbecoming of the positive and the noble (NS.6.53–60). The next scene in which Madam X is seen in a white costume is when her good double, the heroine Shalu, masquerading as Madam X, is depicted singing a romantic song wooing Inspector Vijay.

Image 5.2 Rekha as Madam X (Photograph: NFAI)

The introduction of Madam X's good lookalike, Shalu, also happens through a song sequence, which serves as a self-stated lyrical introduction to her character and its characteristics. Shalu's entry happens in a five-minute long sequence after more than a third of the film is over. For the first 45 seconds, we just see different parts of her person, starting with the feet, hands, hips, lips, and then her entire figure under a veil, before Shalu's face is revealed to a shower of confetti. Even Madam X is revealed after a 2.20-minute-long prelude that has her articulating her mystery and declaring why she reveals herself to only those she deigns fit for the honour. While the first close-up of Madam X shows her in a state of uncontrollable rage, shouting an order, Shalu's first close-up, which also shows her gazing pointedly at the audience, is highlighted as one that is sharp and observant through complementing lyrics stating, 'whoever crosses my way steers away, cut but by the sharpness of my gaze' (Jaipuri 1994).

Shalu is dressed in a traditional Indian *ghagra-choli* in a predominantly orange hue with ample hints of yellow—colours that the *Natyashastra* associates with pleasurable, positive *rasas* like the heroic and the marvellous respectively. These attributes are then verbalised in the lyrics of the song, where she declares herself to be a sharp and perceptible person who 'while being nice to the good, is not meek-hearted and can be bad to the bad-intentioned like a Rampuri knife' (Jaipuri 1994). Her expertise with knives, while highlighting her street-smart nature, also establishes courage as her dominant character trait. This lends plausibility to her subsequent selection for a daring operation, as she reveals that she 'may look innocent but can turn as potent as a bullet' (Jaipuri 1994). The metaphors that introduce Shalu thus use simple rhyming connections, in contrast to the abstract associations and impossible assertions articulated by Madam X. For example, when asked about how she intends to rescue one of her captured aides from jail, she responds, 'No company in the world has made a lock, whose keys Madam X does not have' (AK 1994). This contrast is further evident when Shalu's above-mentioned lines are compared with some of Madam X's dialogues discussed earlier.

Shalu's introductory song sequence ends with her first meeting with Inspector Vijay, where the lyrics hint at a possible romance between the two. This is conveyed in the song's third stanza, where the *vira rasa* (heroic) theme suddenly turns into *vipralambha shringara* (love in anticipation), as Shalu articulates the anticipation of a girl wanting to fall in love, singing, 'How I wish a big-hearted man came in my dreams and lifted my veil. I would play hard-to-get, I would play coy, I would feel embarrassed and refuse to lift my veil…' (Jaipuri 1994).

Interaction with Men (Friends and Foes)

The real Madam X primarily interacts with three aides—her Man Friday Zaka, her ace accomplice and secret admirer Champak Lal and her mentor/partner-in-crime Mr. X/Mathur, who is later revealed to be the police commissioner of Mumbai. She speaks to each in a matter-of-fact manner, sans any emotion, in accordance with her character 'having no emotional quotient' (Shivdasani 2014). She maintains a guarded distance from her aides that demands fear and perpetuates her hierarchical status. She treats her mentor, Mathur, not as a superior but as an equal, to whom she declares her decisions. She never seeks his opinion but expects and demands his cooperation in implementing her decisions. Loyalty born of fear of harsh retribution drives these interactions. She also displays elements of anger, irritation (over the failure of her aides) and arrogance (in her never consulting anyone on any decision) and evokes the *rasa* of *bibhatsa* when she relishes the act of killing or torturing the harmless kin of her opponents, like Vijay's girlfriend and Shalu's siblings respectively.

Shalu as Madam X, while continuing with the charade of Madam X's daring and arrogance, is also the trigger of pleasurable and positive *rasas* like love and humour, along with compassion for her enemies. She is seen romancing Inspector Vijay and opts for flirting (comic love) instead of fear as a strategy to allay Champak Lal's doubts and retain his loyalty.

Thus, Shalu's Madam X does not compromise her character's inherent positive attributes—of courage, love, humour and compassion—but refashions them to humanise her interpretation of the character. This contributes to and perpetuates, without any blurring, the clear distinction between the heroic and the villainous in their adherence to the Rama and Ravana stereotypes. This is hinted at in Shalu's first interaction with her close aides in her Mafia den, where she says, 'Madam X has changed. Her heart, her values, and her thought processes have changed' (AK 1994).

Vira, or courage manifested through heroic acts, is a positive *rasa* that both Shalu and Madam X share and display through their daring, energetic and courageous behaviour. They both lead their own battles and never shy away from a challenge. Madam X engages twice in hand-to-hand combat with Inspector Vijay, while Shalu grapples with Zaka and has a physical fight with Madam X in the climax scene. But while Shalu fights *only* in self-defence or to protect loved ones, Madam X fights for vengeance, perpetuating the 'she stings like a snake' imagery from her introduction song. She repeatedly gives elaborate speeches on the grave consequences for anyone daring to challenge or confront her.

Madam X's interactions with other men are marked either by her looking down at them or talking to them with herself in the foreground making a direct address to the audience, while the object of her conversation looks up at her from the background. With opponents challenging her on an equal footing, like Vijay, she always maintains eye contact.

Shalu however, when masquerading as Madam X, comfortably adopts a beseeching looking-up-to-her-man posture in the presence of the man she loves, like the female Sasirekha. In spite of being a braveheart, she frequently lets Vijay be the driver of dramatic action. In scenes where the dominant sentiment is that of a non-pleasurable or negative *rasa* like fear and disgust, while Madam X *always* triggers those emotions in the other, Shalu experiences them herself. For example, she is constantly apprehensive that her charade will be revealed (in the presence of Commissioner Mathur or Zaka) and feels guilty when she commits her first act of murder. The three murders that Shalu effects as Madam X—first of Zaka, then Champak Lal and finally Madam X—are depicted as unintended killings, done in self-defence or to protect the weak. Once the act is done, she immediately shifts into the mood states of guilt and regret, in accordance with the compassionate streak highlighting the *daya-vira* (the kind-hearted hero) nature of her character.

Final Face-Off

A final face-off between the hero and the villain, in which the latter is vanquished for the return of order and upholding of justice, shapes the climax of *Madam X*. This, as appropriate for any good-triumphs-over-evil moral drama, revolves around characters with epic ambitions or inspired by the epics. The climax is a 15-minute-long sequence that begins with Champak Lal seeing through Shalu's charade. Using her siblings as hostages, he compels Shalu to take him to the hideout where Vijay has imprisoned Madam X and rescues her. Madam X now wants to exact vengeance on Shalu and her siblings, whom she brings to her den and uses as bait to make Shalu agree to surrender to the law as Madam X. This would then enable the real Madam X to disappear with all her wealth. However, after three dramatic confrontations—first between Shalu and Madam X, next between Shalu and Champak Lal and finally between Shalu and Madam X—Madam X is killed when a gun being snatched between her and Shalu in a lengthy fight accidentally fells Madam X in a shower of bullet fire.

Shalu, in accordance with her character's positive/heroic attributes, kills in self-defence, while Madam X indiscriminately guns down half of a police force, along with a minister leading the group, in the climactic battle. Viewed in the context of a need to evoke or heighten the impact of the positive heroic *rasa* over the negative *rasas* of fear/terror and disgust, in the service of a good-triumphs-over-evil ending, the events in the scene are consistent with the dominant *bhava* traits of the characters. Shalu retains a hero's dominant *rasa* of *vira* throughout, first in her ability to bear the torture inflicted by Madam X with resilience and then as she fights back at an opportune moment. Shalu's compassion is reinforced as she considers a dying Madam X with regret instead of as a joyous victor. She never kills for revenge or pleasure, only to protect the weak and the righteous.

Guided by her thirst of revenge, Madam X undertakes some daring acts, but, when cornered, she does not mind exchanging courage for subterfuge, thus consistently retaining the black streak of her character. When Shalu gets the better of her in their first fight, Madam X tries to disarm her by revealing that her siblings are in her captivity.

Fear of Madam X's actions and disgust at her treachery are the connecting themes throughout. This is highlighted in Shalu's final castigation of Madam X, stating, 'Looking at you, I feel disgusted about myself as I wonder why God gave me the looks of a devil like you' (AK 1994). She then spits on Madam X's face in an extreme reaction of disgust (NS.6.72–73).

When she sees Madam X for the first time, Shalu peeps at her from behind Inspector Vijay, trying to remain unseen, perhaps because she is intimidated by the former's ferocity. Disgust for Madam X's ruthlessness turns that fear into resistance, reiterating the courageous streak in her character. However, once she kills Madam X, we see her revert to pity mixed with fear and disgust that make her avoid looking at Madam X in her dying moments. Fear and disgust are thus the two dominant *rasa* reactions consistently evoked by Madam X from the film's male (Vijay) and female (Shalu) hero characters.

The colours of Shalu and Madam X's costumes in the climax, while complementing their mood states at that moment, are consistent with the character traits that each retained in their respective interpretations of Madam X throughout the film. Madam X appears in her trademark masculine outfits in dark shades. When first seen confronting an angry and disgusted Shalu, she is dressed in dark brown pants and a coat, while Shalu is seen in a blazing red (the complementing colour of the *raudra*/furious *rasa*) *churidar–kurta*. However, when both are dressed as Madam X in the final fight, the Rama–Ravana imagery is hinted at. Madam X is dressed in a black outfit, in contrast to Shalu as Madam X, who dons a *shyama* or light blue outfit akin to Lord Rama's complexion in religious art. Shalu's Madam X further has a blue-green peacock feather in her cap, an exact replication of the feather in the crown of Lord Krishna, the avatar of Lord Vishnu that follows the Rama avatar in Hindu scriptures.

The costume as an integral part of the character-building aspect is reinforced during Madam X's punishing and castigation of Shalu before the climax, not only for daring to impersonate her actions but also for trying to fit into her clothes. Stating that they were no mere clothes but a visual manifestation of her fearful reputation as a ruthless criminal, Madam X tells Shalu:

> Madam X: Tune un juton ko pehnne ki jurrat ki jiski aedhi ke neeche jurm ki duniya palti hai; Tune hamaara wo taaz pehen-ne ki himmat ki, jise banane ke liye humne sainkdon saye kar diye; Kaas ki tu police record me hamara khooni karnama padh leti, hamara libaas pehnne ke bajaye, tu kafan pehen leti… (AK 1994)
>
> (You dared to wear those shoes under whose ankle the world of crime thrives; you aspired to wear that crown to make which I killed many… Wish you had also read my blood curdling exploits in the police records before agreeing to impersonate me; instead of wearing my costume you would have preferred to don the white of the coffin instead!).

Complementing dialogues play an integral role in perpetuating the exclusivity and eccentricity of Madam X, making her a spectacular achievement in *vachika abhinaya*. While the film takes frequent liberties in logical continuity, the emotional consistency is maintained throughout, as discussed with respect to both Madam X and her counterpart Shalu. Logically, after being hit with a shower of bullets, Madam X should have died immediately. But she lives long enough to sign off her epitaph herself with her signature line about being 'an express of death', for one last time, thus satisfying the audience's expectation of a grand exit in logical accordance with her larger-than-life existence throughout. Madam X breathes her last with a thunderous laugh and a grandiose monologue, like demonic characters in classical theatre, as she declares:

> Madam X: Koi hume maarkar hamara ant kya karega, mitne wale nahi hain hum… Zindagi ko apne qaid me liye ghumte hain hum, koi zindagi se hume juda kya karega… (Ha Ha Ha…) Kyunki hum hain maut ke woh express, duniya jise kehti hai Madam X (AK 1994).
>
> (How anyone can put an end to me by simply killing me, because I am not someone whose memory can be easily erased! I have moved around carrying life in my bondage, how can someone free me from living? [Laughs uproariously] Because I am that death heralding express, which the world knows as Madam X!).

The immortality that Madam X claims (as articulated as a creative wish by Shivdasani while conceiving the character) has eventually come to her in a way, in retrospect. It is in the 'continuing recollection of her character among fans of popular Hindi cinema today' (Kumar 2012) and, in the way, Madam X stands out as a memorable performance in the 'eclectic and dense'[23] filmography of actress Rekha, even though the film was not a commercial success at the time of its release. Dressed in black and awash in the red of her own blood (*aharya abhinaya*), raging with fury (*sattva abhinaya*) and making insane claims of immortality (*vachik abhinaya*) with animated gestures (*angik abhinaya*) in the face of sure death, Rekha as Madam X thus ends her performance as a masterclass in the achievement of *samanya abhinaya*. It is a synchronised performance of each of the four types of acting prescribed in the *Natyashastra*, seamlessly blended to leave the memorable *rasa* impact of an inflexibly black or evil persona. The final scene then cuts to Shalu and Vijay singing a love song, marking the fulfilment of her need for love and the lonely Vijay's need for companionship, as the credits declare a happy *The End*.

Conclusion

The *Natyashastra* prescribes and prioritises nine *bhavas* as *sthayis* or constant feelings, which are considered to be primary, permanent and universal to all human beings. In a performance working towards a dramatised achievement of these *navarasas*, they are generally realised through a mix of *rasa*-representing character types, often dominated by at least one of these primary emotions. For instance, in *Mayabazar*, the beautiful Sasirekha, embodying elements of the *rati bhava* in her mood, costumes and behaviour, triggers the sentiment of *sringara* in her young beholders. Abhimanyu, through his energetic and valorous acts, becomes an on-screen trigger for actions evoking the *vira rasa* in the audience, just as the illusionist Ghatotkacha triggers *hasya* and *adbhuta*, the villainous Shakuni evokes the sentiment of *bibhatsa* and Krishna, through his artful bringing of calm in the lives of the disturbed protagonists and their relatives, becomes a source of *shanta rasa* for all. Similarly, in *Madam X*, while Shalu and inspector Vijay constantly engage in courageous activities that make for the narrative's *vira-rasa*-evoking moments, Madam X becomes a consistent catalyst for acts of the *bhayanaka* and the *bibhatsa rasas,* albeit with an ample touch of the *adbhuta*—in the nature of her dressing and the manner of her exalted speech, full of metaphors and similes—which makes her the film's biggest attraction.

Each character profile, while personifying a singular *rasa* type, also intermittently displays glimpses of most of the other primary feelings natural to all human beings. But it is in the discrete *bhavas* of a masculine Ghatotkacha-as-Sasirekha, in contrast to the feminine Sasirekha, that *Mayabazar* perpetuates the idea of different *bhavas* for different genders. Occasionally the male Sasirekha does became an agent for the evocation of the sentiment of wonder, given her character as an illusionist, but she definitely does not display the *rasas* exclusive to the female Sasirekha, such as pity and fear. The female Sasirekha strictly restricts herself to a stock set of feelings comprising of love, pity, fear and wonder, evoking the *sringara, karuna, bhaya* and *adbhuta rasas* respectively, while the male Sasirekha gets to broaden the *rasa* set by calling into play acts and expressions of valour, comedy, anger and disgust that trigger the *vira, hasya, raudra* and *bibhatsa rasas* respectively.

In the clear absence of any negative *rasa*-evoking *bhava* (such as anger, fear or disgust) in the actions or the personality of Shalu, and in their exclusive manifestation in the villain Madam X, the film reaffirms the prescribed *bhava* segregation for good and bad characters. The range of attributes of an evil Madam X never enters or explores even a hint of the pleasurable *rasas*, limiting her mood states to portraying the negative/non-pleasurable *bhavas* of *raudra, bhaya* and *jugupsa* only. Even when elements of a positive *rasa* like *vira* are triggered through Madam X, the manifestation is always negative as they are fed by negative *bhavas* like rage and senseless violence. Similarly, Shalu as Madam X occasionally does commit a necessary killing, but what immediately follows is her guilt, whereas Madam X murders without compunction. Shalu, in a way, is a relatively more layered character, but there is a clear demarcation of traits (sadistic enjoyment of violence, unbridled rage, etc.) and body language (bulging eyes, hyperbolic speech, costumes in dark shades) that she never appropriates, just as Madam X is never seen joking or sharing kindness even with her aides. Shalu as the positive Madam X thus not only softens the edges of Madam X's negative *bhavas* but also, like Sasirekha, never compromises the seven graces (beauty, beautiful/pleasing disposition, beauteous luminosity, propriety, serenity, maturity and civility) of the ideal woman, despite being forced to play her part in a more violent and action-oriented space. Though a Mafia boss, she still has compassion for her enemies, rarely loses her calm when tortured and even sings a love song that enables her to portray the three graces of *sobha* (glowing in the experience of love), *kanti* (radiating in a state of expectant love) and *dipti* (heightened *kanti*) (NS 24.22–29)—which are exclusive to a heroine in love.

In actress Savithri's differentiation of the two Sasirekhas through specific *rasa*-enhancing *bhavas* complementing and identifying the 'masculine' and the 'feminine', *Mayabazar* makes its strongest case for a possible acknowledgement of categorising universal human emotions on the basis of gender. In actress Rekha's differentiation of the evil Madam X from her good double, through a selection of *rasa*-enhancing *bhavas* that separate and celebrate the good from the bad, *Madam X* both endorses and perpetuates the *Natyashastra*-recommended *bhava* traits that are to be used to differentiate the hero from the villain.

The ability of an actor to maintain distinction in the *angika, sattvika, vachika* and *aharya* traits of his/her extremely diverse characters, for maximum impact and to enable differentiation between black and white characters, can be reviewed as an achievement and not a limitation. The basis for such an achievement lies in not diluting the characterisation by a need to explore the 'grey'. This is not simply the perpetuation of a stereotype but a complex aesthetic achievement in consistent characterisation that is steadfast in its *rasa* state and *bhava* traits throughout. In a popular art like cinematic melodrama, a codifying text like the *Natyashastra* recommends that certain *bhavas* will have the most impact when represented by a certain gender or character type. This is a general guideline for a performance and its review, which is based on common human experiences. However, by letting one actor be the vehicle for the *rasa*—articulating both the masculine and the feminine and the good and the bad—*Mayabazar* and *Madam X*, despite belonging to two different eras, regions and genres of filmmaking, evidence faith in a good actor's ability to break stereotypes.

Notes

1 Mehta 1995: 37.

2 Interview with Deepak Shivdasani in Mumbai on 14 September 2014.

3 'The epics and myths of the country, would seem to present the most widely acceptable base for the artistic development of the Indian cinema' (Das Gupta 1993: 125).

4 'The emotion belongs to the body because of immediate effect on it, expression follows emotion, and grace accompanies expression. *Bhava* is so called because it makes the audience to feel because of words, gestures, etc. (NS 24.10–11)' (Rangacharya 2010: 185).

5 NS 24.22–29

6 NS 24.30–39

7 'In our cinema, we project our emotions. We are basically very loud people. Even for someone doing subtle acting, he or she has to be more expressive, [especially] at least in the song sequences' (Kapoor 2013).

8 According to the *Natyashastra*, an emotion is best conveyed or felt the most when the words, tone and gestures that constitute or feed it are all *samana*, i.e., equal or most suited to each other, for the outcome to be celebrated as a work of *samanya abhinaya* (NS 24.1–8).

9 In acting, the reactions (*anubhavas*) to a cause (*vibhava*) could be conveyed as mere automatic gestures, such as speaking in a breaking voice to convey sorrow (*vachika abhinaya*) or trembling of body parts to show fear (*angika abhinaya*), without involving the inner performer. Only when the reaction is in sync with the internalised state of being of a character is the true *sattvikabhava* conveyed. 'An actor who has understood/imbibed the inherent *sattva* (emotional) graph of an elevated hero like Rama or Sita, will react with relatively less gestures and more internalised emotion than while playing a common man, in the context of similar provocations' (Subrahmanyam 2010: 50).

10 Dwivedi 2012

11 'The popular [North Indian] play [*Mayabazar*] found its way to cinema thanks to Baburao Painter who made it thrice as a silent movie (1919, 1921 and 1923) with his prodigy V. Shantaram as Lord Krishna. The first talkie version of *Mayabazar* directed by Nanubhai Vakil came in Hindi in 1932. R. Padmanabhan made a Tamil movie in 1935 and the next year P.V. Das brought it to Telugu cinema… Though there were several movie versions in various Indian languages, the 1957 Vijaya Productions' *Mayabazar* is still considered the best for its all-round excellence' (Narasimham 2015).

12 The poll was conducted and published by CNN-IBN (May 2013).

13 The dialogue and songs of the original Telegu version of *Mayabazar*, which is the reference film in this chapter, were written by South Indian cinema's 'wizard of words' (Narasimham 2015) Pingali Nagendra Rao. He has been credited for the film's songs and dialogue as PNR.

14 The *Natyashastra* lists six types of laughter for actors depending on the nature of their characters—*smita* (gentle smile) and *hasita* (slight laughter) for noble men and women, *vihasita* (open laughter) and *upahasita* (ridiculing laughter) for common men and women and *apahasita* (obscene laughter) and *atihasita* (boisterous laughter) for the loud and demonic characters.

15 The character name Madam X has been written without italics to distinguish it from the film *Madam X*.

16 The dialogue writer of *Madam X*, Anwar Khan, has henceforth been cited by his initials AK, and not just his surname Khan, to avoid any confusion with scriptwriter Salim Khan, who will continue to be cited by his surname. All the English translations of AK's Hindi/Urdu dialogues are by me.

17 Though four individuals are credited for the costumes of Madam X, according to director Deepak Shivdasani, it was actress Rekha who designed them and acquired permission from an international fashion magazine for her character's unusual hat designs, while the film's official designers only aided their stitching process (Shivdasani 2014).

18 The Stanislavski principle on characterisation, popular in acting schools in the West, teaches actors to 'feel and express' (Mishra 2010: 99).

19 This is a concept introduced and discussed in the previous chapter.

20 *Madam X*, according to filmmaker Deepak Shivdasani, was not a flop, as commonly assumed, but a *comme ci*, *comme* ça return-on-investment venture (Shivdasani 2014).

21 Urdu poet and two-time Filmfare Best Lyrics Award winner, Hasrat Jaipuri, started his film career in the last 1940s, writing songs for hit Raj Kapoor films. *Madam X* was one his last major film projects where he wrote all the songs.

22 AK 1994.

23 Rekha was one of Indian cinema's leading actresses from the 1970s to the early 1990s, acclaimed for her performances in popular and parallel cinema with a filmography of over 300 films. *Madam X* remains one of her most unconventional, often remembered, loved and loathed on-screen characterisations.

6

Rasa in Performance: Draupadi's Insult and a Plea for Vengeance in Nine Emotions

> For all those who say that the Indian audience is no longer attracted to the traditional styles of storytelling they should watch the entertainment content on Indian television. Ninety percent of what is consumed by audiences on a daily basis on TV, at a much more prolific rate than cinema, is not only theatrical in its style but also belongs to an earlier era of filmmaking[1].
>
> Chandraprakash Dwivedi, director–actor

> I am a young guy making the Mahabharata[2]. After Mahabharat (2013–2014), the old style of making periodicals and costume dramas will no longer work in India. We have thus set a benchmark in a way. Normally TV soaps are written in the simplest possible manner to appeal to the lowest common denominator as people are not supposed to be thinking while watching TV. Our thought was to also attract those who want to engage with some thoughts and philosophies. The crux was to entertain people and through that give a message[3].
>
> Siddharth Tewary, director–producer, TV and OTT

Introduction

In the 100th anniversary year of the Indian film industry, as debates, aspirations and global impact achievements of a century of Indian on-screen entainment were getting reviewed in the context of emergent viewership trends, its oldest genre—the mythological—made an ambitious comeback. *Mahabharat* (Swastik Productions, 16 September 2013–16 August 2014) was the most expensive fiction series ever aired on Indian television. The series was telecast from Monday to Friday at a primetime evening slot on Star Plus[4]. Its creative director, 35-year-old business graduate turned filmmaker Siddharth Tewary, is a young representative of the current millennium's filmmaking generation. He has worked with Euro-American technicians, is a viewer of international cinema, experiments with new technologies in filmmaking and 'has never been a conscious student of the Sanskrit theatre or studied about its *rasa*-evoking prescriptions from drama' (Tewary 2014). Yet, for the dramatisation of the most expensive, high-risk-themed[5] series on Indian television, which aimed to set a benchmark for costume dramas in on-screen entertainment, Tewary opted for a traditional Indian format of storytelling that is perceived to be melodramatic[6] and 'that prioritises a multiple-emotion-evoking narration over one that focuses on one or a few emotions in service of a relatively linear, character-driven style of storytelling' (Shah Rukh Khan 2012)[7]. According to Tewary:

> Action without emotion is zero! However, if you are making the *Mahabharata* for the West [i.e. the USA and Europe] you cannot make it the way we have done. You have to understand that their lifestyle and culture is different and condition your telling accordingly. For instance, there, if something does not fit you in a store you do not give it for alteration, you go for the next option that fits best. There the shops shut at 6 pm, here business picks up after 6 in the evening. I could just go on about the differences… Fact is that our worlds are different. If you are making *Mahabharata* for that world, you might do it the way Peter Brooks adapted the epic[8], but it did not appeal to me. I am a massy guy in my head so too much intellectualisation does not work for me. A show has to talk to me, make me think, but in an entertaining way, it has to move me emotionally (2014).

Tewary's *Mahabharat* garnered the highest TVTs (Television Viewership in Thousands) for a mythological show in the present millennium on Indian satellite television (detailed in Table 6.1). It is the only televised version of the epic to have enjoyed a full run since B.R. Chopra's landmark 1988 adaptation for India's national broadcaster Doordarshan, after three other TV series on the epic were pulled off air midway due to lack of viewership. It also is the only Indian television series in current times to enjoy repeat telecasts beyond its regular run, with dubbed re-telecasts on six regional language television channels (Bengali, Marathi, Odia, Malayalam, Tamil and Telegu), and serialised international broadcasts in Indonesia (ANTV, starting March 2014) and Mauritius (MBC Digital 4, starting December 2015). From its first episode, *Mahabharat* became the most popular mythological show of the time on Indian television and entered the top five fiction show listings after its episodes on the game-of-dice event (Table 6.1).

Table 6.1 A Comparative Review of *Mahabharat*'s TVT Ratings

The viewership ratings of a few sample weeks from the *Mahabharat* TV series' more-than-a-year-long run on Star Plus is compared with proportionate TVTs of leading shows in other popular Indian television genres like the historical, reality shows and socials. The *Mahabharat* series can be seen to have enjoyed a consistent lead over the subsequent mythological show, *Devon Ke Dev Mahadev* (Life OK). The numbers within brackets next to a show's rating points (column 2) indicate its overall ranking among all shows telecast on Indian General Entertainment Channels in that particular week.

Dates	*Mahabharat* (Star Plus) No.1 Mythological	No.2 Mythological	No.1 Historical/ Costume Drama	No. 1 Reality Show	No.1 Social	No.1 Channel TVTs[9] (In millions)
8–14 Dec 2013	3.6 (4)	N/A	*Jodha Akbar*: 4.9 (1)	*Comedy Nights with Kapil*: 3.6 (1) *Bigg Boss 7*: 2.8 (3)	*Diya Aur Baati Hum* 5.7 (1)	Star Plus: 579 Colors: 449 Zee TV: 439
12–18 Jan 2014	**3.6 (4)**	*Devon Ke Dev Mahadev* 3.3 (2)	*Jodha Akbar* 9.8 (1)	*Comedy Nights with Kapil* 5.2 (1) *India's Got Talent* 3.7 (2)	*Diya Aur Baati Hum* 6.4 (1)	Star Plus: 626 Zee TV: 471 Colors: 467

Dates	***Mahabharat* (Star Plus) No.1 Mythological**	**No.2 Mythological**	**No.1 Historical/ Costume Drama**	**No. 1 Reality Show**	**No.1 Social**	**No.1 Channel TVTs[9] (in millions)**
9–15 Feb 2014	7.5 (3)	*Devon Ke Dev Mahadev* 2.9 (3)	*Jodha Akbar* 11.6 (1)	*Comedy Nights with Kapil* 9.1 (1) *India's Got Talent 5* 6.6(2)	*Diya Aur Baati Hum* 13.3 (1)	Star Plus: 702 Colors: 504 Zee TV: 457
9–16 Mar 2014	3.0 (4)	*Devon Ke Dev Mahadev*: N/A	*Jodha Akbar* 5.0 (1)	*Comedy Nights with Kapil* 3.9 (1)	*Saath Nibhana Saatiya* 5.9 (1)	Star Plus: 727 Zee TV: 501 Colors: 466
6–12 Apr 2014	9.1 (2) *Cheer Haran episodes*	*Devon Ke Dev Mahadev* 2.4	*Jodha Akbar* 9.3	*Comedy Nights with Kapil* 9.1	*Diya Aur Baati Hum* 13.4 (1)	
13–19 Apr 2014	7.7 (3)	*Devon Ke Dev Mahadev* 2.1 (6)	*Jodha Akbar* **10.5 (1)**	*Comedy Nights with Kapil* 8.5 (1) *Fear Factor*: 7.3 (2)	*Diya Aur Baati Hum* 14.5 (1)	Star Plus: 790 Colors: 433 Zee TV: 473
11–17 May 2014	6.0 (4)	*Devon Ke Dev Mahadev* 1.7 (7)	*Jodha Akbar* 8.9 (1)	*Comedy Nights with Kapil* 5.5 (1) *Khatron Ke Khiladi* 5.3 (2)	*Saath Nibhana Saathiya* 9.8 (1)	Star Plus: 681 Zee TV: 394 Colors: 367
8–14 Jun 2014	6.5 (3)	*Devon Ke Dev Mahadev* 1.9 (7)	*Jodha Akbar* 7.7 (1)	*Comedy Nights with Kapil* 5.9 (1) *Jhalak Dikhhala Jaa* 5.6 (2)	*Diya Aur Baati Hum* 9.4 (1)	Star Plus: 626 Zee TV: 376 Colors: 366

Dates	*Maha-bharat* (Star Plus) No.1 Myth-ological	No.2 Myth-ologi-cal	No.1 Histor-ical/ Costume Drama	No. 1 Reality Show	No.1 Social	No.1 Channel TVTs[9] (in mil-lions)
13–19 Jul 2014	9.4 (2) (9.1) *Abhimanyu Vadh*	*Devon Ke Dev Ma-hadev* 2.0 (3)	*Jodha Akbar* 9.3 (1)	*Comedy Nights with Kapil 6.8 (1) Jhalak Dikhhla Jaa* 5.6 (2)	*Diya Aur Baati Hum* 10.5 (1)	Star Plus: 712 Zee TV: 436 Life OK: 361
10–16 Aug 2014	**(9.1) 8.5 (3)** *End of War*	*Devon Ke Dev Ma-hadev* 1.7 (3)	*Jodha Akbar* **7.5 (2)**	*Comedy Nights with Kapil* 6.9 (1) *Jhalak Dikhhla Jaa* 4.8 (3)	*Diya Aur Baati Hum* 10.7 (1)	Star Plus: 689 Zee TV: 453 Colors: 411

The ratings peaked in the week depicting the disrobing of Queen Draupadi in the court of King Dhritarashtra, which is the climactic sequence within the game-of-dice event. A moment of high drama with immense consequences that eventually lead to the Mahabharata war, this significant sequence in the game-of-dice event has henceforth been referred to by its reference term in the epic, the *Cheer Haran* sequence. Since viewership rating statistics are a recognised yardstick in the television industry for ascertaining the popularity of a television show, I have concluded the previous chapter's arguments for a *rasa*-based analysis of Indian acting with evidence from television. This becomes necessary, since television is the most-consumed medium of on-screen entertainment in India, after cinema.

Having discussed the distribution, working and evocation of the *rasa* imperative in an entire narrative's plot construction (Chapter 4) and in the dominant mood states and traits of a character throughout a film (Chapter 5), this chapter focuses on the intricacies and nature of multiple-*rasa* achievements within the smallest narrative unit of a filmed story—i.e., a sequence or a scenario. It discusses how the knowledge and awareness of the *bhavas* and *rasas* can help identify and review the success of a range of expressions in a multiple-emotion-conveying performance of an Indian actor. This type of performance is often erroneously under-appreciated or dismissed as melodramatic. Indian drama categories of review will also be explored to understand why, according to the *Natyashastra*, not every stylised dramatic presentation with song, music and expressive performances is a melodrama and how the knowledge and nature of *rasa* evocation can help distinguish melodrama (as understood in the Indian drama context) from a good drama. Just as every *masala* film is not *Sholay*, similarly dismissing every emotive act that is accompanied by song, hyperbolic dialogue or music as melodrama is too simplistic and inadequate. Mukesh Singh, one of the episode directors[10] of *Mahabharat* explains:

> It is wrong to generalise that the Indian audience only likes melodrama and that all the performances in Indian films and television shows are melodramatic. There is a term in the *Natyashastra* called *raso-ut-patih* [the birth of a *rasa*]. If a person watching a drama is not able to feel anything then there is no *rasoutpatih*. When actors acting in a scene are not behaving according to the situation, by being either over the top [this could be closest to what is understood as 'melodramatic' in the context of traditional Indian drama appreciation] or by under playing or underperforming [this is a common complaint of Indian audiences against realism-driven European/Indian parallel cinema performances][11] the emotional state of a character in their performed actions and reactions, then they are not going to touch your heart. And if a performance is not touching your heart, then there is no *rasa*. An actor has to understand the situation and play accordingly. When their interpretation is completely in sync with the situation and the emotion graph of a character, that is drama [this is the highest/most admired form of performance, which a critic unaware of the *rasa* theory or the art of *rasa*-evocation is prone to erroneously under value as melodrama] (Singh 2014).

In the above observation perhaps lies an insight into why Tewary's *Mahabharat* became popular with Indian audiences, while Ekta Kapoor's equally ambitious *Kahaani Hamaaray Mahaabhaarat Ki* (The Story of our Mahabharat, 9X, 2008) failed 'for being too loud or melodramatic with inconsistencies between its actor performances' (Shukla 2014), and Chandraprakash Dwivedi's *Ek Aur Mahabharat* (Zee TV, 1997) was taken off air after only 14 episodes for being too subtle/realistic in comparison to the stylised/dramatic acting expectations from epic characters. According to the *Natyashastra*, the performer and the audience, the actor and the viewer, are necessary participants and accomplices—*sahrydayas*—in the *bhava*-generated and the *rasa*-realised experience, as discussed in Chapter 4. A viewer, or a critic ignorant of the style, nature and the history of influences on a performance, and the context of a character, will not be able to fully relish its *rasa*. For instance, without the knowledge of the specific set of emotions expected to be prioritised in a dramatic performance with epic motivations (as discussed in Chapter 5), one will not be able to identify and appreciate the layers of intricate *bhavas* being conjured in the fleeting facial expressions of an actor's interpretation. Such a viewer or a critic will continue to misread the complexities in an expressive art form as exaggerated and unreal.

This book, through multiple case studies and interviews, has established how the expectations from a dramatic art or an aesthetic performance can vary between cultures. This chapter, through a detailed analysis of every passing mood/*bhava* state and their corresponding *rasa* reactions/expressions on a protagonist's visage within one particular dramatic scenario, discusses the emotive range and impact of an actor's performance in a highly dramatic sequence. It explains how even within a character's seemingly singular *rasa*-dominating performance, a complex play of fleeting emotions (often missed) can be noticed and appreciated by a *sahrydaya* (empathetic) viewer with an awareness and knowledge of the *rasa* theory, leading them to experience true *rasoutpatih*. This is done through a freeze-frame study of the range of expressions employed by actress Pooja Sharma (who plays Queen Draupadi) in the *Cheer Haran* sequence. The frames and the reactions they represent identify the myriad emotive layers in her complex dramatic performance and aid an appreciation of how Draupadi is able to retain and evoke a consistent character sentiment throughout the sequence. *Bhava* consistencies of other major characters and the use of *Natyashastra*-recommended personality enhancing colour in costumes is also identified. Finally, an understanding is offered, based on interviews with the cast and crew of *Mahabharat*, of the conscious and subconscious processes at play on a contemporary Indian shooting location, which work towards the goal of providing the audience with a sumptuous relishing of *rasa* through a roller-coaster multi-emotion experience akin to a good *masala* film. This chapter, while contributing to the dissertation's uniting argument regarding the influence and relevance of the *rasa*-evocation idea in Indian on-screen entertainment, reveals how competent storytellers use its 'eternally relevant recommendations' (Singh 2014) in actual practice to enhance the appeal of a dramatic experience.

The Mahabharata: An Epic in Nine *Rasas*

Mukesh Singh, the on- set episode director of the *Cheer Haran* sequence says:

> *Yanna Bharate, tanna Bharate* (what is not in the *Mahabharata*, is not in India) thus goes the introduction of the epic. I would rather say that whatever does not exist in the *Mahabharata*, does not exist anywhere in the world. All the types of emotions, characters and characteristic nation states existent in the world are described in this story. Any human emotion or character that you can imagine, you will find in the *Mahabharata*. Any story that consists of all the nine *rasas* is called a *mahakavya*, and that's why the *Mahabharata* is called a *mahakavya*. Other stories that have one, two or fewer number of *rasas* are called *kavyas* (2014).

If the *Mahabharata* is a *mahakavya* evoking the nine *rasas*, its *Cheer Haran* sequence is a micro manifestation of that dramatic promise. What starts as a sorrowful event of extreme disgust—the molestation of a lady by the male members of her family on a public platform—ends up leaving its audience with a feeling of wonder and the victim in a state of calm. In this traversing from an extremely negative emotion to one of positive elation lies the dramatic appeal of the sequence in its ability to let a dramatist or director explore the possibility of evoking multiple *rasas* in the audience. According to Tewary:

> The *Mahabharata* is the biggest *masala* story in the world. There is pathos, and there is wonder in the same sequence—that is the beauty

> of the epic. You cannot think of a better story in your lifetime. Just look at the way the story connects. What happened years ago connects to events right in the end… That way the *Mahabharata* is a tremendous potboiler drama, the biggest soap opera ever, superbly written with great conflicts (2014).

The makers of *Mahabharat* reinterpret and present the action in the sequence in such a manner that they are not only able to achieve the above-mentioned *rasas* but offer a sumptuous serving of all the *navarasas* to retain audiences throughout its 14 episodes, despite their prior knowledge of the story. According to Tewary:

> You will find many versions of the epic across India and more if you venture into South-east Asia. People retelling it as a story too add their own interpretations. It has had public and personal interpretations, so I thought I will make my own interpretation, try and ask questions and do whatever appeals to me. I have stuck to the basic crux, but we have taken little creative liberties in how we want to tell it because it is an epic poem into which people have been writing out their interpretations. Veda Vyasa [the original author of the Sanskrit epic *Mahabharata*] and the subsequent writers did not give us a screenplay; they had just written a poem. You have to decipher it, understand it and make your own version. That is why I think people have liked this perspective (2014).

In Tewary's version, the *Cheer Haran* sequence is presented as its makers' comment on and 'support to the public and media outrage across India that followed the Delhi gang rape incident of 16 December 2012' (Jain 2014). These new elements of confrontation and dramatic twist are introduced to serve all the *rasas*, most of which are evoked by characters embodying at least one each from the nine permanent mood sentiments. The scene's heroine and protagonist Draupadi, however, gets to evoke most of the nine sentiments to varying intensities as is permissible within and consistent with her character's dominant *bhava* trait of a courageous heroine.

This chapter explores in detail the five episodes (Ep. 153–157) from Draupadi's entry to her exit in king Dhritarashtra's court, specifically focusing on the *Cheer Haran* sequence within the game-of-dice event.

The entire game-of-dice event in the television series makes for nearly 280 minutes of dramatised content, in the longest on-screen depiction of the event in an Indian cinematic or television adaptation of the Mahabharata. It thus allows ample narrative opportunity for the show's makers and immense performance possibility for its talented actors to showcase a gamut of conflicting emotions to sumptuous *navarasa* impact.

Summary Overview of the *Cheer Haran* Sequence

The game-of-dice event begins with the Pandavas—five sons of Pandu—and their common wife Draupadi entering the court of Pandu's elder brother, King Dhritarashtra of Hastinapur, after having accepted his invitation to a celebration in their honour. This is the only moment when Draupadi is shown in a state of joy (as bliss born of contentment) and presented as a vision of resplendent *sringara*, as manifested in her character's choice of tasteful clothing, make-up and adornments.

The occasion is the eldest Pandava, Yudhistira, being declared the emperor of the entire Bharatavarsha (then existing Indian subcontinent). The reception is organised by Dhritarashtra's son and crown prince, Duryodhana, the first cousin of the Pandavas. The Pandavas have been warned by Dhritarashtra's prime minister, their uncle Vidur, to be on guard. But they still accept the invitation, secure in the assurance of the strength of their dharma (righteousness). The highlight of the celebration is a game of dice, where the opposing players, Duryodhana and Yudhistira, agree to play as stakes possessions that they are or can be proud of[12], beyond inanimate possessions. The intention of Duryodhana and his scheming uncle Shakuni is to rob the Pandavas of their kingdom through trickery. The prime motive behind the setting up of the game, however, is the insult of Draupadi. As the scene unfolds, that insult is manifested as a disgusting act against the modesty of a woman and the deliberate humiliation of a lady who is the princess of one nation (Panchal), the empress of another (Indraprastha) and the eldest bride of a third (Hastinapur). This is done by getting Yudhistira to first pawn and lose his personal wealth, then his kingdom, followed by his brothers and finally himself and Draupadi as slaves to Duryodhana.

Duryodhana then orders Draupadi, who is residing with his mother, Queen Gandhari, to come to Dhritarashtra's court. Draupadi denies his messenger's request, stating that she is nobody's slave, and argues that no one other than herself has the right to barter her freedom. An enraged Duryodhana deputes his younger brother Dushasana to bring Draupadi and commands that on encountering further resistance, he should forcibly drag her to the court.

Until that point in the television series, Draupadi has been presented as a dutiful daughter, caring friend, loving wife and beautiful princess covertly and overtly desired by kings and princes. She has been a passive recipient of affection and attention, but the *Cheer Haran* sequence is a turning point in her character's journey and the epic's drama. It is Draupadi's moment of greatest histrionic impact in the multi-plot epic's narrative that celebrates myriad heroes. She is not only the focus of the *Cheer Haran* sequence but also of one of the most dramatic action moments in the epic so far. The nature of her reactions establishes her as a *virangana* or a heroine, with courage as her character's dominant emotional trait. Hence, unlike Gandhari, who is a compassionate heroine, or Subhadra, who is a romantic heroine, Draupadi is a courageous heroine, whose reactions are aimed at evoking the *vira rasa* fuelled by righteous anger towards any act of injustice. According to Tewary:

> Born of fire, Draupadi is fire [personified]... Unquestioned submissiveness just does not go with her character. She wears red because she is not someone you can push, shove or ignore. She stands for independence; she never allowed the entry of any of the other wives of the Pandavas into her palace. She is somebody with fire, you touch her and she will burn you, but that aspect to her is revealed only after the *cheer haran* sequence not right after her birth (2014).

Portraying Courage Through Multiple Emotions

The 'Indian epics have been open to interpretations in their retellings' (Ramanujan 1999; Tewary 2014), and the *Mahabharat* series is no exception. In creative director Siddharth Tewary's retelling of the

Cheer Haran sequence, Draupadi is the focus of the drama, and not the Pandavas. She is the hero of the scene and is presented as a *virangana*, with courage being her dominant *bhava* (mood state) and *sattva guna* (character trait). However, in Tewary and his team's presentation, the sequence additionally weaves in the mood states of seven other permanent *bhavas*, united under a common arch of *heroism*, consistently feeding the need for a perpetuated evocation of the *vira rasa*. As the game of dice begins in Dhritarashtra's court, Draupadi is shown as constantly being updated about the proceedings. Unlike other film and TV adaptations (e.g., *Mahabharat* 1988), she is not a helpless receiver of bad news; she tries to stop the game when Yudhistira loses his youngest brother and Draupadi's fourth husband, Nakula. In her public chiding of Yudhistira—'How could you lose my husband…' (Bhuta 2014)[13]—is a demonstration of the *rati bhava* that a wife has for her husband. As a loving wife, she rushes to the rescue of her husband, which is a reaction born of love but manifested as heroism as she does not ask for help (yet) but tries to redress the wrong with her still-existing powers as an empress. It is her character's dominant trait of courage that makes her intervene to prevent an injustice, while Queen Mother Gandhari, who too could have stopped the game, instead opts to lament, hoping that other family elders will correct the wrong. Both the ladies have been established as virtuous women, but the different ways in which they react to a similar provocation is a manifestation and reiteration of their respective dominant character traits—courage for Draupadi and compassion for Gandhari.

Draupadi's fearlessness is further established by the fact that she is the only person in Dhritarashtra's court who tries to stop an injustice in a decisive manner and insists that she will not leave the court until the game is abandoned. She eventually has to leave when requested to by Yudhistira and Dhritarashtra quoting rules of propriety. As Yudhistira starts losing one after another of her other husbands and finally himself, in Draupadi (now in her private chambers), we see a change in mood from confidence to dread born of foreboding. The *bhava* expressed is that of fear, and the *rasa* evoked is that of trepidation in the viewer for Draupadi.

When Dushasana barges into her chambers, Draupadi draws a sword and tries to fight him. The *bhava* is that of courage in trying to resist an attack through a duel, and the *rasa* evoked is heroism. She pushes him and heads towards Queen Mother Gandhari's rooms. Her gait reflects her composure; she is not fleeing in fear, though her mood is fearful. In these character-specific, dominant behavioural nuances lies the proof of an actor's ability to generate and maintain a consistent emotion state throughout his/her on-screen presence. This facilitates the audience's ability to feel or experience a perceptible emotion for *rasautpatih*. According to the production-controller of *Mahabharat* Kuntal Shukla:

> Unless an actor is able to identify and grasp the dominant emotion trait of a character, there will be no truth in his/her interpretation of its nature/state of being. Once you get the true emotional nature of a character correctly, and are then given complementing costumes to wear, which you should be able to carry comfortably, the dominant sentiment state of the character automatically gets conveyed (2014).

Before Draupadi can enter Gandhari's room, Dushasana physically stops her and drags her by the hair to Dhritarashtra's court. Natural emotions evoked by such violence against a woman are outrage in the angry, or sorrow in the compassionate, but in the context of its perpetration by a younger brother in-law against his elder sister-in-law, the emotion turns to disgust. This disgust is magnified by the helplessness of the elders of Draupadi's family, especially Bhishma and Drona, who as *atimaharathis*[14], though each singularly capable of protecting Draupadi, opt to do nothing. There is no scope for any element of romance in such a scene, but the feeling of love (as empathy) is fleetingly displayed in a shot-counter-shot sequencing of close-ups as Draupadi's eyes meet those of her third husband, Arjuna, as she is dragged before the Pandavas to the centre of Dhritarashtra's court.

None of the other Pandavas dare to look at Draupadi as she surveys their silence, first with a hope of some form of intervention to relieve her from her ordeal, then with a silent plea for rescue[15], which soon turns to sorrow and eventually disgust over their inaction. Only Arjuna returns her gaze, in which their mutual pain is conveyed and acknowledged. Later in the sequence, when Duryodhana orders her disrobing, Arjuna is the only Pandava who displays some form of protest—he douses the courtroom lights.

Finally, when Draupadi, in a fit of rage, disowns her husbands, it is Arjuna again who initiates a dialogue with her on behalf of all her husbands, asking her to forgive them as a friend, if not as a wife. It is revealed in the Mahabharata towards the end that amongst all the Pandavas, Draupadi loved Arjuna the most. He was also the only man with whom she got to share undivided love for a few moments after he won her hand in her *swayamvara*[16], until the event of her having to marry Arjuna's brothers too. That unstated special bond between Draupadi and Arjuna is constantly alluded in their exchanged looks of empathy and in Arjuna displaying some protest within the permissible limits of his bondage to lessen Draupadi's shame. It is no coincidence that the event's final word of warning from a Pandava prince on the ominous repercussions awaiting the Kauravas for insulting Draupadi is also attributed to Arjuna by the makers of the television series.

Image 6.1 Feeling Compassion for the Fallen, Post the Achieving of an Act of Vengeance—Pooja Sharma as Draupadi and Saurav Gurjar as Bheema are Portraits of Two Very Contrasting Emotions in a Single Frame (Photograph: Mukesh Singh)

Draupadi's *bhava* at this point is one of sorrow as she requests her five husbands, uncles-in-law Dhritarashtra and Vidur, adopted guardian

Drona and the family's eldest member, grandsire Bhishma, to provide her with relief as their rightful duty. She never pleads. She questions their silence, inaction and the merit in their morally weakening interpretation of dharma, with her tone varying from sorrow to anger. She asks:

> If everyone sitting in this court is acting in accordance to their dharma, then is it dharma that is responsible for the insult of a woman? Is it dharma that allows men to exploit women? (Bhuta 2014).

The *rasa* of sorrow is further enhanced when the pleas of the *atimaharathis* are ignored, and they are insulted or forced into silence by Duryodhana. Draupadi watches the debate first with sorrow for the helplessness of the elders in the court, then anger as Karna and Duryodhana insult her and eventually with disgust as she realises the pointlessness of the discussion, where everyone is trying to defend their inaction using self-serving interpretations of dharma. The *daya-vira* (compassionate hero) streak in her heroism is highlighted when her empathy for the helpless elders pleading with Duryodhana for respite makes her command them to be silent and stop degrading themselves further. She then invites Dushasana to fulfil his brother's order to disrobe her, declaring:

> The shine on each of your righteous halos has long ebbed. None of you can protect me anymore. If my sanctity is to be upheld, then the Lord himself will offer me sanctuary. Come Dushasana, test your strength (Bhuta 2014).

Draupadi's inherent courage that had been guiding her reactions of self-defence until now reaches a heightened state of heroism, setting the stage for an unusual act of courage, evoking its most complementing *rasa*, that of wonder, in her ability to achieve personal calm amidst immense external turbulence. She then enters a state of complete *sharanagat* (surrender to the divine), akin to a true devotee, closes her eyes and prays to Lord Krishna for rescue. Her face is lit up to manifest and elicit *vismaya*/wonder regarding the calm she can gather amidst such turbulence, as the series leads its audiences to one of the epic's biggest spectacles. The *rasa* of wonder is now evoked as yards of sari cloth start cascading down from all sides to cover Draupadi, as Dushasana keeps pulling her never-ending sari, until he collapses from exhaustion.

Deep in prayer and oblivious to the action or the spectacle around her, when Draupadi finally opens her eyes after the miracle of the unending sari ends, her face radiates an expression of complete calm. Actress Pooja Sharma at that moment is an image of one of the most difficult *bhavas* to portray in acting, that of inner peace.

Depicting a state of no emotion, she then admirably extends that accomplishment first to the *angika* (gestural) and *sattvika* (emotional) aspects of her act and then to the *vachika* (verbal), as she begins speaking in a controlled tone of raging emotion to curse Dhritarashtra's court. From a state of calm, she metamorphoses into a picture of rage, bathed in the halo of a goddess born, stating:

> I am no more a human, but death incarnate. I am the death of every evil being in this court of sin. Today I have wept the tears of all the unfortunate women in the world. This entire court will now be swept away (Bhuta 2014).

At this point, Draupadi's mother-in-law Kunti and Queen Mother Gandhari rush into the well of the court and try to calm her. Next, Arjuna appeals to her to regain her self-control, and Draupadi is shown remembering Krishna's advice to never let go of restraint. That realisation releases her from her superhuman (goddess-like) state of trance, allowing her to regain her human identities of princess, queen and bride. Memories and the emotion of humiliation return too, which change her *bhavas* from anger to sorrow (as self-pity), and she breaks down in the arms of Kunti. Kunti is the first person she allows to touch and console her in the entire sequence. King Dhritarashtra, chided by his wife, Queen Gandhari, and terrified of Kunti's angry warnings and Draupadi's curse, pleads for Draupadi's forgiveness and requests her to ask for a boon. She first asks for the independence of her husbands and then the return of their kingdom. Duryodhana objects and another debate commences, over which a disgusted Draupadi, angered by the indecisiveness of the men, curses them, stating:

> Beware, you upholders of dharma! Duryodhana will definitely pay for his sins, but before that everyone present here who let that sin happen without protest too will be punished for their silence (Bhuta 2014).

Draupadi then walks out with a victor's gait, with courage and confidence strategically framed within a halo of fire, as the lone embodiment of the *vira rasa* in a room full of shamed male heroes and villains. Shukla reviews Sharma's performance in the *Cheer Haran* sequence as a true work of *samanya abhinaya*, where all the four aspects of acting complement each other to generate *rasa*. He says:

> I was very impressed with Pooja's voice modulation. Born from the holy *yagna*[17] fire, Draupadi by nature, is a fiery personality. Hence, she does not have to shout to convey her anger. Even if she is silent, the energy of her persona is reflected in the very nature of her being, and felt by the audience. This is how a good actor's performance normally generates the feeling of *rasa* in the audience. A mastery of the *bhavas* is essential in a medium that works with close-ups. In this serial the camera does not act—you will not find the zip, zap and zoom movements that you see in other serials, in our *Mahabharat*. Either the camera or the actors should move, both should never move simultaneously, especially while conveying an emotion (Shukla 2014).

The on-set director of the sequence opines that only when an actor achieves complete identification with a character can he/she generate *rasoutpatih*. He says:

> I was amazed by the emotive capabilities of so young an actor and the way she [Pooja Sharma] had managed to portray so many *bhavas* in that one sequence. If you are trying to show I am sad, or trying to show you are happy… there is no *rasoutpatih*. You have to feel the happiness inside. Feel *vira rasa* inside, feel *bibhatsa* (disgust) inside, feel *raudra*

> (anger) inside, you do not have to try to show—'okay now I am feeling *bibhatsa* (disgusted)'; just feel it. If you try to show, it is melodrama, if you feel what you are showing, then that is drama. That was the idea of Bharat *muni* (Singh 2014).

The success of *rasoutpatih* in Sharma's performance is further evidenced in the manifestation of the *rasa* of sorrow in her co-actors in the scene, who were the first to witness her performance. They reacted with spontaneous tears. According to Tewary:

> The *Cheer Haran* was a difficult sequence to shoot because everyone was crying on the sets. The actors playing the Pandavas were actually crying over the helplessness of their characters. They could feel it, sitting there, and not being able to do anything (2014).

Crew and cast members responding with the desired emotional reaction to a sequence is often the first unofficial test that directors rely on while shooting. That take is then canned with the hope that it will evoke similar sentiments in the audience as well.

The *Cheer Haran* sequence finally ends in accordance with another *Natyashastra* guideline—a dramatic performance should conclude with a message or education for its viewers. In *Mahabharat*, the *sutradhar* (narrator) of the series, Lord Krishna, makes a direct address to the audience, urging them to contemplate over mankind's repeated exploitation and subjugation of women down the ages. It ends with a warning that 'whenever and wherever any woman is humiliated and exploited in some form or the other the seed for a battle, or another *Mahabharat*, is sown' (Bhuta 2014). Krishna's critique is a conscious addition by the makers of the series, aimed at finishing the scene in a heightened state of the *vira rasa*. This is offered in the assurance of definite punishment for the perpetrators of a heinous crime by none other than God himself. According to Sourabh Raaj Jain, who plays the character of Krishna in the show:

> What happened with Draupadi is not a solitary, but a repeating incident that we have been encountering day after day in our news and media space. Today, it is a trauma that everyone could relate

> to. The thought of Krishna's monologue after the *Cheer Haran* was related to the Nirbhaya incident. The learning in the thought was that *Mahabharats* [like violently culminating scenarios] will keep happening if these kind of things are going to happen. The high TRPs are perhaps because everybody today can relate to these types of incidents. So even if someone is watching our *Mahabharat* for entertainment, if he ends up learning something, then that would make a huge difference to the society. Bharat *muni*'s entire purpose behind creating the *Natyashastra* was to highlight the need for enlightenment with entertainment... (2014).

The *Cheer Haran* sequence thus marks its second end (after Draupadi's exit) also in the *vira rasa* as Krishna warns of retribution for those committing crimes against women, after a sumptuous serving of the *bibhatsa, bhayanaka, raudra, karuna* and *adbhuta rasas*, interspersed with events that offer a spattering of the *sringara* and *hasya*.

Rasa Achievements in Character Acts

The performance of the hero of the scene, Draupadi, is consistent throughout with the courageous trait *in* her character. Its impact is heightened in the sequence's grand denouement with an act of wonder/*adbhuta* (which also is the *vira rasa's* most complimenting *rasa* state, according to the *Natyashastra*, NS.6.40–42). However, what makes actress Pooja Sharma's interpretation of Draupadi in *Mahabharat* a histrionic achievement is her ability to evoke a gamut of *rasas* through manifestations of seven other permanent *bhavas* (except *hasya*) in a sequence—*fear-love-grief-anger-disgust-wonder-calm-anger/valour*—that, in the nature of their manifestation, contribute towards establishing her character's dominant *rasa* of a *virangana*/brave heroine. Since the *rasas* are an outcome of permanent sentiments that are fundamental and universal to all human beings, a well-etched character having nuance is bound to trigger them. 'All heroes and anti-heroes have the same permanent sentiments. It is the treatment that an actor gives to a character that makes it different' (Mishra 2010: 102). According to Shukla:

> Every character is a summation or product of the *navarasas*. Situations trigger *rasas*. If I am [a product of both positive and negative *rasas*], then I can choose to be a sinner, a rapist, or a good person. All the *rasas* are in me, so I can be anyone or react in anyway. It all depends on whether my reaction to a provocation is positive or negative. Krishna used his valour to try to drape Draupadi in infinite yards of saris. Dushasana used his valour to keep on pulling the unending saris until he fell from exhaustion. But since Krishna's show of strength was for a good cause, it evoked the *rasa* of compassion, while Dushasana's strength was spent on evoking something disgusting. A good drama is thus a mix of characters evoking different *rasas,* and hence every character happens to embody at least one dominant *rasa* (2014).

Based on the reactions of some of the leading characters in the *Cheer Haran* sequence, Singh says, 'Bheema represented the *raudra ras*a, Arjuna *vira*, Yudhistira[18] *shanta*, Duryodhana and Dushasana *bibhatsa*, while Karna was a combination of various *rasas*' (Singh 2014). Thus, the *Cheer Haran* sequence does not only have characters embodying the various *rasas*; even their behaviour towards Draupadi is conditioned by a diversity of individual emotions triggered by her character. Her questions evoke the *rasa* of *bibhatsa* in Karna, as it is born of a belief system that equates a woman marrying five men to a prostitute. In Duryodhana, they evoke the *raudra rasa* because his reaction to Draupadi is conditioned by the memory of a past insult. Among the elder courtiers, like Bhishma and Vidur, it evokes the *karuna rasa*, while the Pandavas' reactions of helplessness frequently tip over into anger that is manifested in the many oaths of future retribution by Bheema and Arjuna. Yudhistira, true to his character's dominant *bhava* of *sama*, remains silent throughout, as a *paatra*[19] containing the *shanta rasa*. The clearly identifiable sentiments of the different characters in the *Cheer Haran* sequence, their dominant character *bhavas* and *rasas* and their mood-appropriate clothing colours are briefly summarised below, highlighting, again, an Indian drama's broad adherence to *Natyashastra* prescriptions (see Table 6.2).

Table 6.2 *Bhava*-Coordinated Costumes for Heightened *Rasa* Impact

Name of the Character	**Dominant Character Emotions (*Bhavas*) Expressed**	**Dominant *Rasa*/s Evoked by their Actions**	***Rasa*-Specific Costume Colours as Recommended by the *Natyashastra***	**Colours of the Costumes worn in the *Cheer Haran* Scene**
Duryodhana	Anger-Disgust	Disgust	Blue	Dark Blue and Red
Shakuni	Fear-Disgust	Fear and Disgust	Black and Blue (respectively)	Black
Dushasana	Anger-Disgust	Fear and Disgust	Black and Blue	Dark Blue
Karna	Anger-Disgust	Disgust and Surprise	Blue and Light Orange/Yellow	Light Orange
Bhishma	Sorrow	Sorrow	Pigeon Grey	Ash Colour
Dronacharya	Anger-Sorrow	Anger and Sorrow	Red and Pigeon Grey	Red
Vidur	Courage-Sorrow	Courage and Sorrow	Orange and Pigeon Grey	Orange
Draupadi	Courage-Anger	Heroism and Anger	Orange and Red	Red
The Pandavas		Pity		
Yudhistira	Calm-Sorrow	Pity and Disgust[20]	Pigeon Grey and Blue	Blue and Yellow
Bheema	Heroism-Anger	Anger and Pity	Red and Pigeon Grey	Orange and Yellow
Arjuna	Heroism-Love-Anger	Heroism and Pity	Orange and Pigeon Grey	Cream and Yellow
Krishna	Sorrow-Anger-Heroism	Heroism and Wonder	Orange and Yellow	Yellow

Bhava/Rasa Training for *Mahabharat*

Most of the actors playing the lead characters in *Mahabharat* had to undergo an acting workshop to prepare for their roles, where they were made aware of the acting guidelines in the *Natyashastra*. Saurav Gurjar, an Indian national-level kick-boxing champion making his debut with the character of Bheema reveals:

> We were taught about *bhava* and *rasas* in an acting workshop that we had to undergo before the commencement of actual shooting. But unlike most other actors in my age group, I was aware of it, since I had studied in a Hindi medium school where these concepts were taught to us. Knowledge of the *rasas* is important for every actor, but it is even more helpful for those acting in a mythological because one has to go through the displaying of a greater roller coaster of emotions in this genre. I believe, that any actor who wants to make a mark in his career, should attempt to act in an adaptation of the *Mahabharata* at least once, because it has all the *rasas* and characters with every possible *bhava* (Gurjar 2014).

The roller-coaster acting that Gurjar is referring to is basically the stylised form of *Natyadharmi* performance that the *Natyashastra* extensively discusses, especially in the context of epics with larger-than-life characters. According to Shukla:

> Unlike the regular *saas–bahu* (family socials) type of drama in close-ups, the drama in a mythological has to be achieved in collaboration with all the actors and their acting styles happening in the same wave length, which is why a common workshop becomes necessary as was done with this *Mahabharat*. Otherwise, actors with varying calibers will bat at varying wavelengths like what happened in Ekta Kapoor's *Kahaani Hamaaray Mahaabhaarat Ki* (its actors Ronit Roy, Jaya Bhattacharya, Anita Hassanandani… all were on different wavelengths) because of which it could never connect with the audience. One even needs a different posture and modulation to deliver the dialogue in a mythological. Doing an epic series is a group art, and the actors in this serial have been successful to a great extent in generating the right *bhavas* and *rasas*. Many times, when we were shooting at the outdoors, I have seen so many viewers falling at the feet of Saurabh Jain, [the actor who plays Lord Krishna]. Ye unke bhaav utpan karne ki ability ke success ka proof hai ki wo serial ke bahar bhi apne liye darshakon mein bhakti ras ka bhav generate kar rahe hain (This is a proof of the success of the actor in expressing the true *bhava* of his divine character

through his performance that even outside of the show, he is able to generate the feeling/*rasa* of devotion among his viewers) (2014).

Actor Sourabh Raaj Jain credits his character's popularity to its ability to evoke the *navarasas* that make him both human and relatable, and hence contemporary. According to Jain:

> The concept of the *navarasas* is extremely relevant and something every actor should be aware of and know how to evoke to become a versatile actor. Krishna embodies the *navarasas* and the *chausath kalas* (64 arts). So, if you are portraying Krishna always as that smiling, twinkling character, then where are the *rasas* and the *kalas*? Why does Krishna have that slightly heavier make-up than his contemporaries? Because fine dressing too was part of one of his *kalas*; and so was his embodying the whole diversity of human emotions... That was the image I was working to achieve in my interpretation of Krishna. We were definitely conscious about how to make our Krishna different from previous portrayals, how to make him contemporary. In our creative discussions we realised that in spite of being a God he was born in a human form and I personally believe that Mahabharata is history, not mythology. So, all the emotions that come with the human species have to be with him as well. That focus on bringing out that human side of God, eventually became the most endearing difference of our Krishna (2014).

The self-reviews of Gurjar and Jain provide insights into the benefits of the knowledge of *bhavas* and *rasas* in the enhancement of their craft courtesy of their training under *Natyashastra* guidelines. Shukla, who has worked as a crew member on successful television shows across popular TV genres like the social and the mythological, says:

> Every actor and director working in India is consciously or unconsciously following the prescriptions of Bharat *muni.* Those who are untrained actors, they learn and perform by watching the trained actors. Those who are trained, are taught about sage Bharata's *Natyashastra*, while also being exposed to Aristotle's ideas on acting. The difference between the two is like that between a tabla (an Indian drum) and a drum. Both are leather instruments, but while the tap on a *tabla* will make its Indian listener spontaneously

> shake a limb to a rhythm that's recognised from within, the same reaction does not happen to a drum's beat. Fact is that we have got used to things that are emotive or strike an emotional chord within us. Take our cinema for instance. Any film that has been successful from *Baazigar* (Abbas Mastaan 1993) to *Delhi Belly* (Abhinay Deo 2011), have at the fundamental level been very strong at evoking emotions. Sage Bharata's ideas enjoy universal resonance, be it in certain aspects of Aristotle's theory or the visual pleasures of *The Godfather* (Francis Ford Coppola 1972). It is these *navarasas* that makes our cinema different from other world cinemas (2014).

A creative openness towards a fusion of influences while retaining the Indian core in interpretation is arguably echoed in Shukla's very choice of words as he seamlessly flits between English and Hindi, acknowledges Greek and Indian philosophies on aesthetics and employs examples from Bollywood and Hollywood. In these illuminating reviews by creators of drama, both behind and in front of the camera, and on good and bad acting, along *rasa*-based parameters, it is revealed that within a stylised performance lies an intricate art form—one that is arrived at through intense training and a studied or guided knowledge in traditional Indian performance aesthetics.

Constructing *Rasa* in Post-Production

Rasa is evoked in filmed content at two levels. The first is on the set itself, among the crew and onlookers present during the shooting of a sequence. The second is in the conscious decisions taken by its makers to make deliberate changes to conventional shooting practices and in the heightening of a sequence's emotional impact through editing choices made during post-production. According to Tewary:

> On television and even within our *Mahabharat* TV series, we normally do not shoot the plot of an episode or an event in the linear way in which it appears on telecast. One sequence from one episode and another from another episode can often get shot on the same day and then joined on edit. But we shot the *Cheer Haran* sequence as a linear narrative. It took us a month to write the sequence.

> Next, we sent the script to the sets and asked every actor to read it, including the technical crew working on the episodes. Then we had a discussion with everyone on why this is the most important sequence and discussed each character's emotional journey through the whole sequence and told them to ask any relevant question pertaining to their role. So, it was not like [as is the common practice for shooting on television] the actors were coming to the set on the day of the shot and asking and understanding about their scene for that day... My way of working is to not memorise the lines, but to feel it, in order to be able to add value to the emotion while speaking. I wanted people to feel how that girl who was being dragged felt, so the entire dragging sequence was done as one long take for the viewers to feel Draupadi's emotion and I also shot the scene in close-ups on her face at 100 frames in slow motion to heighten that feeling and convey each of the emotions [e.g., the changing *bhavas* in freeze frames as discussed above] that she was feeling as the sequence was happening. Even the way she was thrown [into the well of the court], and the way a lone spotlight was made to fall on her when she makes that decisive line asking all to "shut up" and the way she changed the emotion in her voice for that moment, that entire environment and the synchronisation of emotions of everybody who was standing in that frame is what I think made it so impactful. I really felt at that moment that we had actually shot something worthwhile (2014).

Saurav Gurjar opines:

> We shot that sequence over nine days, and for those nine days even off the sets we all were in a somber mood. For the first few episodes we all were literally crying. Any compassionate human being, whether he can help or not, will definitely feel pained on hearing a woman's calls in distress. In the initial days of shoot, the tears would naturally come in each of us, but once the shooting started getting stretched, we did use glycerin (2014).

To evoke that worthwhile experience of *rasoutpatih* on the set and sustain it in a television audience that watches the scene much later, with myriad distractions, calls for a post-production heightening of *rasa* through editing. The choice of which *bhava* reactions of the actors to use is part of a conscious technical manipulation. On the editing table, they are put together in a sequence, with emotive shot-counter-shots, and the action is re-organised around the entire event to achieve the desired *rasas* at an optimum level of engagement. The aim is to make the audience feel for Draupadi, like Gurjar stated above, and compel them to return every night throughout the week-long telecast of the *Cheer Haran* sequence until they witness her vindication. According to Tewary:

> On TV, we do not have the advantage of the undiluted hold of the 70mm. Here the concern is about whether the eyes of an actor are talking or catching attention? Is the emotion right? Is the performance right? How are they portraying the writing visually? Any form of entertainment, any story without emotion will not work. Nobody is interested in two people fighting. Action without emotion is zero. My biggest agenda is to always catch the emotion and get its graph right. I have to understand each person's emotions as to who would be doing what, and whose close-ups need to be put in and for how long in the final edit from the entire shoot. This is an important call as it is on the script table and the edit table, where a serial or a film is made (2014).

For instance, the character Karna's reaction towards Draupadi may have been motivated by his disgust for her having five husbands, but the way it is edited and presented in the *Cheer Haran* sequence evokes the *rasa* of disgust towards him in the audience. Repeated close-ups of tears falling from the eyes of the helpless Pandavas or the righteous male elders in the court like Bhishma, Vidura and Drona may seem melodramatic, but they effectively contribute to the sequence's potential to evoke *karuna rasa* in the audience. Both Duryodhana and Shakuni react with disdain to Draupadi's faith in the almighty to protect her. Yet, the series' directors, to further enhance the impact of the *adbhuta rasa* with a sense of temporary closure, insert another miracle not mentioned in the original text: all the menfolk who watched the 'wrong in silence' (Tewary 2014) are stripped of their ornaments and upper garments. In this dramatic detour from the core text, the show's makers create a possibility for the evocation of the only other *rasa* missing in the entire event, *hasya* as righteous joy. As the men in Dhritarashtra's court behold the scene in awe, fleeting moments of mirth are constructed around the conspiracy's two main architects—Duryodhana, who is suddenly caught gaping vacantly, while a visibly perturbed Shakuni is given an extra spin as he is disrobed, conjuring hints of the *hasya rasa*. This unexpected comic moment is hinted at in Krishna's faint smirk before he effects the partial disrobing of the men in Dhritarashtra's court. A teary-eyed Krishna is another departure from the previous on-screen avatars of Krishna in the *Cheer Haran* sequence, wherein he is often seen beaming in the creation of a spectacular rescue. Instead, Krishna's character in the Tewary's *Mahabharat* expresses a felt *rasa* reaction of *compassion* for Draupadi's sorrow[21]. Tewary explains:

> According to some versions of the Mahabharata, Krishna never came and Draupadi was actually disrobed. But we took the call of going with the popular perception otherwise somebody would have burnt our office. The guiding thought however was to get the emotions right. If the emotions are wrong then you cannot tell a story right, it's over. If God came and gave her the sari, could it happen that He just came there, gave the sari and everyone just stood like that and said—"Wow"! It could not have happened like that; there had to be a take to it. We had to show something to today's viewers that whenever you do something like this to a woman this is going to happen. Our writer Mihir Bhuta suggested that the *angavastra* (upper garments) of the male characters should go, to which Aarav Chawdary, [the actor who plays Bhishma] suggested, "Why only the *angavastra*, every male ornament should go as well". So, on the set, during shooting, we decided to disrobe everybody and it ended up being a huge talking point, courting tremendous audience appreciation (2014).

Conclusion

The increase in online and DVD access to various world cinemas (especially Euro-American) and their alternate styles of storytelling among Indian audiences and filmmakers, especially in the experimental and independent Indian cinema spaces, may fuel the notion that Indian on-screen entertainment is abandoning its traditional storytelling roots and dramatic styles. Yet, if viewership is the recognised yardstick of the popularity of a film or television show, 'the *masala* genre of movies consistently topping annual Indian box-office blockbuster charts'

(Vijayakar 2016; Koimoi.com Team 2016), and the nature of shows leading the GEC ratings (Table 6.1) tells a contradictory story. A review of the most successful box-office hits of Hindi cinema in the first decade of the new millennium based on their *rasa*-generating ability also indicates the continuing adherence to the evoking of the *navarasas* as a *masala* formula format.

Image 6.2 In Yet Another Sanskrit Drama Tradition of Beginning a Performance with an Invocation of the Gods, Every Morning, Prayers are Offered to Lord Ganesha before the Commencement of the Day's Shooting on the Sets of *Mahabharat*. Episode Director Mukesh Singh is Seen with Folded Hands, Second from Right. (Photograph: Piyush Roy)

Image 6.3 Creative Director Siddharth Tewary (in the Centre, Sixth from Left), Production Controller Kuntal Shukla (Fifth from Right) and Author-Critic Piyush Roy (Second from Right), on the Sets of *Mahabharat* in Umargam in Gujarat, India with Crew Members. (Photograph: Swastik Productions)

While observing the shooting on the sets of *Mahabharat*, I noticed one of the series' episode directors, Loknath Pandey, asking his actors before the retake of a fight/war sequence, '*aur* energy *lao, aur* emotions *lao*...' ('Bring more energy into your act, show more emotions...') (Pandey 2014). Energy is *utsaha*, emotions are *bhavas*. The names of the terms have changed but the expectation remains the same. According to Shukla, 'This knowledge comes from his memory of good things that he has seen or good dramatic experiences he has enjoyed in the past. This is why, the Indian acting style is different from the West because we still knowingly *or* unknowingly are 100 per cent following the dictates of Bharat *muni*' (Shukla 2014). Filmmaking techniques have evolved, but the ultimate goal of telling a filmed story remains the same; the aim is to achieve a level of emotion and the creation of a feeling, or *rasa*, in the audience, as discussed by creative director Siddharth Tewary or prodded from his actors by episode director Pandey. Both of them had not read the *Natyashastra* at the time. The show's production controller Kuntal Shukla and senior episode director Mukesh Singh, however, had both been students of Sanskrit drama. They credit the high TRP ratings of the *Cheer Haran* sequence to the way it was written, conceptualised and presented to evoke all the *navarasas*. According to Singh, 'This sequence evokes all the *rasas*. Nothing is left. It has *karuna*, it has *adbhuta* (in the way Krishna saves Draupadi), it has *bibhatsa* in the act of a man trying to molest a woman in front of her kin, it has *vira rasa* in the conduct of Draupadi throughout or the oaths for vengeance taken by Bheema and Arjuna in the end...' (Singh 2014). Tewary reviews the impact of the *Cheer Haran* scene, stating, 'In that one *cheer haran* scene there is anger, pathos, sense of wonder...' (Tewary 2014). If one compares the comments of Tewary and Singh, they both talk about similar goals and identical parameters for the success of a scene or a show. Only the terms used are different: the *navarasas* become *masala*, singular terms for emotion like *karuna* and *adbhuta* are exchanged for their English language counterparts of pathos and wonder. This shared knowledge of the expectations from and attributes of a good performance allows different sets of creative people from different generations and schools of filmmaking to be able to work together towards realising the ideal in an entertainment show that also enlightens the audience. Simultaneously, the core, uniting argument of this dissertation, the need for and relevance of a *rasa*-theory-based studying of Indian on-screen performances, direction and allied creative achievements, is once again reaffirmed.

By taking the scope of research and review from cinema to television, this chapter further extends the applicability of *rasa*-based criticism. Finally, this chapter broadens the discussion in the second section of the book on how to use a *rasa* template that applies to plot and character generalisations to dissect and distinguish the often-ignored emotive layers within individual dramatic performances. Most importantly, this chapter moves beyond a theory-based review and evidencing of *rasa* achievements in a finished creation, to explore its conception, modification and evocation on a shooting location as a drama-creating work activity in progress. By using extensive analytical interviews with actors, directors and crewmembers at work, it considers the actual recording and review of the *rasa*-evoking processes in practice, both on location and post-filming in editing studios.

Image 6.4 On the Sets of *Mahabharat*: Sourabh Raaj Jain as Krishna (in the Chariot in the Centre) Gets Ready to Shoot for the War Sequence Against a Green Screen (Photograph: Piyush Roy)

Not every member from the cast and crew on the sets of *Mahabharat* may use Sanskrit drama terms like *bhava* and *rasa*, but they consciously or subconsciously work towards their achievement, as is evident in the analysis of the performances and presentation in the service of a particular *rasa*. This indicates how even on a contemporary Indian drama set populated predominantly by a cast and crew of 20–30 year olds, a two-thousand-year-old concept continues to teach and guide actors. It aids them in maximising the emotion generated by their work, while offering those outside fresh insights into the emotion-evoking strategies of modern Indian content makers. This once again reaffirms the conscious and subconscious flow of *rasa* realisation within Indian art forms and its best artists and works.

Image 6.5 On the Sets of *Mahabharat*: From Left to Right—Actor Shaheer Sheikh Portraying Arjuna; Author and Critic Piyush Roy; Actor Aham Sharma Portraying Karna; Series Creative Director Siddharth Tewary and Actor Sourabh Raaj Jain Portraying Lord Krishna (Photograph: Swastik Productions)

Notes

1 Interview with Chandraprakash Dwivedi in Mumbai on 27 June 2013.

2 The original Sanskrit epic will continue to be referred to as Mahabharata. The 2013–2014 TV adaptation of the epic telecast on Star Plus India will henceforth be referred to as *Mahabharat.*

3 Interview with Chandraprakash Dwivedi in Mumbai on 22 July 2014.

4 Star Plus is a Hindi language general entertainment channel, owned by 21st Century Fox's Star India, which got wholly owned by The Walt Disney Company India from 2019.

5 Three television adaptations of the Mahabharata (between 1997 and 2008), before Tewary's version on Star Plus, had been abandoned midway due to lack of viewership.

6 A show like *Mahabharat* would normally be categorised or reviewed as a melodrama, going by the conventional understanding of 'melodrama' to be a dramatic work that exaggerates plot and characters in order to appeal to the emotions, often with strongly stereotyped characters. Language, behaviour or events which resemble melodramas are also called *melodramatic*. In (Western) scholarly and historical musical contexts, *melodramas* are dramas of the 18th and 19th centuries in which orchestral music or song is used to accompany action.

7 It can alternately be interpreted that the expectation from an ideal drama/cinema in the Indian context (i.e., a sumptuous evocation of myriad *rasas*) is different from the idea of the ideal in the Western/Euro-American context or parameters of film criticism, which celebrates an isolated engagement with fewer or a singular *rasa*.

8 Peter Stephen Paul Brook is an English theatre and film director based in France who had directed a nine-hour-long stage play adaptation of the Mahabharata with an international cast of actors. This was first performed in 1985. This was later abridged and showcased as a six-hour-long TV miniseries and a TV film in 1989.

9 Television Viewership in Thousands (indiantelevision.com: Mahabharat 2013–2014).

10 In any mega-episode-spanning mammoth television serial like the *Mahabharat*, different episode directors are employed on a shooting location or set to simultaneously shoot multiple sequences of a single episode. Different episode directors are also employed to shoot indoor and outdoor sequences. Their individual content is then sent to the editing studio, often a few kilometres away in the nearest city (e.g., Mumbai for the *Mahabharat* TV series, which was shot in Umargam in the neighbouring state of Gujarat) for final editing and re-fashioning into a logically narrated sequence that is then sent to the channel to be telecast. This final making of an episode is overseen by a creative director, like Tewary, who ranks above the episode directors in the hierarchy of television content makers.

11 Rajabali 2004: 183

12 This is a strategic subterfuge planned by Duryodhana's uncle Shakuni for a possible staking of individuals.

13 Mihir Bhuta, a popular writer in Gujarati and Hindi theatre and Hindi film and TV industry, wrote the dialogue of *Mahabharat*. They became a highlight of the TV series for their thought-provoking insights emphasising the contemporary relevance of the epic's eternal struggle stories and moral dilemmas. Since the *Cheer Haran* sequence was aired towards the series'

telecast phase in 2014, the dialogues from those episodes have been cited as (Bhuta 2014). The translations are mine.

14 *Atimaharathi* is a warrior capable of fighting 12 Maharathis (a warrior capable of fighting 60,000 warriors) simultaneously. Rama, Lakshmana, Vali, Ravana, Hanuman, Bhishma, Drona, Ashwatthama, Karna, Arjuna, Balaram, Jarasandha and *devas* like Indra were *atimaharathis* according to the epics.

15 Draupadi is never seen begging for help from anyone, in true consistency with the *virangana* trait/courageous nature of her character. She instead chides Yudhisthira for staking her honour in a game of dice and demands intervention from those valorous courtiers in Dhritarashtra's court known for their righteousness (Bhishma and Drona) or sagacity (Vidur).

16 A ritual contest that frequently occurs in the Mahabharata, where eligible grooms undergo a contest of prowess to win a princess as a bride. It was a common marriage custom among the royalty in ancient India.

17 A *Vedic* ritual of sacrifice

18 The meaning of Yudhisthira's name—one who is constant/calm in a state of war i.e., *yudh-me-sthir*—itself indicates calmness to be his character's dominant trait.

19 'The word "*paatra*" [used for a character] in Sanskrit also means a vessel from which you can drink anything. Drinking salted buttermilk from it, makes the vessel salty to taste. Sweet milk makes it sweet. Use the 'paatra' to drink the juice of fruits or alcohol. As long as it is filled with something, it remains as if it is made to contain only that. The mind of the actor is like an empty vessel. You can fill it with the feelings of any character. After doing a role, as the actor gets off the stage, his mind becomes empty again, like the vessel that is emptied after use' (Mishra 2010: 101–102).

20 Though the character of Yudhisthira is calm and righteousness personified throughout the epic, the game of dice is the only sequence where his actions (like putting his family members at stake) and subsequent non-action and restraining of his brothers from mitigating Draupadi's insult based on a flawed and self-serving interpretation of dharma evoke disgust.

21 'In all the *Cheer Haran* sequences that we have seen on-screen so far, Krishna is always seen smiling while generating those endless saris for Draupadi. But our Krishna is seen and shown to be sad and angry while giving her the sari. Why? Because he is in a human form! If a similar incident happens with your friend will you be smiling while helping her even if you are God? I have always tried to give these little nuances in my interpretation while performing to give that human touch to Krishna' (Jain 2014).

Conclusion

> We need a broader humanist film education. We need to generate a new group of critics and taste makers who can talk about emotion and melodrama freely. People, who are not so schooled in the Western idea of neo-realism, and that's what they are looking for everywhere. They should be able to see the melodrama in its true context and not as a failure... And if they do, then they will get the central idea of masala, of mix, of something that can be both inwards and outward and that you don't have to choose and appreciate the fact that getting both of this at once, better captures the flavour of being alive[1].
>
> Mark Cousins, critic, curator and filmmaker

> Sometimes it's best to leave an actor where he is best accepted. John Wayne never got off his horse in his entire career, nor did Charlton Heston from his chariot. Sean Connery was best known as 007, as was Shah Rukh [Khan] for his romantic adventures[2].
>
> Amitabh Bachchan, Indian cinema legend and superstar

Mythologist Devdutt Pattanaik, in a comment on Indian civilisation's tremendous appetite for assimilation and localised adaptation of foreign influences, says, 'Whatever comes into India, tends to become Indian' (Pattanaik 2014). The Indian experience and interaction of the seventh art, cinema, has been no different. Conceptualised in the West, and coming into India months after its birth, it has, as discussed, grown into a vibrant and robust cultural form with a signature identity of its own. Under the influence of a civilisation whose scriptures have been orally performed for generations, and where thousand-year-old epic tales and their stylised *rasa*-embodying characters are part of daily life, rituals, references, culture, art and festivities, the medium of cinema has been re-imagined and localised, i.e., it has become Indian. Its Indian attributes, however, suffer a crisis in understanding when experienced in a context beyond that of its core or local Indian viewership. The causes of this have been discussed. An alternate fair and informed perspective has been offered as one of the fundamental outcomes of this book.

All national cinemas have cultural specificities typical to the context of their production, and performances across the world play by distinct styles and rules on how best to engage and move an audience. Conventions of actual practice are formulated and passed down from one generation to the other by incorporating what impacts their audience the most. Every actor/filmmaker always starts as a viewer, and the elements and aspects of storytelling that delighted them the most when they were growing up watching and experiencing cinema as an activity enjoyed communally[3], they try to re-create for their audience.

Emotion is one of the most compelling means of impression and communication in any performative mode of expression, evoked either by an individual or as collaborative effort, as in theatre or cinema. It is also the most abused and misunderstood term, because the degrees of expression of an emotion can vary immensely depending on different influences such as culture, context, class and civilisation that shape the worldview of a viewer and a critic alike. The consequence is an easy generalisation for that which is incomprehensible and uncommon or an arrogant dismissal of the other, often as inferior. The bulk of Indian cinema productions have invariably been dismissed in this manner by majority Euro–American reviewers and curators, select Indian intelligentsia and influential film critics writing in the Indian English media, as evidenced through a fair length of the Indian movie industry's century-plus existence. The recognition of mainstream Indian cinema—popularly but erroneously known as Bollywood—in the late 20th century as an influential cinematic style that has been entertaining nearly half of the global movie-going audience has facilitated its ascendance as a subject for critical academic study in the current millennium. The focus so far has primarily been on studying it as a cross-cultural influence on a diverse and growing viewership across the globe. Indian cinema has also been studied as a representation, no doubt an invaluable one, of India's past and present history and (arguably patronisingly) as an exotic cinematic form to be celebrated or experienced for its emotional hybridity. The role of India's drama traditions in shaping the unique attributes of its narratives, the aesthetic unity in their multi-emotion palette and acting achievements in the stylised and stereotypical performances, especially within the *masala* form of storytelling, is an enigmatic subject, barely addressed as yet in a convincing fashion.

This book contributes towards the cultivation of an understanding of that enigma by introducing and engaging with a systematic appreciation process using tools of reference from the well-known dramaturgical conspectus, the *Natyashastra*. The theoretical framework offered is that of Indian aesthetics' seminal, relevant and still influential *rasa* theory. It has been argued that this is a valuable guide for better appreciation of the melodramatic, stylistic and stereotypical tendencies in India's multilingual modes of cinematic storytelling. Western models of film criticism that privilege the realistic form of the cinematic art have been inadequate in comprehending these aspects, and hence they are unable to generate an empathetic review or a fair understanding of the distinguishing characteristics of Indian cinematic genres. This further warrants the need for referring 'to an indigenously generated and tested model or theory of appreciation for an essentially home-grown variant of an international art form' (Balan 2014).

The deployment of the fundamentals of *rasa* theory, *bhava* and *rasa* in the context of cinema has been explained in the body of this work. An evidence-based argument has been constructed concerning the founding influence of the *Natyashastra* on early movie-making practices in cinemas across India. This is because 'one needs to understand what Indian theatre was all about [in terms of the nature of its origin and ideas on the purpose of its existence, its presentation styles and aesthetic guides for review] to understand why our films are the way they are' (Menon 2015). This theoretical enquiry has been a cornerstone of this book. It studies landmark and representative films from Indian cinema's Silent Era—*Raja Harishchandra* and *Kaliya Mardan*—and the early Talkie Era—*Sita Bibaha* and *Lalita*—from two different moviemaking centres in the West (Maharashtra) and the East (Odisha/West Bengal). It critically engages with one of the greatest achievements from the Golden Age of Indian Cinema from its southern language film industries, *Mayabazar*, a landmark and influential Hindi film *Sholay*, a cult/B-movie representative of its East–West fusion experiments from the 1980s and 1990s, *Madam X* and a critically acclaimed popular post-2000 Indian television series, *Mahabharat*. Amongst them, the study sample has covered the span of a hundred years of Indian on-screen entertainment across genres, eras and mediums of consumption (film to television) from all the four major filmmaking regions in India (central/north, west, south and east). Along with identifying hitherto ignored *Natyashastra* prescriptions in early Indian filmmaking, it has been revealed how the evocation of *rasa* was an integral aesthetic aim, defining the purpose of the auteurship of the father of Indian cinema, Dadasaheb Phalke. By using film reviews from India's regional language media, it has been shown how the evocation of *rasa* has been an important aesthetic expectation and concern in early attempts at film criticism. This challenges a comfortable and an often-repeated erroneous academic position that links the origin attributes and styles of all Indian cinema to the Parsi theatre, as an immediate predecessor.

Analytical discussion on how to acknowledge a *rasaeur*, a term coined to describe a director who not only manages to evoke the *navarasas* in his film but is also able to unite its meaning/suggestion under a single dominant *rasa*, is further expanded in the context of the auteurship of Phalke as a *rasaeur* of the *adbhuta*. Using Phalke's notes and articles from pre-independence Indian journals and newspapers discussing the influence of the *Natyashastra* on his work and detailed interviews with a sample of 38 technicians, actors and filmmakers across age, region, industry and significant periods of Indian film history, practical insights from stakeholders within the Indian film craft have been described. Some of the interviewees, including veteran stars and technicians in their 80s and 90s who, following years in retirement, had almost vanished from public memory, have been accessed for the purpose of academic enquiry to get first-person experienced insights into the aesthetic traditions shaping India's pre-independence Talkie Era and the post-independence Golden Age. In their shared perspectives on the need for *rasa* evocation as the desired purpose of all on-screen entertainment, the existence of a common aesthetic tradition for India's diverse language cinemas is reinforced. These findings aim to address the scepticism often expressed concerning the influence and applicability of *rasa* theory by many leading academic experts of Indian cinema[4]. Thereby, it is stressed that there should be greater engagement with the practical creators of an art form and their approach to the processes of production that extends beyond accepted academic interpretations of their creations. The nature of established academic assessment of Indian cinema, especially based on globally accepted norms, can be problematic, misleading and even disparaging to an art form if the standards of acceptance or parameters of review are oblivious or insensitive to the idioms of culture and tradition shaping local creativity. Unfortunately, even the reviews of Indian films in popular national media, especially in the English language, continue to be assessed through the lens of Western film reviews based on Euro-American templates of film criticism.

This book has endeavoured to repudiate the patronising and negative reviews of three of Indian cinema's most misunderstood narrative idioms—the multiple-emotions-evoking *masala* form of narration, the plethora of stylised/stereotypical characterisations and its predilection for expressive performances and melodrama[5]. Detailed analysis of a diversity of common film scenarios (e.g., dance sequences in *Lalita*, a fight scene in *Sholay*, a high drama event in *Mahabharat*, etc.) and character performances using the *bhava* and *rasa* paradigms have been explored. These are used to extend the usage of the aesthetic appreciation templates offered by the *rasa* theory as a guide to ascertain the merits, nature and extent of *rasa* realisation in plot construction, characterisation and performance. This is accomplished in the context of an entire narrative's plot development and a schematic scene by scene breakdown and analysis of the landmark and much-analysed Hindi film *Sholay* through a fresh review perspective. The intricacies and the identification of multiple *rasa* evocations within the smallest narrative unit of a filmed story, i.e., a single sequence, is offered from the *Mahabharat* TV series.

By means of a varied sample of song- and dance-featuring music sequences and dialogue-highlighting drama scenes, this book facilitates identification of the layers of expressed and suggested emotions within song-, dance- and dialogue-driven scenarios and performances. The success of an acted performance in its ability to achieve unity within the four types of equally important aspects of *abhinaya*(s) as suggested by the *Natyashastra*—the *angika* (bodily gestures/physical), *vachika* (speech/verbal), *aharya* (costumes/ornamental) and *sattvika* (emotions/emotional)—is discussed through a diversity of character achievements across genres. The dressing up of characters in costumes that complement their dominant *bhava*/mood states as prescribed by the *Natyashastra* and the use of specific colours in the mise en scène to heighten the *rasa* impact of an on-screen action have been noted in examples from film and television. However, the extent to which the choice of colour can enhance and impact the on-screen emotion can be further explored.

The concepts of *bhava* and *rasa* have been further used in the book to discuss acting achievements within seemingly stylised or stereotypical acts based on their adherence to expected behaviours of the good and the bad or the masculine and the feminine as prescribed by the *Natyashastra*. Such characterisation may make some characters look stereotypical, but through an analysis of three lead performances in *Mayabazar, Madam X* and *Mahabharat*, it is explained how competent actors have been able to make them sharply personalised and contextualised throughout the span of a film. This knowledge and awareness of *bhavas* and *rasas* will help acknowledge and appreciate the layers of expressions portrayed in the multiple-emotion-conveying performance of an Indian actor. This has been done through an analysis of every passing mood/*bhava* state and the corresponding *rasa*-evoking reactions/expressions on a protagonist's visage through a freeze-frame of close-ups.

Appreciation is generated for a well-stylised act, or a successful stereotype, through an elucidation of the processes that lead to its achievement. These have been shown through actor and director interviews to have been achieved through intense training and a studied knowledge of intricate and demanding traditional performance guides. This training has been argued to equip an Indian actor to rise to the challenges of both stylised and realistic acting, as is evident in the filmography of the actors discussed in the book such as Savithri, Sanjeev Kumar, Jaya Bhaduri, Amjad Khan and Rekha. Whether a 'lack in its training makes it difficult for someone schooled only in realistic acting from attempting a convincing stylised interpretation'

(Kher 2015), as argued by acting-guru and actor Anupam Kher, is, however, subject to further investigation and research.

In contrast to the preoccupations of a predominantly rational and realism-oriented idiom of film criticism, a *rasa*-based analysis thus brings the focus of critical attention back to emotion and its various modes of expressive articulation. Simultaneously, the *rasa* theory's acknowledgement of understanding art in the context of the culture—of its creators, their created characters and their behaviour—is a valuable recommended tool for reviewing stereotypical and stylised performances. Stereotype, as highlighted by Amitabh Bachchan, is integral to all genres of filmmaking. These often seem stylised when the on-screen behaviour of characters to universal action triggers tends to differ between national cinemas as a result of their incorporation of region-specific nuances on dressing, talking, gesturing or expressing. These are also shaped by local ideas and expectations on ideal behaviour as per gender, role, position of influence, context of a character and the like, which define the style differentials within stereotypes.

To move audiences by appealing to their ability to feel is arguably more universal and hence more impactful than appealing purely to the intellect, due to an emotive appeal's possibility to *also* impress a range of viewers from varied educational and regional cultural backgrounds. Realism is a debatable prism to judge value, as highlighted by director Siddharth Tewary (2014) and argued by actress Vidya Balan, because 'the reality or the experiences shaping the daily life of a person in India, may not be the same as the reality of someone in the Western world' (Balan 2014). On the contrary, the *navarasas* representing universal human emotions are felt and recognised throughout the human race, albeit to varying degrees. It is perhaps for this reason that Indian cinema has so easily achieved a dominant position in the entertainment culture, not only throughout South Asia but also across the Middle East, North Africa, Russia, Eastern Europe, Central and Southeast Asia.

By arguing for a universally recognised attribute like emotion, whose achievement is measured primarily by a narrative or a performance's ability to convey feeling or evoke a desired emotion in the audience, the *rasa* theory offers a potentially more inclusive model of aesthetic criticism to fill the gap lamented by Mark Cousins in the opening quote. Moreover, emotion as a tool for aesthetic appreciation can also help to look beyond an increasing preference towards reviewing films, especially in popular *Natyadharmi* cinematic genres like Sci-fi, fantasy, adventure, epics, etc., on their technical advancements and quality of presentation that embellish an on-screen narrative's outer package. These are primarily based on the level of advancement in technologies of production, the use of better-quality CGI-generated visuals, ambitious narrative backdrops, increased pace of narration and the like. A review that prioritises performance and emotion and also deals with a story's core can help ascertain an on-screen narration's success in cohesively connecting the above-mentioned elements to felt impact. The methodology offered on how to review, understand and appreciate foundational cinematic attributes such as plot construction, performances and directorial achievement from an exclusively emotional perspective does not, however, exclude the possibility of considering alternative perspectives. How this template can be used to appreciate acting achievements, plot denouement and unity aspects of realistic narratives can be explored through further research.

Philip Lutgendorf, in his path-breaking essay *Is there an Indian Way of Filmmaking* (2007), has viewed the entry of the exhaustive corpus of Indian cinema into global film studies at the beginning of the 21st century as a fit cause for 'systemic realignment... an Einsteinian paradigm-shift introducing new ways of thinking' (Lutgendorf 2007). This book concludes that the inclusion and engagement with *rasa* theory in contemporary film studies is the next logical step towards acknowledging the narrative, dramatic and performative diversity within that corpus. As a tool of film criticism, the *rasa* theory challenges the sacrosanct First-World codes for identifying a good film and allied misplaced notions that impose a putative aesthetic hierarchy on all cinematic genres and styles. It also is an invaluable interpretative model that enables us to appreciate the diversity within an Indian cinematic corpus of more than 50,000 films, to facilitate a more informed decision about the good, the bad and the beautiful within it from the cinematic perspective.

Even in the new and rapidly growing 21st-century content consumption platforms such as OTT (over-the-top) media, in the Indian context, films and film songs (especially on YouTube)—classics and contemporary—continue to be a major source of entertainment, along with cumulative repeat telecasts of popular TV shows like the *Mahabharat* series (streaming on Disney+Hotstar, as of 2021) analysed in Chapter 6. A cursory review of the content and presentation of India's first Netflix original web series, *Sacred Games* (Netflix 2018/2019), reinforces the continuing influence of the *masala* structure and *rasa*-evoking elements like grand dialogues, dramatic acting and multi-genre, popular-star-driven plots with liberal references to Indian epic stereotypes in character motivations and journeys in most web series made in India[6]. The above narrative elements and influences can be evinced in varying degrees in subsequent popular or acclaimed web series across a diversity of OTT platforms, such as *Sacred Games Season 2* (Netflix 2019), *City of Dreams* (Disney+Hotstar 2019), *Aashram* (MX Player 2020), *Asur* (Voot 2020), *Paatal Lok* (2020) and *Tandav* (Amazon Prime Video 2021). However, the predominantly integral presence of lyrical/musical scenes and abundance of dance sequences in similar content of yore is being increasingly exchanged for song-less parallel cinema structures, albeit still consistent with the *Lokadharmi* style as discussed in the *Natyashastra*. This, while assuring the possibility of reviewing existing OTT content too using *bhava*/*rasa* principles, calls for further research using more TV shows and web series samples to bring validation through a greater variety of content across new and emerging platforms from the traditional to the digital.

An awareness of the concepts of *bhavas* and *rasas* in acting and the *rasa* methodology's expository techniques and their possibilities at interpreting a range of acting can be further explored and imitated by people studying other melodramatic or misunderstood world cinemas[7] that celebrate style, stereotype and emotion. It can also help us better appreciate the drama achievements in non-realism-prioritising on-screen genres, namely animation, epic fantasies, costume dramas, musicals, family drama, classic films to contemporary telly melodramas, spectacular OTT achievements and the like. This will establish the foundations for a humanist film education that will enhance our pleasure from the myriad storytelling possibilities to be found within global cinema and television.

Notes

1 Interview with Mark Cousins in Edinburgh on 23 February 2014

2 Cover story interview with Amitabh Bachchan for the July 2011 issue of *Stardust*

3 This is especially relevant in the context of Indian film-viewing habits as echoed by a range of interviewees from its diverse regional cinemas, spanning eight decades of movie-watching memories between them (Begum 2013; Benegal 2015; Ghosh 2014; Menon 2015; Nair 2013).

4 Dwyer and Patel (2002), Rajadhyaksha (2003), Lal and Nandy (2006)

5 In this book, the term 'melodrama' has been used as per its understanding as a Western performance review term. It therefore refers to a dramatic presentation interspersed with songs, dance and music and has sensational portrayals appealing to heightened emotions and a narrative world generally populated by clearly divided good and evil characters. The understanding of 'melodrama' as a review term in the context of an Indian/Sanskrit drama review, however, can be for significantly different performance attributes (or their lacunae) as discussed by TV director Mukesh Singh (2014). But whenever used in this book, the term 'melodrama' stands for its Western/Euro–American connotations.

6 For instance, each episode title of the first season of *Sacred Games* is named after characters or events from the epics (Mahabharata) or the puranas, such as Aswathama, Halahala, Atapi Vatapi, Brahmahatya, Sarama, Petakalpa, Rudra and Yayati.

7 This could include a majority of films from the rest of the Indian subcontinent, Nollywood (Africa), the Middle East and the Third World.

Reference List

Abrams, Nathan, Ian Bell and Jan Udris. 2001. 'Authorship.' In *Studying Film*, 155–173. London: Arnold.

Aggarwal, Mamta. 2015. '15 Famous Saints of the Medieval India.' *HistoryDiscussion.Net*. Accessed 15 March 2016. http://www.historydiscussion.net/religion/15-famous-saints-of-the-medieval-india/714.

Aggarwal, Vidhu. 2010. 'The Anti-Colonial Revolutionary in Contemporary Bollywood Cinema.' *CLCWeb: Comparative Literature and Culture*, 12(2): 1–10.

Anjaria, Ulka and Jonathan Shapiro Anjaria. 2008. 'Text, Genre, Society: Hindi Youth Films and Postcolonial Desire.' *South Asian Popular Culture*, 6(2): 125–140.

Arnold, Alison E. 1991. 'Hindi Film Git: On the History of Commercial Indian Popular Music.' PhD Diss., University of Michigan.

Banker, Ashok. 2001. *Bollywood*. New Delhi: Penguin Books.

Barnow, E and S. Krishnaswamy. 1980. *Indian Film*. Oxford: Oxford University Press.

Basu, Anustup. 2011. 'The Eternal Return and Overcoming "Cape Fear": Science, Sensation, Superman and Hindu Nationalism in Recent Hindi Cinema.' *South Asian History and Culture*, 2(4): 557–571.

Bhansali, Sanjay Leela, dir. 2002. *Devdas*. Eros International, 2003. 2:54. DVD.

Bharata. 1961 (200BC–200AD). *The Nāṭyaśāstra: A Treatise on Hindu Dramaturgy and Histrionics*. Translated by Manomohan Ghosh. Calcutta: The Asiatic Society of Bengal.

———. 1967 (200BC–200AD). *The Nāṭyaśāstra*, vol. 1. Translated by Manomohan Ghosh. Calcutta: Granthalaya.

———. 1987 (200BC–200AD). *The Nāṭyaśāstra*. Translated by a board of scholars. New Delhi: Sri Satguru Publications.

Bhat, Asawari. 2012. 'Glimpses of Natyashastra.' *Hsss.Iitb.ac.in*, 16 March 2012. Accessed 20 March 2012. http://www.hss.iitb.ac.in/courses/HS450/notes2.htm.

Bhatkal, Satyajit, dir. 2001. *Chale Chalo: The Lunacy of Film-Making*. Excel Home Videos, 2007. 02:21. DVD.

Bhatt, G.K. 2004. 'Bharatamuni.' In *Indian Literary Criticism Theory and Interpretation*, edited by G.N. Devy, 5–14. Hyderabad: Orient Longman.

Bhimsingh, A., dir. 1974. *Naya Din Nai Raat*. Universal Home Entertainment, 2010. 02:12. DVD.

Bhugra, D. 2005. 'Mad Tales from Bollywood: The Impact of Social, Political, and Economic Climate on the Portrayal of Mental Illness in Hindi Films.' *Acta Psychiatr Scand*, 112: 250–256.

Bhushan, Nyay. 2008. 'Bollywood Billions: Indian Distribution and Production Change with the Times.' *Film Journal International*. Accessed 1 April 2012. http://www.filmjournal.com/filmjournal/contentdisplay/newsandfeatures/features/movies/e3i72ce5cb5941da1cd05399b795709e311.

———. 2016. 'Hollywood Movies Make Major Gains in India.' *The Hollywood Reporter*, 30 March 2016. http://www.hollywoodreporter.com/news/hollywood-movies-major-gains-india-879282.

Blanchard, Dan. 2007. 'Spiritual Aspects of Hindustani Indian Classical Music.' *Jadedragon.com*. Accessed 15 March 2012. http://www.jadedragon.com/articles/icm.html.

Booth, Gregory D. 1995. 'Traditional Content and Narrative Structure in the Hindi Commercial Cinema.' *Asian Folklore Studies*, 54: 169–190.

———. 2000. 'Religion, Gossip, Narrative Conventions and the Construction of Meaning in Hindi Film Songs.' *Popular Music*, 19(2): 125–145.

———. 2011. 'Preliminary Thoughts on Hindi Popular Music and Film Production: India's "Culture Industry(ies)".' *South Asian Popular Culture*, 9(2): 215–221.

Bowers, Faubion. 1969. *Theatre in the East: A Survey of Asian Dance and Drama*. New York: Grove Press.

Brunch. 2006. '75 Years of Bollywood Talkies.' *Brunch*, 30 April 2006: 4–15.

Brunow, Dagmar. 2010. 'Thank You, Shah Rukh Khan!' In *Reconsidering Audience Studies: The Reception of Bollywood in Germany*, 30 September 2010–02 October 2010. Vienna: University of Vienna.

Caughie, John. 1981. 'Cahiers du Cinéma.' In *Theories of Authorship*, edited by John Caughie, 35–47. London: Routledge.

Chakra, Shyamhari. 2013. 'Odia Cinema at Seventy-Five.' In *Routledge Handbook of Indian Cinemas*, edited by K. Moti Gokulsing and Wimal Dissanayake, 63–71. New York: Routledge.

Chakravarty, Sumita S. 1998. *National Identity in Indian Popular Cinema 1947–1987*. Delhi: Oxford University Press.

Chatterjee, Saibal. 2006. 'Lyrics Today Aren't Poetry, Just Bad Prose.' *Outlook*, 26 June 2006: 62–63.

Chatterjee, Saibal, Gulzar and Govind Nihalani, eds. 2003. *Encyclopaedia of Hindi Cinema*. New Delhi: Encyclopaedia Britannica.

Chaudhuri, Sohini. 2005. *Contemporary World Cinema*. Edinburgh: Edinburgh University Press.

Chaudhury, Pravas Jivan. 1952. 'The Theory of Rasa.' *The Journal of Aesthetics and Art Criticism*, 11(2): 147–150.

———. 1965. 'Indian Poetics.' *The Journal of Aesthetics and Art Criticism*, 24(1) Autumn: 197–204.

Chopra, Anupama. 2000. *Sholay: The Making of a Classic*. New Delhi: Penguin Books.

Cooper, Darius. 2000. *The Cinema of Satyajit Ray*. Cambridge: Cambridge University Press.

Courtney, David. 2012. 'Filmi Sangeet—The Indian Film Song.' *Chandrakantha.com*, 05 February 2012. Accessed 10 March 2012. http://chandrakantha.com/articles/indian_music/filmi.html.

Daiya, Kavita. 2011. 'Visual Culture and Violence: Inventing Intimacy and Citizenship in Recent South Asian Cinema.' *South Asian History and Culture*, 2(4): 589–604.

Damsteegt, Theo, ed. 2003. *Heroes and Heritage: The Protagonist in Indian Literature and Film*. Leiden: Leiden University, Research School CNWS.

Das, Srijana Mitra. 2006. 'Partition and Punjabiyat in Bombay Cinema: The Cinematic Perspectives of Yash Chopra and Others.' *Contemporary South Asia*, 15(4): 453–471.

Das Gupta, Chidananda. 2008. *Seeing Is Believing*. New Delhi: Viking.

De, Sushil Kumar. 1959. *Some Problems of Sanskrit Poetics*. Calcutta (Kolkata): K.L. Mukhopadhyay.

Deo, Surya. 2013. 'Sita Bibaha: Prathama Cinema Prathama Moksha.' *Dharitri*, 2013.

———. 2015. *Odisha Cinema Gita 1936–1969*. Bhubaneswar: Srujan.

Desai, Jigna. 2004. *Beyond Bollywood: The Cultural Politics of South Asian Diasporic Film*. New York: Routledge.

Desai, Jigna and Rajinder Kumar Dudrah. 2008. *Bollywood Reader*. Maidenhead: Open University Press.

Devy, G.N. 2004. *Indian Literary Criticism Theory and Interpretation*. Hyderabad: Orient Longman.

Dhar, Jasobanta Narayan. 2007. 'The Story and History of Odissi Dance and Sri Geeta Govinda.' *Orissa Review*, LXIII(10) May: 43–44.

Dickey, Sara. 1995. 'Consuming Utopia: Film Watching in Tamil Nadu.' In *Consuming Modernity Public Culture in a South Asian World*, edited by Carol A. Breckenridge, 131–156. Minneapolis: University of Minnesota Press.

Dickey, Sara and Rajinder Dudrah. 2010. 'South Asian Cinemas: Widening the Lens.' *South Asian Popular Culture*, 8(3): 207–212.

Dissanayake, Wimal and Malti Sahai. 1998. *Raj Kapoor's Films: Harmony of Discourses*. New Delhi: Vikas Publishing House.

Dubey, Rachana. 2006. 'It's Yesterday Once More.' *Dnaindia.com*, 12 August 2006. Accessed 12 February 2012. http://www.dnaindia.com/entertainment/report_its-yesterday-once-more_1046912.

Dudrah, Rajinder Kumar. 2006. *Bollywood: Sociology Goes to the Movies*. London: Sage.

Dudrah, Rajinder, Elke Mader and Bernhard Fuchs. 2015. *SRK and Global Bollywood*. Oxford: Oxford University Press.

Dwivedi, Chandraprakash. 2012. *Upanishad Ganga*. Shemaroo, 2012. 21:33. DVD.

Dwyer, Rachel. 2000. *All You Want is Money, All You Need is Love: Sex and Romance in Modern India*. London: Cassell.

———. 2002. *Yash Chopra: 50 Years in Indian Cinema*. New Delhi: Lotus Collection.

———. 2005. 100 *Bollywood Films*. New Delhi: Roli Books.

———. 2010. 'Bollywood's India: Hindi Cinema as a Guide to Modern India.' *Asian Affairs*, 41(3): 381–398.

Dwyer, Rachel and Divya Patel. 2002. *Cinema India: The Visual Culture of Hindi Film*. New Jersey: Rutgers University Press.

Dwyer, Rachel and Jerry Pinto. 2011. *Beyond the Boundaries of Bollywood*. New Delhi: Oxford University Press.

Epstein, Jeremy. 2004. 'World Domination by Box Office Cinema Admissions.' *GreenAsh.net*. Accessed 02 April 2012. http://greenash.net.au/thoughts/2011/07/world-domination-by-box-office-cinema-admissions/.

Farrell, Gerry. 1993. 'The Early Days of the Gramophone Industry in India: Historical, Social and Musical Perspectives.' *British Journal of Ethnomusicology*, 2(1): 31–53.

Ganesan, Sivaji. 2007. *Autobiography of An Actor*. Edited by T.S. Narayana and translated by Sabita Radhakrishna. Chennai: Sivaji Prabhu Charities Trust.

Ganguly, Deepa. 2012. 'Rasa: Serenity, Valor, Love.' *UNT Digital Library*. Accessed 10 April 2012. http://digital.library.unt.edu/ark:/67531/metadc3347/.

Garga, B.D. 2012. 'Dadadsaheb Phalke: The Premier Pioneer.' In *Silent Cinema in India: A Pictorial Journey*, edited by B.D. Garga, 42–63. New Delhi: HarperCollins.

Garwood, Ian. 2006. 'The Songless Bollywood Film.' *South Asian Popular Culture*, 4(2): 169–183.

GECs News Headline. 2013. 'Mahabharat.' *indiantelevision.com*, 09 September 2013. Accessed 01 June 2016. http://www.indiantelevision.com/keyword/mahabharat.

Gehlawat, Ajay. 2006. 'The Bollywood Song and Dance, or Making a Culinary Theatre from Dung-Cakes and Dust.' *Quarterly Review of Film and Video*, 23: 331–340.

Gerow, Edwin. 1977. *Indian Poetics*. Wiesbaden: Otto Harrassowitz.

———. 2002. 'Rasa and Katharsis: A Comparative Study, Aided by Several Films.' *Journal of the American Oriental Society*, 122(2): 264–277.

Ganti, Tejaswini. 2004. *Bollywood: A Guidebook to Popular Hindi Cinema*. London: Routledge.

Ghosh, Kartik Kumar. 1985. 'Odia Chalachitra.' In *Golden Jubilee Celebration of Oriya Film Industry Souvenir*. Cuttack: Film Development Corporation of Orissa.

Ghose, Goutam, dir. 2010. *Moner Manush*. Dhoom Video, 2010. 02:26. DVD.

Gnoli, Raniero. 1956. *The Aesthetic Experience According to Abhinavagupta*. Roma: Stampato.

Gokulsing, K. Moti and Wimal Dissanayake. 2004. *Indian Popular Cinema: A Narrative of Cultural Change*. Stoke-on-Trent: Trentham Books.

Gowariker, Ashutosh, dir. 2008. *Jodhaa Akbar*. UTV Home Entertainment, 2008. 03:34. DVD.

Grissom, Harriette D. 2007. 'Feeling as Form in Indian Aesthetics.' *The Free Library*. Accessed 10 April 2013. https://www.thefreelibrary.com/Feeling+as+form+in+Indian+aesthetics.-a0186951066.

Guneratne, Anthony R. 1997. 'Religious Conflict, Popular Culture and the Troubled Spectators of Recent Indian Film.' *Contemporary South Asia*, 6(2): 177–189.

Gupta, Manjul. 2010. *A Study of Abhinavabharati on Bharata's Natyasastra and Avaloka on Dhananjaya's Dasarupaka*. New Delhi: Gyan Publishing House.

Habegger-Conti, Jean. 2010. 'Filming by Tabish Khair.' *Transnational Literature*, 2(2): 1–2.

Hansen, Kathryn. 1991. *Grounds for Play: The Nautanki Theatre of North India*. Los Angeles: University of California Press.

Harris, Jordan Scott. 2008. 'Sholay (India, 1975).' *apetrifiedfountain.blogspot.co.uk*, 23 April 2008. Accessed 14 May 2015. http://apetrifiedfountain.blogspot.co.uk/2008/04/sholay-india-1975.html.

Hiriyanna, M. 1997. *Art Experience*. Mysore: Kavyalaya Publishers.

Hirzer, Petra. 'Fandom beyond Borders and Boundaries: Peru in Love with SRK.' In *SRK And Global Bollywood*, edited by Rajinder Dudrah, Elke Mader and Bernhard Fuchs, 182–199. New Delhi: Oxford University Press.

Hogan, Patrick Colm. 2003. 'Rasa Theory and Dharma Theory: From the Home and the World to Bandit Queen.' *Quarterly Review of Film and Video*, 20: 37–51.

———. 2008. *Understanding Indian Movies: Culture, Cognition, and Cinematic Imagination*. Texas: University of Texas Press.

———. 2009. 'Hindi Cinema as a Challenge to Film Theory and Criticism.' *Projections*, 3(2): v–ix.

Hood, John W. 2000. *The Essential Mystery: Major Filmmakers of Indian Art Cinema*. London: Sangam Books.

IMDb. 1990. 'User Reviews: Reviews & Ratings for Sholay.' *Imdb.com*. Accessed 15 May 2016. http://www.imdb.com/title/tt0073707/ratings.

IMDb. 2007–2016. 'Ram Gopal Varma Ki Aag: User Reviews.' *imdb.com*. Accessed 23 April 2016. http://www.imdb.com/title/tt0473310/reviews?ref_=tt_urv.

IndiaNetzone. 2011. 'Kalicharan Pattnaik.' *indianetzone.com*, 17 November 2011. Accessed 17 November 2015. http://www.indianetzone.com/51/kalicharan_pattnaik.htm

Iordanova, Dina, Juan Goytisolo, K. Gàjendra Singh, Rada [Sbreve]e[sbreve]ić, Asuman Suner, Viola Shafik and P. A. Skantze. 2006. 'Indian Cinema's Global Reach: Historiography Through Testimonies.' *South Asian Popular Culture*, 4(2): 113–140.

Jadhav, Ravindra Harishchandra, dir. 2011. *Balgandharva*. Fountain Music, 2011. 02:04. DVD.

Jain, P.C. and Dr Daljeet. 2005. 'Delight of Senses: The Indian Way of Seeing It.' *Exotic India*, October. Accessed 22 February 2012. http://www.exoticindiaart.com/article/rasa/.

Jain, Rajeev Kumar, Tanu Rai and Indrani Bose. 2013. *60th National Film Awards 2012: The Official Catalogue*. New Delhi: Directorate of Film Festivals, Government of India.

Jha, Lata. 2015. 'Sholay 40 Years On: Remembering Minerva Theatre.' *Mint*, 13 August 2015. Accessed 22 April 2016. http://www.livemint.com/Consumer/hRPf7h8ebJyNXrwJQ5q2dM/Sholay-40-years-on-Remembering-Minerva.html.

Jha, Subhash K. 2005. *The Essential Guide to Bollywood*. New Delhi: Roli Books.

———. 2014. 'Sholay 3D Review: Dhoom 3 Pales in Comparison to

Ramesh Sippy's Classic.' *Firstpost*, 07 January 2014. Accessed 07 May 2015. http://www.firstpost.com/bollywood/sholay-3d-review-dhoom-3-pales-incomparison-to-ramesh-sippys-classic-1325955.html.

Jones, Matthew. 2009. 'Bollywood, Rasa and Indian Cinema: Misconceptions, Meanings and Millionaire.' *Visual Anthropology*, 23(1): 33–43.

Joshi, Namrata. 2006. 'Hum Se Cinema.' *Outlook*, 26 June 2006: 66–69.

Joshi, Sam. 2004. 'How to Watch a Hindi Film: The Example of Kuch Kuch Hota Hai.' *Education About Asia*, 9(1): 22–25.

Kabir, Ananya Jahanara. 2010. 'The Kashmiri as Muslim in Bollywood's "New Kashmir films".' *Contemporary South Asia*, 18(4): 373–385.

Kabir, Nasreen Munni. 1999. *Talking Films: Conversations with Javed Akhtar*. New Delhi: Oxford University Press.

———. 2001. *Bollywood: The Indian Cinema Story*. London: Channel 4 Books.

———. 2006. 'Play That Back.' *Outlook*, 26 June 2006: 70–71.

———. 2013. 'Milestone 100.' *Time Out Mumbai*, 9(18). 26 April–09 May. Mumbai: Paprika Media.

Kamal, dir. 2013. *Celluloid*. Horizon Audio & Video, 2013. 02:09. DVD.

Kane, P.V. 1994. *History of Sanskrit Poetics*. New Delhi: Motilal Banarsidass.

Kapoor, Kapil. 2006. 'Abhinavagupta on Bharata's Theory of Rasa.' In *Abhinvagupta: Reconsiderations*, edited by Makarand Paranjpe and Sunthar Visuvalingam, 144–183. New Delhi: Samvad India Foundation.

Katz, Ruth and Arvind Sharma. 1977. 'The Aesthetics of Abhinavagupta.' *British Journal of Aesthetics*, 17(3): 259–265.

Kaur, Raminder and William Mazzarella, eds. 2009. *Censorship in South Asia: Cultural Regulation from Sedition to Seduction*. Bloomington: Indian University Press.

Kaur, Ravindra. 2002. 'Viewing the West through Bollywood: A Celluloid Occident in the Making.' *Contemporary South Asia*, 11(2): 199–209.

Kesari. 1913. 'Mr. Phalke's Moving Pictures. Newsletter from Bombay.' *Kesari*, 06 May 1913.

———. 1913. 'Interview with Phalke.' *Kesari*, 19 August 1913.

Kesavan, Mukul. 2012. 'Attitude Bollytude.' *Outlook*, 04 June 2012: 12–16.

Khokar, Ashish Mohan. 2010. 'The Dance History Column.' *narthaki.com*, 30 July 2010. Accessed 16 November 2015. http://www.narthaki.com/info/tdhc/tdhc20.html.

Khosla, Raj, dir. 1971. *Mera Gaon Mera Desh*. Shemaroo, 2013. 02:28. DVD.

Koimoi.com Team. 2016. 'Bollywood's Top Worldwide Grossers.' *Koimoi.com*, 03 March 2016. Accessed 08 April 2016. http://www.koimoi.com/box-office/bollywoods-top-worldwide-grossers/.

Krishna.com. 2002. 'About Krishna.' Accessed 22 March 2016. http://www.krishna.com/about-krishna.

Krishnamoorthy K. 1974. *Anandavardhana's Dhvanyaloka: Critical edition with Introduction, English Translation & Notes*. Dharwar: Karnataka University.

———. 1974. *Essays in Sanskrit Criticism*, 2nd ed. Dharwar: Karnatak University.

———. 1988. *Abhinavagupta Dhvanyāloka-locana*. New Delhi: Meharchand Lachhmandas Pulications.

Kumar, Ranjit Keval. 2011. 'Crossovers and Makeovers: Contested Authenticity in New Indian Cinema.' PhD Diss., University of Wollongong. Accessed 05 April 2012. http://ro.uow.edu.au/theses/3417.

Kumar, Shikha. 2012. 'Hum Hai Maut Ki Woh Express, Duniya Jise Kehte Hai Madam X.' *dnaindia.com*, 14 October 2012. Accessed 14 March 2016. http://www.dnaindia.com/entertainment/report-hum-hai-maut-ki-woh-express-duniya-jise-kehte-hai-madam-x-1752198.

Lal, Vinay and Ashis Nandy, eds. 2006. *Fingerprinting Popular Culture: The Mythic and the Iconic in Indian Cinema*. New Delhi: Oxford University Press.

Lal, Vinay. 1992. 'Indian Poetics and Western Literary Criticism.' *Indian Literature*, 147: 101–107.

Lancaster, Clay. 1957. 'Reviewed Work(s): The Aesthetic Experience According to Abhinavagupta by Raniero Gnoli.' *Artibus Asiae*, 20(2/3): 220–222.

Lele, Jayant. 1980. 'The Bhakti Movement in India: A Critical Introduction.' *Journal of Asian and African Studies*, 15:1–15.

Leone, Sergio, dir. 1965. *For a Few Dollars More*. Produzioni Europee Associati, 2005. 02:12. DVD.

———. 1968. *Once Upon a Time in the West*. Paramount Home Entertainment, 1969. 02:46. DVD.

Lutgendorf, Philip. 2007. 'Is There an Indian Way of Filmmaking?' *International Journal of Hindu Studies*, 10: 227–256.

Tewary, Siddharth, dir. 2013. *Mahabharat*. Swastik Productions, 2013–2014. Star Plus.

Malhotra, Sheena and Tavishi Alagh. 2004. 'Dreaming the Nation: Domestic Dramas in Hindi Films Post-1990.' *South Asian Popular Culture*, 2(1):19–37.

Manto, Saadat Hasan. 2010. *Stars from Another Sky: The Bombay Film World in the 1940s*. New Delhi: Penguin India.

Marchand, Peter. 2006. *The Yoga of the Nine Emotions*. Vermont: Destiny Books.

Martin-Jones, David. 2006. 'Kabhi India Kabhie Scotland.' *South Asian Popular Culture*, 4(1): 49–60.

Maruthur, Navaneetha Mokkil. 2011. 'Re-viewing Her Nights: Modes of Excess in Indian Cinema.' *South Asian Popular Culture*, 9(3): 273–285.

Masand, Rajeev. 2014. 'Salim-Javed on Sholay.' *YouTube.com*, 13 January 2014. Accessed 15 January 2015. https://www.youtube.com/watch?v=0nL_otl0Jho.

Mason, David. 2006. 'Rasa, "Rasaesthetics" and Dramatic Theory as Performance Packaging.' *Theatre Research International*, 31(1): 69–83.

Masson, J.L. and MV Patwardhan. 1970. *Aesthetic Rapture: The Rasadhyaya of the Nāṭyaśāstra*. Poona: DCRI.

Massey, Reginald. 1992. 'From Bharata to the Cinema: A Study in Unity and Continuity.' *ARIEL: A Review of International English Literature*, 23(1): 59–71.

Mazumdar, Ranjani. 2003. 'The Bombay Film Poster.' *Film International*, 4: 13–18.

McCarthy, Niall. 2014. 'Bollywood: India's Film Industry by The Numbers [Infographic].' *Forbes.com*, 03 September 2014. Accessed 26 January 2015. http://www.forbes.com/sites/niallmccarthy/2014/09/03/ bollywood-indias-film-industry-by-the-numbers-infographic/#27ded3cf7bf0.

McDougall, William. 1948. *An Introduction to Social Psychology*, 29th ed. London: Methuen.

Mehta, Parvinder. 2011. 'Predicaments of History and Mimetic Agency: Postcolonial Return, Repetition and Remediation in Rang De Basanti.' *South Asian Popular Culture*, 9(3): 299–311.

Mehta, Vijaya. 1995. 'The Indian Performer.' In *Rasa: The Indian Performing Arts in the Last Twenty-five Years*, edited by Ananda Lal and Chidananda Dasgupta, 35–38. Calcutta: Anamika Kala Sangam Research and Publications.

Memsaab. 2009. 'Made of Awesome: Filmindia and Baburao Patel.' *WordPress.com*. Accessed 30 March 2012. http://memsaabstory.wordpress.com/2009/06/16/made-of-awesome-filmindia-and-baburao-patel/.

Miller, Barbara Stoler. 1977. *Love Song of the Dark Lord: Jayadeva's Gitagovinda*. New York: Columbia University Press.

Minai, Cassidy. 2013. 'Odissi Dance in Odia Films: Including a Rare Dance in Lalita (1949)!' *cinemanrityagharana.co.uk*, 28 November 2013. Accessed 15 November 2015. http://cinemanrityagharana.blogspot.co.uk/2013/11/odissi-dance-in-odia-films-including.html.

Mishra, Braj Vallabh. 2010. 'Bharat Muni's Natya Shastra: Vast and Subtle in Bharat Muni's Edifice of Acting.' In *Acting in Everyday Life*, edited by Kishore Namit Kapoor. Mumbai: Colour's Touch.

Mishra, Vijay. 2002. *Bollywood Cinema: Temples of Desire*. London: Routledge.

———. 2009. 'Spectres of Sentimentality: The Bollywood Film.' *Textual Practice*, 23(3): 439–462.

Mitra, Chandan. 2006. 'It's Bombay, My Jaan.' *Outlook*, 26 June 2006: 56–60.

Mokashi, Paresh, dir. 2009. *Harishchandrachi Factory*. UTV Motion Pictures, 2009. 01:36. DVD

Moorthy, Rani. 2011. 'Acting Out the Laws of Man(u), and My Part in Their Downfall.' *South Asian Popular Culture*, 9(1): 7–14.

Morcom, Anna. 2001. 'An Understanding Between Bollywood and Hollywood? The Meaning of Hollywood Style Music in Hindi Films.' *British Journal of Ethnomusicology*, 10(1): 63–84.

Morcom, Anna. 2007. *Hindi Film Songs and the Cinema*. Hampshire: Ashgate Publishing.

Mukherjee, Sujit. 1999. *A Dictionary of Indian Literature: Beginnings*, vol. 1. Hyderabad: Orient Longman.

News 18. 2013. 'Mayabazar' is India's Greatest Film Ever: IBNLive Poll.' *Ibnlive.in.com*, 12 May 2013. Accessed 08 August 2013. https://www.news18.com/news/india/mayabazar-is-indias-greatest-film-ever-ibnlive-poll-608772.html.

Nagarajan, A.P, dir. 1964. *Navarathri*. Moserbaer, 2008. 02:41. DVD.

Naficy, Hamid. 1994. 'Veiled Vision/Powerful Presences: Women in Post-Revolutionary Iran.' In *In the Eye of the Storm: Women in Post-Revolutionary Iran*, edited by Mahnaz Afkhami and Erika Friedl, 131–150. New York: Syracuse University Press.

Nair, P.K. 2011. 'Phalke Factory: In the Age of Silence.' *phalkefactory.net*, 25 December 2011. Accessed 13 July 2013. http://wiki.phalkefactory.net/index.php?title=IN_THE_AGE_OF_SILENCE/.

Narasimham, M.L. 2015. 'Blast from the Past: Mayabazar (1957).' *The Hindu*, 30 April 2015. Accessed 30 May 2016. https://www.thehindu.com/features/friday-review/mayabazar-1957/article7159111.ece.

Narasimhiengar, M.T. 1908. 'The Vyakti-Viveka of Mahima-Bhatta.' *Journal of the Royal Asiatic Society of Great Britain and Ireland*, January: 63–71.

NDS Studio. 2009. 'History of Bollywood.' *Bollywoodtourism.com*. Accessed 10 March 2012. http://www.bollywoodtourism.com/bollywood-history.

National Film Archive of India. 1989. 'Silent Films 1913–1934.' 75th Glorious Year of Indian Cinema.

Nowell-Smith, Geoffrey. 1967. *Visconti*. London: Secker & Warburg.

Ojha, Rajendra. 1988. *Screen World Publication's 75 Glorious Years of Indian Cinema: Complete Filmography of All Films (Silent & Hindi) Produced Between 1913–1988*. Bombay: Screen World Publication.

Pandey, K.C. 1959. *Comparative Aesthetics Vol. 1: Indian Aesthetics*. Varanasi: Chowkhamba Sanskrit Series Office.

Patankar, R.B. 1980. 'Does the "Rasa" Theory Have Any Modern Relevance?' *Philosophy East and West*, 30(3): 293–303.

Patnaik, Kalicharan, dir. 1949. *Lalita*. Great Eastern Movietone Ltd. Personal Archive, 01:22.

Pattanaik, Devdutt. 'When Audience Was a Customer.' *Mid-Day*, 30 August 2015–10 September 2015. http://devdutt.com/articles/applied-mythology/society/when-audience-was-customer.html.

Pendakur, Manjunath. 2003. *Indian Popular Cinema: Industry, Ideology and Consciousness*. Cresskill, N.J.: Hampton Press.

Phalke, Dadasaheb. 1917. 'Indian Cinema: I.' *Navyug*, Bombay: November 1917.

———. 1917. 'Indian Cinema: II.' *Navyug*, Bombay: December 1917.

———. 1918. 'Indian Cinema: III.' *Navyug*, Bombay: February 1918.

———. 1918. 'Indian Cinema: IV.' *Navyug*, Bombay: September 1918.

Phalke, Dadasaheb, dir. 1913. *Raja Harishchandra*. National Film Archive of India, 2012. 00:40. DVD.

———. 1919. *Kaliya Mardan*. National Film Archive of India, 2012. 00:47. DVD.

Phalke Summanwar, Sharayu. 2012. *The Silent Film*. Pune: Indian Connect.

Prabhupāda, Swami. 2014. 'Chapter 3: Karma-Yoga.' In *The Bhaktivedanta Book Trust International, Inc*. vedabase.net, 10 February 2014. Accessed 15 March 2015. http://vedabase.net/bg/3/19/.

Prasad, Madhava M. 1998. *Ideology of the Hindi Film: A Historical Construction*. New Delhi: Oxford University Press.

———. 2001. 'Melodramatic Polities?' *Inter-Asia Cultural Studies*, 2(3): 459–466.

———. 2003. 'This Thing Called Bollywood.' *Presented at Unsettling Cinema: A Symposium on the Place of Cinema in India*, May 2003. Accessed 20 March 2012. http://www.india-seminar.com/2003/525/525%20madhava%20prasad.htm.

Punathambekar, Aswin. 2008. 'We're Online, Not on the Streets: Indian Cinema, New Media and Participatory Culture.' In *Global Bollywood*, edited by Anandan P. Kavoori and Aswin Punathambekar, 282–299. New York: New York University Press.

Puri, Om. 2006. 'No Songs and Dance About It.' *Brunch*, 30 April 2006: 14.

Raghavan, V. 1940. *The Number of Rasas*. Adyar: Vasanta Press.

Raghavendra, M.K. 2006. 'Structure and Form in Indian Popular Film Narrative.' In *Fingerprinting Popular Culture: The Mythic and the Iconic in Indian Cinema*, edited by Vinay Lal and Ashis Nandy, 24–50. New Delhi: Oxford University Press.

Raheja, Dinesh and Jitendra Kothari. 1996. *The Hundred Luminaries of Hindi Cinema*. Delhi: India Book House Publishers.

———. 2004. *Indian Cinema: The Bollywood Saga*. London: Aurum Press.

Rajabali, Anjum. 2003. 'The Unimportance of Scriptwriting.' In *Encyclopaedia of Hindi Cinema*, edited by Saibal Chatterjee, Gulzar and Govind Nihalani, 309–324. New Delhi: Encyclopaedia Britannica.

Rajadhyaksha, Ashish. 1997. 'Indian Cinema: Origins to Independence.' In *The Oxford History of World Cinema*, edited by Geoffrey Nowell-Smith, 398–408. Oxford: Oxford University Press.

———. 1997. 'India: Filming the Nation.' In *The Oxford History of World Cinema*, edited by Geoffrey Nowell-Smith, 678–689. Oxford: Oxford University Press.

———. 2003. 'The "Bollywoodization" of the Indian Cinema: Cultural Nationalism in a Global Arena.' *Inter-Asia Cultural Studies*, 4(1): 25–39.

Rajadhyaksha, Ashish and Paul Willemen. 1999. *Encyclopaedia of Indian Cinema*. London: British Film Institute; New Delhi: Oxford University Press.

Ram, Kalpana. 2011. 'Being "Rasikas": The Affective Pleasures of Music and Dance Spectatorship and Nationhood in Indian Middle-Class Modernity.' *Journal of the Royal Anthropological Institute*, (N.S.): 159–175.

Rama Rao, Tatineni. 1966. *Navaratri*. Prasad Art Productions. 02:45. *YouTube.com*, 03 December 2016. Accessed 25 December 2016. https://www.youtube.com/watch?v=6Gbvtff3YM4.

Ramanujan, A.K. 1999. 'Three Hundred Ramayanas: Five Examples and Three Thoughts on Translation.' In *The Collected Essays of A.K. Ramanujan*, edited by Vinay Dharwadker, 131–160. Delhi: Oxford University Press.

Rangacharya, Adya. 1966. *Introduction to Bharata's Nāṭyaśāstra*. New Delhi: Munshiram Manoharlal Publishers.

———. 2010. *The Natyasastra: English Translation with Critical Notes*. New Delhi: Munshiram Manoharlal Publishers.

Rangoonwalla, Firoze. 1979. *A Pictorial History of Indian Cinema*. England-Hong Kong: Hamlyn.

Rangoonwalla, Feroze and Vishwanath Das. 1970. *Indian Filmography: Silent and Hindi Films (1897–1969)*. Bombay: J. Udeshi.

Rangoonwalla, Firoze, ed. 1970. *Phalke Commemoration Souvenir*. Bombay: The Phalke Centenary Celebrations Committee.

Rangoonwalla, Firoze, ed. 1970. 'Phalke's Evidence Before the Indian Cinematograph Enquiry Committee of 1927–1928.' In *Phalke Commemoration Souvenir*, 72–77. Bombay: The Phalke Centenary Celebrations Committee.

Rao, Venkat. 2014. *Cultures of Memory in South Asia: Orality, Literacy and the Problem of Inheritance*. New Delhi: Springer.

Rawson, Philip. 1967. 'An Exalted Theory of Ornament: A Study in Indian Aesthetics.' *The British Journal of Aesthetics*, 7(1): 31–40. https://doi.org/10.1093/bjaesthetics/7.1.31.

Ray, Satyajit. 1976. *Our Films, Their Films*. Kolkata: Orient Longman.

Rayan, Krishna. 1965. 'Rasa and the Objective Correlative.' *British Journal of Aesthetics*, 5(3): 246–260.

Reddy, K.V, dir. 1957. *Mayabazar*. Universal Home Entertainment, 2010. 03:04. DVD.

Roy, Amit. 2015. 'Unifier Who Cried Often.' *The Telegraph*, 20 October 2015. Accessed 21 November 2015. http://www.telegraphindia.com/1151020/jsp/nation/story_49016.jsp#.VxSxn_l96hc.

Roy, Piyush. 2010. 'Pseudos or Shams? The Truth About the Arts Brigade.' *Stardust*, May 2010: 31–40.

———. 2012. 'Our Films, Their Critics.' *Orissa Post*, 12 February–18 February: 8.

Roy, Piyush. 2013. 'Narratives of Disgust.' *Deep Focus Cinema*, 1(3): 30–39.

———. 2014. 'A Story About Song and Dance.' *Orissa Post*, 22 June–28 June: 7.

———. 2014. 'Our Mahabharat Has Upped the Benchmark for TV Content in India.' *southasianistblog.com*, 13 August 2014. Accessed 14 March 2015. https://southasianistblog.com/2014/08/13/our-mahabharat-has-uppedthe-benchmark-for-tv-content-in-india/.

———. 2015. 'Gaps & Silences in Indian Film Criticism.' *Orissa Post*, 05 April–11 April: 11.

———. 2016. 'Sholay's Abiding Aesthetic Appeal.' *Orissa Post*, 07 February–13 February: 5.

Rushdie, Salman. 1996. *The Moor's Last Sigh*. London: Vintage.

Sabharwal, Jyoti and Vyjayantimala Bali. 2007. *Bonding: A Memoir*. New Delhi: Stellar Publishers.

Sankaran, A. 1929. *Some Aspects of Literary Criticism in Sanskrit or The Theories of Rasa and Dhvani*. Mylapore: University of Madras.

Sarma, N.N. 1994. *Panditaraja Jagannatha: The Renowned Sanskrit Poet of Medieval India*. New Delhi: Mittal Publications.

Sarrazin, Natalie. 2008. 'Celluloid Love Songs: Musical Modus Operandi and the Dramatic Aesthetics of Romantic Hindi Film.' *Popular Music*, 27(3): 393–411.

Sarris, Andrew. 2010. 'Director Categories from The American Cinema: Directors and Directions 1929–1968.' *theyshootpictures.com*, 02 August 2010. Accessed 25 March 2012. http://www.theyshootpictures.com/sarriscategories.htm

Sarris, Andrew. 1968. *The American Cinema: Directors and Directions 1929–1968*. New York: Dutton.

Schechner, Richard. 2001. 'Rasaesthetics.' *The Drama Review*, 45(3): 27–50.

Schwartz, Susan L. 2004. *Rasa: Performing the Divine in India*. New York: Columbia University Press.

Screen Writers. 2009. 'Then and Now.' *ScreenIndia.com*, September 2009. Accessed 02 February 2012. http://www.screenindia.com/news/then-and-now/522755/.

Sharad150. 2007. 'Blasphemy!' imdb.com, 01 September 2007. Accessed 10 April 2015. http://www.imdb.com/user/ur15828330/.

Sharad Rajgopal, Shoba. 2011. 'Bollywood and Neonationalism: The Emergence of Nativism as the Norm in Indian Conventional Cinema.' *South Asian Popular Culture*, 9(3): 237–246.

Share Pics Hub. 2015. 'Lord Radha Krishna Beautiful Painting. Shree Radha Krishna Lovely Images." Accessed June 30, 2016. http://sharepicshub.blogspot.co.uk/2013/03/lord-radha-krishna-beautiful-painting.html.

Sharma, Abhas. 2012. 'Those Were the Movies.' business-standard.com, 26 May 2012. Accessed 01 November 2013. http://www.business-standard.com/article/beyond-business/those-were-the-movies-112052600042_1.html.

Sharma, Abhishek, dir. 2014. *The Shaukeens*. Shemaroo, 2014. 02:04. DVD.

Sharma, Mukunda Madhava. 1968. The Dhvani Theory in Sanskrit Poetics. Varanasi: Chowkhamba Sanskrit Series Office.

Sharma, Seshendra. 2002. 'Poetics, East and West.' sffworld.com, 10 March 2012. Accessed 05 October 2013. http://www.sffworld.com/authors/s/sharma_seshendra/articles/poeticseast4.html.

Shivadasani, Deepak, dir. 1994. *Madam X*. Nishita Productions. 01:59.

Shresthova, Sangita. 2003. 'Strictly Bollywood? Story. Camera, and Movement in Hindi Film Dance.' Graduate Diss., Massachusetts Institute of Technology.

Shrivastav, Shabdita. 2012. 'No Actor is Bigger than Their Role or a Script.' *NG.com*, 17 March 2012. Accessed 02 April 2012. http://www.naachgaana.com/2012/03/19/no-actor-is-bigger-than-their-role-or-a-script/.

Singh, Bhim. 2008. *Odia Chalachitra ra Agyanata Adhayay*. Cuttack: Seetaleswari Prakashani.

Singh, Bhrigupati. 2003. 'WHAT Sort of an Object is Cinema in India?' Presented at Unsettling Cinema: A Symposium on the Place of Cinema in India, May 2003. Accessed 20 March 2012. http://www.india-seminar.com/2003/525/525%20the%20problem.htm.

Sippy, Ramesh, dir. 1975. Sholay. Eros Entertainment, 2007. 03:24. DVD.

Skillman, Teri. 1986. 'The Bombay Hindi Film Song Genre: A Historical Survey.' *Yearbook for Traditional Music*, 18: 133–144.

Sreekantaiyya, T.N. 2001. *Indian Poetics*. Translated by N. Balasubrahmanya. New Delhi: Sahitya Akademi.

Srinivas, Lakshmi. 2005. 'Imaging the Audience.' *South Asian Popular Culture*, 3(2): 101–116.

Srinivas, S.V. 2010. 'Breaking the Rajini Myth.' *Open*, 02 October 2010. Accessed 03 April 2012. http://www.openthemagazine.com/article/cinema/breaking-the-rajini-myth.

Stadtler, Florian. 2005. 'Cultural Connections: Lagaan and its Audience Responses.' *Third World Quarterly*, 26(3): 517–524.

Subrahmanyam, Padma, dir. 2010. *Bharatiya Natyashastra: A Study of the Ancient Treatise on Dramaturgy*. Prasar Bharati, 06:02. DVD.

Subrahmanyam, Padma, Sudharani Raghupathy and S. Sarada Bharatanjali. 2010. *Bharatiya Natyashastra, Natyopasana: Secrets of Shastras Revealed by Gurus*. New Delhi: Doordarshan Archives.

Subramani, Anurag. 2013. 'Sholay From Chaos to Super-Duper Event (in Glorious 70 mm … with Stereophonic Sound).' *The Event, the Subject and the Artwork*, 16 (Spring). Accessed 02 October 2015. https://www.doubledialogues.com/article/sholay-from-chaos-to-super-duper-event-in-glorious-70-mm-with-stereophonic-sound/.

Sunil, Princy. 2005. 'Rasa in Sanskrit Drama.' *The Indian Review of World Literature*, 1(1). Accessed June 10, 2009. http://worldlitonline.net/july-05/Contents.htm.

Thomas, Rosie. 1995. 'Melodrama and the Negotiation of Morality in Mainstream Hindi Film.' In *Consuming Modernity Public Culture in a South Asian World*, edited by Carol A. Breckenridge, 157–182. Minneapolis: University of Minnesota Press.

———. 2008. 'Indian Cinema: Pleasures and Popularity.' In *The Bollywood Reader*, edited by Rajinder Kumar Dudrah and Jigna Desai, 21–31. New York: Open University Press.

Tieken, Herman. 2000. 'On the Use of Rasa in Studies of Sanskrit Drama.' *Indo-Iranian Journal*, 43: 115–138.

Vajdovich, Gyorgyi. 2010. 'Shah Rukh Khan's Pioneer Role in Introducing New Production, Distribution and Marketing Techniques in Globalised Bollywood.' Presented at International Conference on Shah Rukh Khan and Global Bollywood, University of Vienna, Vienna, 30 September–02 October.

Varde, Ashwin, ed. 2000. *The 100 Greatest Films*. Mumbai: Magna Graphics.

Vasudevan, Ravi. 2000. *Making Meaning in Indian Cinema*. New Delhi: Oxford University Press.

———. 2011. 'The Meanings of Bollywood.' In *Beyond the Boundaries of Bollywood*, edited by Rachel Dwyer and Jerry Pinto, 3–29. New Delhi: Oxford University Press.

Vatsyayan, Kapila. 2007. *Bharata The Nāṭyaśāstra*. New Delhi: Sahitya Akademi.

Verma, Meenakshi and Sobia Khan. 2011. 'Hollywood Studios Fox Star, Viacom18, Walt Disney Keen to Produce Films in Regional Languages in India.' ET Bureau, 31 August 2011. Accessed 01 March 2012. http://articles.economictimes.indiatimes.com/2011-08-31/news/29949374_1_regional-language-bhojpuri-ravi-kishan.

Vijayakar, Rajiv. 2016. 'Sultan: The Classic Hindi Film Returns.' *Bollywood Hungama*, 16 July 2016. Accessed 17 July 2016. http://www.bollywoodhungama.com/movies /features/type/view/id/10952.

Virdi, Jyotika. 2003. *The Cinematic ImagiNation: Indian Popular Films as Social History*. New Brunswick, N.J.: Rutgers University Press.

Wright, Neelam Sidhar. 2015. *Bollywood and Postmodernism*. Edinburgh: Edinburgh University Press.

Yadav, Anubha. 2001. 'An Evolving Present within a Past: A History of Screenwriting Practices in Popular Hindi Cinema.' *Journal of Screenwriting*, 2(1): 41–59.

Yale University. 2012. 'Shah Rukh Khan at Yale University as Chubb Fellow (official video).' *YouTube.com*, 15 April 2012. Accessed 15 March 2016. https://www.youtube.com/watch?v=q0OaOnT8res.

Zankar, Anil. 2003. 'Heroes and Villains: Good Versus Evil.' In *Encyclopaedia of Hindi Cinema*, edited by Chatterjee Saibal, Gulzar and Govind Nihalani, 355–366. New Delhi: Encyclopaedia Britannica.

List of Interviews

Alter, Tom. Personal interview (in English). 24 August 2013.

Bachchan, Amitabh. Personal interview (in English). 6 July 2011.

Balan, Vidya. Personal interview (in English). 11 June 2014.

Begum, Shamshad. Personal interview (in Hindi/Urdu). 9 September 2013.

Benegal, Shyam. Personal interview (in English). 15 July 2015.

Cousins, Mark. Personal interview (in English). 23 February 2014.

Deo, Surya. Personal interview (in English). 7 July 2014.

Dwivedi, Chandraprakash. Personal interview (in Hindi/English). 27 June 2013.

Dwyer, Rachel. Personal interview (in English). 19 January 2014.

Ghosh, Gopal. Personal interview (in Odia). 6 July 2014.

Gokhale, Vikram. Personal interview (in English). 1 May 2013.

Gordon, Anu. Personal interview (in English). 21 April 2014.

Gurjar, Saurabh. Personal interview (in Hindi/English). 26 July 2014.

Jain, Sourabh Raaj. Personal interview (in Hindi/English). 25 July 2014.

John, Ali Peter. Personal interview (in Hindi/English). 9 September 2014.

Kamal. Personal interview (in English). 4 May 2013.

Kapoor, Kishore Namit. Personal interview (in Hindi/English). 17 May 2013.

Khan, Salim. Personal interview (in Hindi/Urdu/English). 6 September 2013.

Khan, Saroj. Personal interview (in Hindi/English). 7 July 2015.

Kher, Anupam. Personal interview (in English). 27 May 2015.

Malini, Hema. Personal interview (in Hindi/English). 15 August 2013.

Menon, Anjali. Personal interview (in English). 10 June 2015.

Mukherji, Srijit. Personal interview (in English). 29 July 2015.

Mohapatra, Nirad C. Personal interview (in English/Odia). 13 June 2013.

Nair, P.K. Personal interview (in English). 8 May 2013.

Nanda, Prashanta. Personal interview (in English). 7 September 2013.

Pandey, Kamlesh. Personal interview (in English). 10 October 2013.

Pattanaik, Devdutt. Personal interview (in English). 10 July 2015.

Pujari, Sarat. Personal interview (in Odia/English). 27 June 2013.

Rajamouli, S.S. Personal Interview (in English/Telegu). 8 December 2012; 12 August 2015.

Shivdasani, Deepak. Personal interview (in English). 14 September 2014.

Singh, Mukesh. Personal interview (in Hindi/English). 25 July 2014.

Swaroop, Kamal. Personal interview (in English). 11 July 2013.

Shukla, Kuntal. Personal interview (in Hindi/English). 24 July 2014.
Tandon, Lekh. Personal interview (in Hindi/English). 10 July 2015.
Tewary, Siddharth. Personal interview (in English). 22 July 2014.
Vijayakar, Rajiv. Personal interview (in English). 15 August 2012.
Vishwanath, K. Personal interview (in English). 17 August 2015.

Glossary

A

Aascharya	Surprise
Abhidhanakosha	A lexicon that lists names
Abhinaya	Acting or histrionic representation
Abhisarika nayika	A heroine driven by love or infatuation, who let's go of the shyness expected of her gender and takes the initiative to meet her lover
Adhbuta	Marvellous
Adhunik	A modern social drama in the Odia language, mostly translated from its Bengali genre counterparts
Aharya	Costumes/Ornaments
Alankara	Means of embellishment
Amrutamanthan	The churning of the ocean
Anand/Ananda	Joy/Bliss
Angavastra	Upper garments
Angika	Bodily gestures and physical movements
Anubhavas	The consequents/Verbal, physical and emotional reflexes or reactions to an action trigger
Apahasya	Vulgar/obscene laughter
Apsaras	Celestial maidens and nymphs
Apun	A colloquial reference to the self in Mumbai's Hindi lingo
Artha	Wealth
Ashta-nayikas	A collective name for the eight types of heroines who represent the eight different mood states of a woman in love as described in the *Natyashastra*
Atahasya	Boisterous/loud laughter
Atimaharathi	A great warrior, as mentioned in the epics, who is capable of fighting 7,20,000 warriors simultaneously

Audarya	A sense of civility or respect in all situations
Ayojaka	Conceptualiser

B

Bhakti	Devotion
Bhagavata Mela	A folk theatre form from Tamil Nadu
Bhagavata Tungis	An enclosed place (specific to Odisha) where a group of performers sing phrases from the Gita
Bhajan	A devotional song
Bhangi	Gestural acting
Bharatanatyam	One of the eight classical dances of India; its origin has been sourced to temple-dancing traditions in South India
Bhava	An emotional mood or state of mind
Bhavai	A folk theatre form from Gujarat
Bhavayanti	To originate
Bhay/Bhaya	Fear
Bhayanaka	Fearful
Bhoga	Food offered to the gods
Bibhatsa	Odious
Biryani	Flavoured rice cooked with meat or vegetables

C

Champu	A genre in Indian literature that originated in Sanskrit poetics. It consists of a mixture of prose and poetry, where the prose is interspersed with verses.
Chanda	A style of rendering poetry typical to Odia literature where the verses stress on rhythm
Chausath kalas	The 64 different traditional arts, a mastery of which formed an integral part of the development of a cultured individual in ancient India
Chitra purvaranga	A stylised dramatic presentation embellished with song and dance
Chittavrittis	Cognitive/mental tendencies
Cheer haran	The act of disrobing of a woman

Churidar-kurta	Traditional clothing worn by women in North India, it comprises a long shirt worn over loose trousers
Cinéma vérité	True/Truth cinema; this was a French film movement of the 1960s that showed people in everyday situations with authentic dialogue and naturalness of action.
Comme ci, comme ça	A return-on-investment venture

D

Dakhini nacha	A local dance form prevalent in East India that is seen as a predecessor of its extremely stylised classical dance form, Odissi
Dana vira	A hero famed for his generosity
Dashkathia	A group folk dance from Odisha where the performers use a pair of sticks
Dastaan	Epic Persian adventure sagas
Daya vira	A compassionate hero
Desi	A colloquial term referring to something Indian
Devadasi	A temple dancer
Devaloka	Land of Gods
Dharma	Righteousness
Dharma vira	A hero who fights for the establishment of law, righteousness and other noble values
Dhairya	Serenity/Patience/Fortitude
Dhvani	Suggestion/The meaning of an art form
Dipti	A heightened state of expectation of love
Doshas	Faults or lacunae, [here] in context to one's character
Dwapara Yuga	One of the four *yugas* the Earth timeline has been categorised into in the Hindu scriptures

G

Gambhirya	Serenity
Gandharva	Reference to a type of musical theatre in which young boys essayed the female parts on stage

Gandharvas	Celestial musicians
Ghazal	A song of love in the Urdu language
Ghagra-choli	Traditional outfit worn by Indian women consisting of a long skirt and a corset-like blouse
Ghrna	Disgust
Gita Govinda	Jaideva's 12th century CE epic poem depicting the love between Radha and Krishna
Gitinatya	A musical drama form typical to East India
Gopis	Village maidens

H

Hasa	Mirth
Hasita	Slight laughter
Hasya	Comic
Itihasa	History; it is also a reference to 'mythological' epics like the Ramayana and the Mahabharata that are considered to be documents of ancient Indian history

J

Jashn	A performative folk form from Kashmir
Jatra	Professional theatre form prevalent in the eastern parts of the Indian subcontinent, primarily (undivided) Bengal, Odisha and Assam
Jugupsa	Disgust

K

Kama	Sex/Lust
Kanti	A beauteous state of being in expectation of love
Kalahantarita	An impatient heroine separated from her lover over a quarrel
Karmayogi	A selfless doer who carries on without worrying about the fruits of his/her labour
Karuna	Pathos/Compassion
Katha	A story; can also refer to the telling of a story
Kathak	A classical Indian dance form from North India

Kathakali	A highly expressive traditional Indian dance from Kerala
Kathakas	Bards cum storytellers
Kavya	A poem
Khandita nayika	A heroine enraged with her lover for cheating on her
Kimbadanti	Story from local mythology or folk lore
Kirtan	A continuous rendering of devotional songs in a group setting
Kirtankar	A person who leads or sings in a *kirtan*
Koodiyattam	Stylised theatre from Kerala, where the main characters speak in Sanskrit, while the side characters speak in Malayalam
Kroadha	Anger

L

Lalita	Sportiveness (not to be confused with the protagonist of *Lalita*, the film)
Lasya	Grace
Laya	Rhythm
Leela	Divine play
Lila	A play; can also refer to a musical theatre form of Odisha
Lokadharani	A realistic drama performed to natural acting featuring ordinary characters

M

Madhurya	Moderation/Self-possession
Makhan chor	One who steals and eats cream; a term of endearment referring to the child avatar of Lord Krishna and his love for cream
Maargi	Classical theatre
Mahabharata	The world's longest epic poem revolving around an ancient war between cousins
Mahakavya	An epic poem evoking all the nine *rasas*

Malikas	Song form from Odisha featuring elements of *chanda* and *champu* (see above)
Mangalsutra	An auspicious necklace presented to a bride at her wedding as an indication of her marital status
Masala	Reference to an Indian film form that mixes the attributes of dominant Hollywood genres such as musical, comedy, action, melodrama, etc. in one film
Maya	Illusion
Mayavi	A magician or an expert at creating an illusion
Moksha	Liberation
Mausi	Aunt
Mise en scène	The set design aspects of a theatre or film production
Mukta mancha jatra	Open air theatre

N

Nataka	Play
Natya	Dance drama
Natyacharya	A teacher of theatre trained in the traditions of the *Natyashastra*
Natyadharmi	A stylised play with song and dance elements featuring larger than life characters from the epics
Natyakaar	Another term for a *natyacharya* in the Odia language
Natyashastra	The Sanskrit drama treatise written by Bharata *muni*
Natyaveda	Another reference to the *Natyashastra* as the fifth Veda
Natwari	The dance performed by Krishna on the hood of snake Kaliya
Nautanki	A highly dramatic performance full of exaggerated emotions
Navarasa	The nine universal human emotions according to the *Natyashastra*
Nayaka/Nayika	Hero/Heroine

Nirdeshaka	Director
Nirveda	Detachment
Nrityanatya	Dance drama

O

Odissi	Stylised 20th-century version of a classical Indian dance performed to *Natyashastra* guidelines. It was revived from elaborate dance-depicting architecture motifs on the temples of Odisha, especially Konark.

P

Pala	A sung folk form when performers sing to devotional poems
Paatra	A Sanskrit term used to describe a character; in some Indian vernaculars it refers to a vessel
Praglabhya	Maturity
Prajojoka	Producer
Prema rasalilas	A dance-drama portraying various aspects of love
Proshitabhartruka	A heroine missing her sojourning husband/lover
Purana	A record of ancient events
Purusartha	Purpose of life; Hindu scriptures list *dharma, artha, kama* and *moksha* as the four *purusarthas.*

Q

Qawaali	Sufi devotional song form performed in a group

R

Raga	A traditional melodic pattern or mode in Indian music
Ranga	Colour
Ramayana	The oldest Sanskrit epic from India that depicts the story of Lord Rama
Ramleela	A North Indian folk form depicting tales from the Ramayana
Rasa/ Rasas	Emotions/Sentiments

Rasalila	A musical dance drama depicting tales of Radha and Krishna
Rashtra-debata	A deity worshipped by an entire kingdom/state
Rasika	An empathetic spectator with an evolved taste for appreciation
Rasautpatih	Also spelt as *rasoutpatih*, it refers to the moment of the birth of a *rasa* or the experiencing of a *rasa* by a *rasika*.
Rati	Love
Raudra	Furious

S

Sadharanikarana	The universalisation of an emotion
Sahrydaya	A viewer in a similar emotion state or total identification with the drama situation of a performer or on-screen character
Samana/Samanya	Of equal measure/sharing similar or equal attributes
Sambhoga	The experiencing of a joyous state of love in union
Sangeet natak	A song and music predominating theatrical form typical to western India, especially Maharashtra
Sattva guna	Character trait
Sattvika	State of emotion/Pertaining to emotions
Sattvikabhava	Involuntary emotional reactions
Seva	Service offered as a ritual to an elder patron, king or a deity
Shanta/ Shanti	State of calm/Peace
Sharanagat	A state of complete surrender to the divine
Shastra	A guiding text or a book of codes
Shero-shayari	A rhetorical and stylised poetic articulation of ideas and stories
Shoka	Sorrow
Shyama	Light blue
Smriti	Scriptural knowledge that was remembered and passed on by generations of sages and the learned before being written or codified

Smita hasya	Modest smile
Sobha	Beauty radiated as a radiant glowing state of being post the experiencing of love
Sringara/sringaar	The erotic/romance
Sruti	Scriptural knowledge heard directly from the God or gods
Stamba	A shocked state of being rooted to a spot
Sthayibhava	Permanent emotional mood states of the mind
Sthairya	Steadiness
Suddha purvaranga	A simple drama presentation depicting daily life featuring ordinary characters
Suchaka	Originator
Sutra	Code or a text on rules
Sutradhar	Narrator
Svadhinabhartruka	A heroine with a husband who, captivated by her beauty, is perpetually by her side in near-complete subjugation to her charms
Swang	Performance style from the Punjab region of the Indian subcontinent
Swadana	The act of partaking or relishing
Swadeshi	Made in India or in one's own country
Swaraj	Self-rule
Swayamvara	A ritual contest where eligible grooms (often princes and royalty) undergo a contest of prowess to win a princess as a bride

T

Tamasha	Entertainment/Spectacle
Tandava	Shiva's cosmic dance
Tala	Rhythm timing; also a unit of measurement for time and space
Tatvagyana	An emotional state of detachment born within one's self from the awareness or knowledge that the world is an illusion
Tejas	Spirit
Terukkuttu	Folk theatre form in South India

U

Upahasya	Ridicule
Upahasita	Ridiculing laughter
Upanishads	Sacred Hindu texts containing the essence/end chapters of the *Vedas*. They focus on themes like the nature of God, paths to salvation, etc.
Utsaha	Energy

V

Vachika	Verbal or pertaining to speech
Vasakasajja nayika	A heroine all dressed up, eager for union with her lover
Veda	The oldest scriptures in Hinduism, these are considered to be revelations seen by/revealed to ancient sages after intense meditation
Vedic	Pertaining to or recommended by the *Vedas*
Veer/Vir	A hero
Vibhavas	Determinants or the words, causes and actions leading to the happening of actions and events in a way that they generate certain *bhavas*
Vidushaka	Jester
Vihasita	Open laughter
Vilasa	Graceful bearing
Vipralabdha nayika	A heroine deceived by her lover
Vipralambha bhava	The sorrowful/lovesick mood state of waiting for a lover
Vira	Heroic
Viraha	Sadness born of separation from a loved one
Virahotkanthita	A heroine distressed by separation
Virangana	A heroine with courage as her character's dominant trait
Vismaya	Astonishment
Vyabhicaribhavas	The 33 transitory mental states mentioned in the *Natyashastra*

Y

Yagna — A *Vedic* ritual of fire sacrifice

Yagnakund — The sacred altar for performing a *yagna*

Yuga — A unit of time used for measuring the Earth's age/period of existence in Hindu scriptures

Z

Zamindar bari — Palatial residences of landowning lords mostly in rural settings

Index

E

F

G

H

I

About the Author

Piyush Roy is an Indian National Film Award winning critic–columnist and an international author, curator, filmmaker and professor in film, media and aesthetics studies.

Appreciating Melodrama: Theory and Practice in Indian Cinema and Television is Roy's fourth published book. Previously, he has authored two fiction works, *Never Say Never Again* (2007) and *Alexander—An Epic Love Story* (2008), and an online novel series, *The Millennium Batch* (2020). He made his nonfiction debut with *Bollywood FAQ: All That's Left to Know About the Greatest Film Story Never Told* (2019).

Former editor of popular film magazine, *Stardust*, and film weekly, *StarWeek,* Roy brings over two decades of work experience in media and entertainment journalism; he has worked at senior reporting positions with *Hindustan Times* and *The Indian Express* and been published in *The Times of India Crest Edition* and *Speaking Tree*, *The Asian Age*, *Society* magazine, *Screen* and *The New Indian Express*. He is the writer of a near-decade-long popular film column, Sunday Talkies, with *Orissa Post* and has authored over 1000 media publications.

Honoured with 'Special Mention' for Best Critic at the 60th Indian National Film Awards (2013) by the President of India, Pranab Mukherjee, he was invited by Queen Elizabeth II and The Duke of Edinburgh to the UK–India Year of Culture's official inauguration at the Buckingham Palace in 2017, an event that featured eminent Indians from the nation's civil society, politics, sports, arts and culture to commemorate 70 years of Indian independence. He was also conferred the Sir William Darling Memorial Prize (2014) by the Principal, University of Edinburgh 'for enhancing the reputation of the University through his conduct, example and scholarship'.

An advisory board member of Global University Film Awards, Hong Kong, he has been a jury member of Power Brands Bollywood Film Journalists' Awards and Star Writers Program, a talent hunt for television content writers organised by Star TV India Pvt. Ltd. He is the

Founder–Festival Director of Edinburgh Festival of Indian Films and Documentaries (2016–2017) and made his museum gallery showcase debut as a poet and photographer with a unique pan-Indian photo-poetry exhibition, 'The Collector of Characters', on the theme '70 years of the Indian independence' at the Assam State Museum in 2017.

In the filmmaking world, his debut documentary feature, *Pleasures Prejudice & Pride: An Indian Way of Filmmaking* (2018), has been the focus of dedicated seminar screening tours across global universities. His latest film, an experimental feature called *Amrtāh: The Author of Time* (2021), is inspired by ideas, insights and learner–teacher interactions in The Upanishads, and he is presently working on a documentary trilogy exploring multifaith pilgrim journeys across spiritual traditions.

Having taught at higher education institutions in the UK and India (such as Indian Institute of Mass Communication Dhenkanal, Indian Institute of Management Ahmedabad, The Kohima Institute, MIDAS Pune, Jain University Bengaluru and The University of Edinburgh, Scotland), he is the Founding Dean and Professor at the School of Liberal Arts and Sciences, RV University, Bengaluru.

Website: www.piyushroy.com